"*Barbara has vast experience in teaching learners of all levels of Net experience—or lack of it. She has become an expert in explaining technical issues in words that even the severly nontechnical reader can understand. What Barbara Ling has produced is a seminar-in-a-book to bring you up to par in a surprisingly short time.*"

—From the Foreword by Joyce Lain Kennedy,
Syndicated columnist, *Careers Now*

"*Poor Richard's Internet Recruiting is a must have guide for employers! Barbara Ling understands the dynamics of the Internet and has shown us how to harness that power for our recruiting needs. It gives you the edge you need to recruit hot prospects in today's competitive human resources market.*"

—Marrianne Williams, Editor, Outfront News,
A FrontPage Learning Community, http://www.outfront.net/

"*WOW, what an unbelievable resource! Full of great ideas, examples, and internet bookmarks... Any company looking to hire employees through the Internet MUST get this book.*"

—Joel Weiner, Webmaster,
http://www.MoreTraffic4U.com/

"*My colleagues and I have devoured all the Poor Richard series of books, and put many of their insights into practice for our clients. Poor Richard's Internet Recruiting we'll be using too—but for ourselves!*"

—Brian Millar, Creative Director
http://www.myrtle.co.uk/

"*I have long been a fan of Barbara Ling and always watch for her postings because she gives excellent advice on Internet recruiting. This book is absolutely awesome! Barbara does seminars, but having her book is like having Barbara right beside me leading me step by step to do everything right for recruiting! It's a MUST read for anyone new to recruiting, and even seasoned pros (like me!) will learn from it.*"

—Terri Robinson, President, Robinson & Associates,
http://www.recruit2hire.com/

"*Do you want to recruit on the Internet or be recruited thru it? This is the book for you! I found this book full of extremely helpful information. It does not matter if you are a veteran of the net or a neophyte this book has all the information that you need, laid out in a way that is practical and easy to understand. It is obvious that Ms. Ling is both familiar and passionate about her subject and her enthusiasm comes across to the reader. I liked the way she pointed out both the advantages and pitfalls of using the net, and more importantly how to avoid the pitfalls.*"

—Thomas A McKean,
Independent Consultant

POOR RICHARD'S INTERNET RECRUITING

Easy, Low-Cost Ways to Find Great Employees Online

by
Barbara Ling

Poor Richard's Internet Recruiting:
Easy, Low-Cost Ways to Find Great Employees Online

SAN#: 299-4550
Top Floor Publishing
8790 W. Colfax #107
Lakewood, CO 80215

Feedback to the author: feedback@topfloor.com
Sales information: sales@topfloor.com
The Top Floor Publishing Web Site: http://TopFloor.com/
The Poor Richard Web Site: http://PoorRichard.com/
Cover design/illustration by Marty Petersen, http://www.artymarty.com

Library of Congress Catalog Card Number: 00-105954

ISBN: 1-930082-01-0

03   02   01   6 5 4 3 2 1

Dedicated to my husband, Moses Ling.
My life, my love, my heart

ABOUT THE AUTHOR

Barbara Ling has been an active participant on the Internet and a thought-provoking newsgroup poster since 1988. On the job, she rose from the ranks in AT&T from a network tools developer to become the lead Unix/NT network administrator for two districts, acquiring skills in systems engineering, Web site creation, and development and training. She also wrote several user manuals on the software and platforms she taught.

Barbara first approached recruiting in 1995. She fast realized that her skills in this area fell into the "how do we locate candidates?" arena, and quickly developed a list of rules to follow when prospecting for quality professionals. As a result of her insight and writing skills, she soon became a columnist for online recruiting at the *Boston Herald,* where her work can be seen once a week.

Her first book, *The Internet Recruiting Edge,* was published in 1998 and has received top billing in all recruiting industry publications, including *Staffing Industry, The Fordyce Letter, Inc. Magazine*'s review of online recruiting, and more. It has now been updated to its fifth edition. Her other books include *Avoiding the Contractor From Hell,* available at http://www.contractorhell.com/ and *The Real Estate Pro's Internet Edge* at http://www.realestate-resources.com/.

In 1999, Barbara Ling and her partner Alison Clemente kicked off the RISE Internet Recruiting Seminar Series at http://www.riseway.com/, which is currently enjoying tremendous success.

Barbara resides in New Jersey with her husband and family.

ACKNOWLEDGMENTS

Throughout my life, I have had the great good fortune of meeting, working with and learning from the following people. Tony Byrne is the most phenomenal trainer the recruiting industry has ever know, he gave me a chance when hardly anyone else would. Alison Clemente has been my partner in RISE Internet Recruiting Seminars; her ability to create incredible futures is unmatched.

The project editor, copyeditors, publisher, and owner of Top Floor Publishing-respectively, Jerry Olsen, Fred Kloepper and Hilary Powers, Missy Ramey, and Peter Kent—shared ideas and creativity that made writing *Poor Richard's Internet Recruiting* a joy. Meanwhile, Joann Woy, as proofreader, and Liz Cunningham, as indexer, helped make this book all that it could be. I have also benefited immeasurably from the Studio B Computer Book Publishing mailing list, and am most grateful for the nuggets of wisdom fellow mailing list members provide. I also want to extend a special thanks to Joyce Lain Kennedy for contributing the Foreword.

Colleagues from the recruiting industry have been a blessing. Bill Vick, Minnie Ahlstrand, and Glenn Whitten from Recruiters Online were my first clients in Internet recruiting; increasing their site visibility over eightfold jump-started my skills in Internet publicity. To this day, I continue to learn from them. Other fellow professionals, including Brian Weis from Recruiters Network, Diane Propsner from Galileo Consulting, Andrew Hammer from Top Echelon, David Manaster from the ERExchange, and Richard Posey from CareerMarketplace, have provided cherished working relationships, friendship and insights over the years. And of course, the thousands of recruiters themselves, who participate in the Recruiters Network, ERExchange, *Inc. Magazine*, and Recruiters Coffeeshop forums—I truly appreciate the opportunity of being part of such great communities.

My colleagues in the iManager team back when I was a techie at AT&T—Terry Zappula, Ed Horch, Mary Ellen Ferrara, and Diane Boyd—showed me the ultimate perk of teamwork. Never before, and never since, have I worked with a group so imbued with "all for one, and one for all"; it's an experience I have treasured ever since. And David G. Korn, Steve Bellovin, and Bill Cheswick, researchers from Bell Labs, provided me the opportunity to grow my technical skills from the very best. They were incredible teachers to boot, and it was an honor and privilege to learn from them.

The Internet affords people the chance to meet their heroes online. Back in 1995, I exchanged correspondence with Donna Gillespie, author of *The Light Bearer*, one of the most compelling novels of the 20th century. Her book is one that changes lives; I am deeply indebted to her for her encouragement when I decided to try my hand at writing as well.

I could never have accomplished anything near my success without the support of my family. My parents, Ben and Gloria, are the most superb mom and dad on this planet. If I raise my kids half as well as they raised me, I'll be Supermommy! My children—a rambunctious trio—are a blessing and a joy.

And finally ...

Poor Richard's Internet Recruiting is dedicated to my husband, Moses Ling. To my husband—The Bridge Across Forever was just the beginning. I love you the mostest. Always.

CONTENTS AT A GLANCE

TABLE OF CONTENTS

FOREWORD

by Joyce Lain Kennedy

This book is about you and your staffing needs. It reveals the special techniques you can use on the all-purpose Web to find people for your enterprise—finding them faster, cheaper, and smarter.

Chances are you already know how to use the Web to look up stock quotes, sign up for newsletters, and find out what's playing at the Roxy—and how much the tickets cost. You already know how to use the Web to read online newspapers, buy at auction, shop for a house, and find a loan.

Are the skills you use to pull data from the Web transferable from bargain shopping to talent finding? You bet they are! Improvable, but transferable. This means that as an averagely gifted Net user, you have a running start toward becoming a great e-recruiter by applying the tips in this book from a great e-recruiting trainer.

Help From the Pro's Pro

Barbara Ling—arguably the world's leading Internet recruiting trainer—explains in these pages how to fine-tune your all-purpose Web skills to snare the best talents for your staffing needs. For immediate examples of how to find free résumés on the Internet, jump to Chapter 10, "Search Engines and Directories."

But what if you suspect, or even know for sure, that you're way behind the curve in dealing with the Web? Here's your chance to catch up quickly. Barbara has vast experience in teaching learners at all levels of Net expertise—or lack of it. She has become expert in explaining technical issues in words that even the severely nontechnical reader can understand. What Barbara Ling has produced is a seminar-in-a-book to bring you up to par in a surprisingly short time.

Her book is well timed. The cut-above talent you most want to source and hire—in almost any career field—is using the all-purpose Web, too. A-list candidates turn to the Web for job searching, of course, but they also scour it to make sure they don't fog out and fall behind, that they remain current with their industries' late-breaking developments. The quality of people you want to hire recognize that a communications revolution has thrust us into an utterly different kind of life than we knew in the 1900s.

Several years ago recruiter Bill Vick, founder of the pioneering organization Recruiters Online, asked if I knew Barbara Ling, whom he described as "an amazingly talented woman who is writing all these great tips and techniques for cyberspace recruiting." I didn't know about Barbara until then; but since Bill's initial referral, I've observed Barbara's top-notch work and exceptional knowledge of the online recruiting industry. Her seminars are drawing rave reviews far and wide.

Don't miss this chance to benefit from a hefty chunk of Barbara's practical wisdom about recruiting in the Internet Age. This is a useful recruiting book that you'll want to carry with you like a digital personal assistant. The new time has come.

Joyce Lain Kennedy
Syndicated newspaper columnist: *Careers Now*
Author: *Resumes for Dummies, Cover Letters for Dummies, Job Interviews for Dummies*

Why You Want to Recruit on the Internet

Many employers view Internet recruiting to be a task as frustrating as drying up the ocean with an eyedropper. Look at all the hype surrounding it. Monster.com! Hotjobs.com! SpendingLotsAndLotsOfMoney.com! Time is money, and the Internet is just plain *huge*—while all of us and our coffee cups might know about **Yahoo!** at http://www.yahoo.com/ for searching and **eBay** at http://www.ebay.com/ for auctions and **Ivillage** at http://www.ivillage.com/ for communities, how can you zoom directly to the specific, targeted resources where your future employees can be found and still have a dime left to call your own? It's not your specialty, it's not your passion—*you simply need to hire people*. And you want to achieve that at a cost that's less than a Bahamas cruise.

Does the above basically cover your views about Internet recruiting? If so, I've got fantastic news for you! No matter the industry in which you work, high-quality Internet recruiting can be achieved for zero to minimal monetary costs. Don't believe me? Ever hear of the **America's Job Bank** at http://www.ajb.org/?

You can view résumés there for free. How about search engines like **AltaVista** at http://www.altavista.com/ and super ISPs like **AOL** at http://www.aol.com/? Did you know that one of the first documents new users put up on their personal Web site is their résumé? And that you can immediately uncover people actively searching for employment in your industry?

It's true. And this is the book that will show it all to you, step-by-step.

Poor Richard's Internet Recruiting is divided into the following chapters. Each of them has been designed to be a self-contained nugget of knowledge, although I urge you to read from the beginning to the end; you'll uncover more did-you-knows about recruiting and the Internet in general.

Chapters One through Three introduce you to the basics of Internet recruiting. You'll learn that you probably already possess the needed skills to be successful, and how to convince your future employees that your job opportunities are the best available. Additionally, you'll learn how to minimize the efforts needed to get online in the first place.

Chapters Four through Six help you burst out of the starting gate at full gallop by teaching you how to determine your exact needs, write killer job advertisements, and find over a dozen online resources to locate free or low-cost job-posting alternatives where your future employees gather.

Chapters Seven through Nine walk you through, step-by-step, how to get the most benefit possible from industry niche sites, professional organizations, and your local state or city job banks.

Chapters Ten through Thirteen reveal the hidden benefits of search engines (you can use them to locate thousands of free résumés online), colleges, forums, and mailing lists. You'll also find suggestions for community networking and increasing your reach within your targeted future employee network.

Chapters Fourteen through Seventeen teach you how to use newspaper sites (many of your local newspapers will have an online presence too), job fairs, user groups, and Internet classifieds and Web rings. Many employers aren't aware of these resources.

Chapters Eighteen to the end of the book round out your experiences with Internet recruiting by discussing ways of certifying that your future employees aren't lying to you, when to use a recruiter, how to evaluate the traditional boards, and more. By the time you've finished this book, you'll have an excellent education on how to locate employees for free on the Internet.

The Appendix for *Poor Richard's Internet Recruiting* contains lots of valuable resources to aid you in your recruiting endeavors. As you can see, this book is extremely comprehensive yet simple to understand and apply. While reading it, you'll be struck by how much common sense is involved with recruiting online; treat professionals as you'd like to be treated and you'll be off to a great start.

I've been the lead trainer in the Internet recruiting field for several years now. My first book, *The Internet Recruiting Edge*, a guide specifically tailored for recruiters and HR professionals, is the only resource to have won five stars from *Inc.* magazine and is currently in its fifth edition; this year will also see the creation of the special-edition *IT Internet Recruiting Edge* as well. I'm a columnist for the *Boston Herald* and the creator and innovator of the **RISE Internet Recruiting Seminars** at http://www.riseway.com/ as well as **EarPerk!**, the complete, free candidate/recruiter/employer exchange where you can find industry comparisons and more at http://www.earperk.com/.

I know you'll gain great benefits from reading this book! I hope you enjoy reading it as much as I did writing it.

Best wishes,
Barbara Ling
http://www.barbaraling.com
btl@barbaraling.com

CHAPTER ONE

Is Internet Recruiting for You?

The Internet—Isn't It Just for Shopping?

Ah, the Internet. You see it just about everywhere. Simply turn on the TV, or walk past a train station, or pick up your local newspaper—ads for Internet businesses are more common than confetti after the New Year's party. They're everywhere.

If you're like the majority of people who spend more than a minute or two online, you probably have a pretty good idea of how the Internet can work for you. For example, AOL users become familiar with how to use their chat rooms and favorite places. Day traders quickly learn how to *attempt* to create monetary masterpieces with online financial companies such as **DLJ Direct** at http://www.dljdirect.com/ or **Quote.com** at http://www.quote.com/. Frugal individuals always stop by **Priceline.com** at http://www.priceline.com/ before shopping at their local super-markets, and baby boomers browse through **eBay** at http://www.ebay.com/ in search of their favorite childhood Barbie or GI Joe doll. When you think about it, it's quite incredible the amazing abilities you can obtain on the Internet. There are so many facets available that it can boggle the mind.

As the leading trainer in Internet recruiting, I often hear the following exclamation from my students: "Hey, I didn't know you could do that!" or "Wow, it's that easy to find that information online?" The realm of possibilities is so large yet so simple, it can leave people stunned with the ease of it all. Thus, before we jump into the world of finding your future employees online, let's first go over some rather neat things you can accomplish online.

E-commerce

E-commerce is simply the action of buying or selling on the Internet. It's a craze that began a few years ago, but is now ramping up to incredible levels. Whenever you buy or sell anything on the Internet, you're engaging in e-commerce. I remember visiting **eBay** at http://www.ebay.com/ one day when I was drowning in nostalgic memories of my childhood. Figuring what the heck, I searched for some titles by one of my favorite authors, Albert Payson Terhune; I came up with over 30 people selling their old copies for quite reasonable prices. Thus, I'm now rebuilding my old library at home. Who would have guessed it was so easy to locate pieces of my past?

Talent for Auction—*You've heard of auction sites like eBay? Professionals can auction themselves off at similar sites, dedicated strictly to the career and freelance markets.*

The neat thing about eBay is that you can sell virtually anything. Back in 1999, the Internet recruiting industry was rather amused when a group of consultants or programmers tried auctioning themselves off at that site. It turned out to be a harbinger of things to come—later that year saw a great proliferation of talent and freelance sites such as **Monster's Talent Bank** at http://talent.monster.com/, **Techies.com** at http://www.techies.com/, and many others—as depicted in Figure 1.1, for example.

E-commerce manifests itself in many other ways. Have you ever visited **Amazon.com** and bought a book? Now, of course, you can buy much more than that—movies, music, home improvement, and the like—but long ago, books were the most popular commodities. The simple action of pointing, clicking, and buying

Figure 1.1: Guru.com lets skilled professionals market themselves.

a book is e-commerce at its most simple. Places like Amazon.com make it so simple not only to shop online, but also to streamline your gift giving as well. A few months ago, one of my suppliers, Tony from **Ipubco** at http://www.ipubco.com/, went out of his way to ensure my site was trouble-free. I wanted to do something special, so I found out his family's interests and sent a gift package from Amazon.com that contained books his family would consider enjoyable. All of this was done from the comfort of my own home office—I didn't have to leave the house, hop into the car, brave the highways, stand and wait in a line, wrap the gifts, and then patiently wait to send it at the post office.

What Price Ease?—*The convenience of online shopping means that you don't have to leave the comfort of your own home. The same thing holds for Internet recruiting—it can be done at your computer in your time with your schedule.*

Sites like Amazon.com have another interesting offering for the customers. Did you know that you can request to be e-mailed whenever an author of your choosing writes a new book? What a great reminder service! You don't have to visit book sites every day to see if something new comes out—you'll receive notification the moment it happens. It will save you time and aggravation. *It's a service that many job and career sites, too, are now offering to their customers*—professionals can request to be e-mailed whenever a job matching their interests is advertised, and employers can opt to receive résumés of individuals who possess the skills they need.

Another popular application of e-commerce is that of affiliate programs. You might have heard about places like AllAdvantage (Surf the Web! Wheeee!); that's merely one example of a powerful, thriving industry. Remember our visit to Amazon.com? Another offering that Amazon gives its customers is the ability to provide direct links to its products from individual customers (called *affiliates*). Affiliate programs let customers earn residual income resulting from sales. Why, there are even scripts available at places like **Anaconda.net** at http://www.anaconda.net/ that ensure you maximize your commissions from sites like the above, and complete directories for affiliate programs at **Refer-it** at http://www.refer-it.com/ as shown in Figure 1.2.

Free Money—*You can generate continuous residual income by becoming an affiliate with an e-commerce site. Including direct links to their products (for example, computer books if you're in the technical industry) will result in commissions being earned by you when a visitor buys.*

This trend, too, is being seen in Internet recruiting; **CareerCentral** at http://www.careercentral.com/ offers a percentage of a client's sale to the affiliate who referred said client, as does **CollegeRecruiter** at http://www.adguide.com/. Freelancing sites such as **eLance** at http://www.elance.com/ offer similar programs.

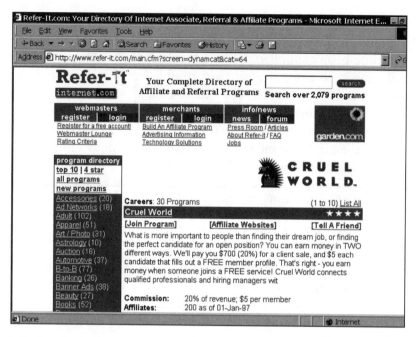

Figure 1.2: Some career sites let you earn money via their affiliate programs.

This example of e-commerce can be beneficial to your Internet recruiting efforts. No matter what industry your business is in, there should be books or software that pertain to it. Just think if you could include such information in a special section of your Web site that would draw future employees like ice cream draws children— not only would you be providing excellent resources, but also earning money on the side. For example, I've designed Web sites for technical recruiters and included a resource center that contained direct links for technical certification training materials from **FatBrain.com** at http://www.fatbrain.com/, Personal Digital Assistants from **Beyond.com** at http://www.beyond.com/, money management books from Amazon.com, and the like. All of these links were coded with the business-owner's referral ID.

One of the things I love about e-commerce is how, when done well, it can (emphasis on the word *can*; alas, many people ignore it) drive ethical behavior on the Internet. Have you ever received unsolicited e-mail of ridiculous offers like "Make 3,452,945 dollars in the next 7 minutes!" or "Golf balls—Cheap!" or other such pie-in-the-sky ideas? Such e-mail, called *spam*, is sent because it's free, easy to do so, and the instigators are always hoping to make it rich somehow, someway. It's impolite and ineffective, however; sending unsolicited e-mail hardly ever works. Yet, many people insist on continuing the practice. Its failure has showcased, more than ever, how targeted marketing (or permission marketing, or opt-in marketing, or ...) instead can work miracles in one's business.

E-commerce ties into this in an effective fashion. The end goal of a businessperson on the Internet is to make money, either directly (sales) or indirectly (sowing the seeds for a great reputation online). Coincidentally, this is what e-commerce is all about.

Great Relationships—*One of the benefits of the Internet is it provides simple ways to network with your communities and customers. The more politeness you show, the more you will stand out from your competitors, and the more people will consider your job opportunities.*

The desire to engage in successful e-commerce has led many smart marketers on the Internet to participate in *long-term relationship building*. You'll see it all the time online:

- Free e-zines for which visitors can sign up and receive special offers or pertinent news every week (and because the visitor signed up voluntarily, it's considered quite okay to include advertisements for your services in these e-zines).
- Tell-a-friend scripts that allow visitors to refer their friends to the site, thus encouraging free marketing.
- Free quizzes or puzzles that keep visitors on the site; generally the longer visitors spend at a site, the more they remember it.
- Forums and discussion boards that encourage a sense of community; often groups of people will start posting regularly and helping out one another.

These are the components that help build a thriving Web site that hosts thousands of visitors a week. The career sites already know this—you only have to visit places like **MyJobSearch.com** at http://www.myjobsearch.com/ or **CareerMag** at http://www.careermag.com/ to see not only employment opportunities and listings, but also plentiful, crucial resources such as message boards as depicted in Figure 1.3 to help job seekers make their new decision. When visitors discover useful information gathered all in one spot, their perception of the site is heightened favorably. Why visit more than one Web site on the Internet if another meets all of one's needs?

Think like a job seeker. What is the site you'd prefer—one that has only jobs, or one that provides information about maximizing one's salary, breaking the glass ceiling, jump-starting the start-ups, relocation links, and the like?

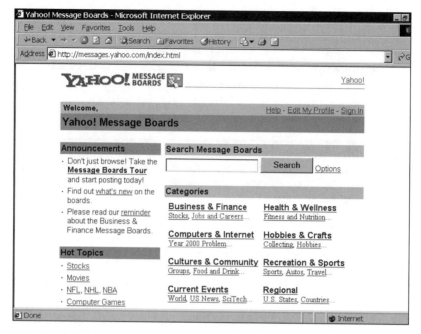

Figure 1.3: Participating in communities makes hiring much easier.

Another use of e-commerce that's becoming popular is membership sub-scriptions to sites. One sees this all the time in Internet recruiting—participating in job/career sites like eQuest, Headhunter.net, and about a gazillion others all cost money; sometimes people can sign up for this online. It used to be that secure access to résumés (and résumés only) was the Golden Child of Internet recruiting—companies could pay thousands of dollars to view these documents. Due to the rise in popularity of Internet recruiting, such sites are now offering other services like job broadcasting, résumé matching, member discounts, and more. The services you can find at a given site should be increasing every day.

Golden Resources—*With thousands of sites out there on the Internet about jobs and careers, how can you stand out from all the rest? The answer is in the services and resources you provide. Everyone can showcase jobs; not everyone can put together quality information that assists professionals in defining their new career.*

The above examples are only a few of the ways e-commerce is benefiting the Internet. Are any of them familiar? If so, you're already way ahead of your competitors; many of these techniques can be applied in Internet recruiting, too.

Stocks

Many, many people use the Internet for their stock purchases and trading. It can be either a fulfilling pastime, or one that encourages you to yank out any hair remaining from the last time the market crashed. I love visiting various and sundry financial boards; the amount of information you can ferret out is staggering. Consider **The Motley Fool** at http://www.fool.com/—you will not only see a rich suite of research tools and advice, but also uncover a thriving community in which virtually every aspect of financial planning and stock investing is discussed. No matter what stock-savvy level you're at, you can always locate resources that will assist you in making your financial decisions.

If your experience with the Internet begins and ends with stocks, you have a firm foundation now for finding employees online. You're familiar with searching for financial quotes; you can now search for résumés instead. You've researched the background of various companies in preparation for investing; it's a simple matter to take these skills and apply them to considering some of the many career/job sites that are on the Internet. You might have set up an account in which all of your financial transactions are stored; with Internet recruiting, you might invest in a service that tracks all of your job orders, the people who have responded to your résumé, and more. You have the basic skills already—now all you have to do is apply them to this new venture.

Day Trading—*Did you know that many job seekers will search for employment opportunities during the day while working at their current position?*

Networking, Classmates, Personals, and Chat

One of the fascinating aspects of the Internet is the anonymity it affords to any and all. Many sites now exist that are dedicated to bringing together people from your past such as **Alumni** at http://www.alumni.net/, **ClassMates** at http://www.classmates.com/, and **Kiss** at http://www.kiss.com/, as well as professionals from your present like **Industry Insite** at http://www.industryinsite.com/, shown in Figure 1.4. These places are very enticing for Internet surfers. Have you ever engaged in AOL's Instant Messaging or ICQ, or perhaps participated in an online chat? The premise is simple—you merely type in your name and click "Chat" or select a person in your contact list and send them a message. It's a real-time version of multiple e-mail.

ICQ and Instant Messaging can be beneficial for business relationships. Every time that I'm online, my customers who have my ICQ number know they can contact me with their questions. This gives them the security of knowing that I'm always

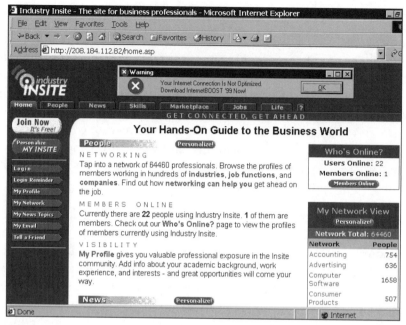

Figure 1.4: Industry Insite is only one site dedicated to professionals' networking.

available when needed. For example, if my clients all of a sudden have a burning need to know how to pump up their job post, they just have to "beep" me online, and I'm on the task at hand.

I See Who?—*ICQ is one of the most useful business tools you can use for staying in real-time touch with your customers (assuming you are always online). It allows clients to "beep" you when they see you are online, enabling you to instantly respond to their questions.*

Is ICQ or Instant Messaging or chats something with which you are familiar? If so, you're well grounded in being able to engage in online dialogues with potential employees, and in knowing how to search or browse for interesting conversations. This is a skill you can then apply when browsing résumés or actively installing a "call me about employment opportunities" button on your Web site.

Travel

One of the most popular uses of the Internet today is scheduling one's travel. There are many, many ways to do this. Virtually all airlines will have an interactive Web site available where you can schedule your flights, rent a car, choose a hotel, and more. Another breed of travel site has emerged, one that gives the customer the ability to compare different fares from many airlines. **Travelocity** at http://www.travelocity.com/

and **Expedia** at http://www.expedia.com/ have destination guides to help visitors make travel decisions, direct links to vacation spots and cruises, fare comparisons, and much more. When you use sites like the previous, *you're actively involved with researching your own agenda.* You know the qualities of the flights or vacations you need—you know when you have to leave, what kind of location you'd enjoy the most, the types of accommodations that would make your time off the most memorable. You're in control of finding the best resources for your needs.

Sherlock Holmes, I Presume?—*It's quite easy to locate industry-niche career and resource sites at which your future employees can be found. It might require some detective skills and logical deductions. Luckily, search engines and other valuable Web sites make this a simple process to undertake.*

If you've done any of the above, you've already learned some excellent skills that are the basis of any successful Internet recruiting campaign. One of the key components for low-cost or free recruiting on the Internet involves actively searching out the best sites for not just plain job-seekers, but people actively looking for careers in *your* industry. These sites, as you'll see later, are plentiful, but you have to know how to uncover them. And once you find them, you'll have the opportunity to decide upon the best possible ways of using them.

Like everything else in this world, travel can be quite annoying and cumbersome. If you're already familiar with sites like Travelocity, you might also be aware of **Ticked.com** at http://www.ticked.com/, depicted in Figure 1.5. This marvelous site is for "ticked-off travelers" and contains goodies on easing business travel like rating available services, providing tips and tricks for discounted fares, and the like. It's a pretty sure bet that if a provider knows it will be discussed and evaluated on another site, it will try to stay on its toes a tad more. Sites that provide knowing commentary can act as incentives for providers to ensure things go as smoothly as possible.

The same thing, you'll discover, holds true for the business world. **Vault.com** at http://www.vault.com/, for example, has thousands of unofficial employee message boards in which both employees and other professionals will vocally express their opinions (quite often, most voraciously). And **Fortune Magazine** at http://www.fortune.com/ has a series of bulletin boards that allow for people to discuss the best companies to work for, what companies are favoring in-state residents only, and the like. Like the travel commentary site, the main thrust for these Web sites is to provide a forum for individuals like you and me to openly debate and discuss the pros and cons of various companies. Depending upon who's posting, these sites can give you a good insider's view on what it's really like to work for a corporation.

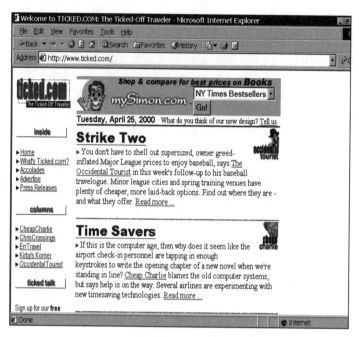

Figure 1.5: Ticked.com broadcasts opinionated commentary; other career sites do as well.

Research

One of the most beneficial aspects of the Internet is the ability to research virtually anything under the sun. Have you ever used it in this fashion? Perhaps you've gone to a search engine like **AltaVista** at http://www.altavista.com/ or directory like **Yahoo!** at http://www.yahoo.com/ and searched for Broadway tickets, Barry Manilow, or MP3. That's researching on the Internet! Depending upon your searching skills, this can be an excellent, effective way of hunting down your quarry online.

One such example could be the following. You've received an unexpected refund from the federal government, and decide to spend that money on a killer sound system. You can visit **Google** at http://www.google.com/ and search for stereo comparisons. You might be returned sites like **SoundStage** at http://www.soundstage.com/, where you'll find reviewers' choices for stereo equipment, and **Stereo Review's** *Sound and Vision* magazine at http://www.soundandvisionmag.com/, where you'll uncover buyer's tips. These sites can give you some excellent ideas and advice about what to look for, within your price range. Once you have this information firmly internalized, you're now an educated consumer who can shop with confidence. Your next step would be to return to Google and search for price comparison—this should return sites that will assist you in comparing prices from numerous sites. Some Web sites returned might be:

EvenBetter
http://www.evenbetter.com/

Price-Watch
http://www.pricewatch.com/

PriceGrabber
http://www.pricegrabber.com/

There, you'll discover rebates, best deals, and other money-stretching opportunities.

Faster, Cheaper, Better—*The Internet allows you to search out retail bargains that will save you time, money, and effort when purchasing. This action can be applied to Internet recruiting; you can also uncover career or job sites that will return you better candidates faster than others.*

While you were accomplishing the above, you might not have realized that you were doing extensive Internet researching. You had a goal in mind, and you undertook searching out resources to help you achieve that goal in as rapid and cost-effective a manner as possible.

Think about other reasons for researching on the Internet. Have you ever needed to find industry information for your business? Buy Broadway tickets? Check out the local *TV Guide* schedule? See what restaurants were located close by your home? The Internet can be an incredible tool that will slice through winding ways of confusion and provide direct guides to the information you need the most.

All of the previous can be applied to low-cost or free online Internet recruiting. Consider our first example; instead of looking for stereo components, perhaps you need to hire Java programmers. In this case, you would research where these people can be found, where the specific Java-oriented job sites are posted, and how you can make the highest return possible from your time invested on the Internet. And yes, you can even find free resources that will aid you in evaluating the torrents of information you'll uncover—EarPerk! at http://www.earperk.com/ is a site that provides comparison shopping for the job-seeking industry.

News

One of the most common resources you'll uncover on the Internet is just plain and simple news. Local news! National news! Industry news! News news! News is something that's dynamic and changing every hour, every minute … it's content that, when installed on a Web site, gives visitors reasons to return again and again.

You've probably seen it on just about every site you've visited. Let's take a typical Internet destination—the portal site, **Yahoo!** at http://www.yahoo.com/. One of the selections you'll notice on the main page is a link for **News**—it will bring you to http://dailynews.yahoo.com/. There, you'll see links for business news, entertainment news, technology news … news about anything and everything you could imagine. But it's not that they created all the news content themselves; many of the articles are reprinted from the Associated Press, ABC, and other venues. Here is a very important quality about news on the Internet—there are several Great Big Mother Of All News-Related Sites that will license their content to subscribers. This means that the wheel isn't being reinvented twice—companies are willing to pay to include quality visitor-attracting material on their site. And not all providers of such services charge big bucks—**Moreover** at http://www.moreover.com/ provides headlines that you can integrate into your Web site for free.

Valuable Free Content—*Dynamic, valuable content is something that compels visitors to return to sites again and again. You can find several sites that will deliver free headlines for your own use; this could be most beneficial in attracting employees.*

Think how this can apply to your own Internet recruiting efforts. Why would different Web sites want to include relevant news? Because that's one component of quality sites that attract visitors and compel them to stick around (while possibly exposing said visitors to various and sundry advertisements, another application of e-commerce). Now, let's consider special industry sites like those for the banking profession. Do you think bankers would find banking-related news that's constantly being updated of interest? The providers of such sites certainly do, and that's why you'll see many industry-related stories and news headlines also appearing on professional organization sites, trade association sites, and special-interest sites. The more reasons that a particular Web site can give for targeted audiences to visit, *the higher the probability that any job or advertisement you post on such a site will be seen by your future employees.*

The Internet and Recruiting

Now that I've given you some examples of how you can apply the knowledge you already might have towards Internet recruiting, let me tie it into your present-day business. As you can see, *Internet recruiting is simply one more way of using the Internet for business-related purposes.* The people whom you want to hire are out there—your quest is to find them in an effective fashion. No matter in what area you need to hire, you will be able to uncover specific sites where your future employees have gathered.

Early in 2000, I gave a RISE seminar down south about effective Internet recruiting. I well remember an insurance recruiter who attended and declared to me in front of my class, "Barbara, it seems to me that Internet recruiting is all just hype! My kind of people don't build computers, they don't use the job boards, they just use the Internet for business, if that. So how can the traditional means of Internet recruiting be effective?"

I love questions like that, because that student was right on the money. Depending upon the industry in which you are hiring, you have specific, different options you can use. Because techies and nerds like me built the Internet, you'll have a much easier time locating these types of professionals because *they leave their mark all over the Internet.* Nontechnical professionals, however, have starkly different experiences and user habits when online—chances are their favorite sites are the consumer-oriented places like **America Online** at http://www.aol.com/. Luckily, sites like that have a simple interface to search for people who are actively seeking new employment. But even in this instance, you'll see that more and more specialty career niche sites are being created, such as **4InsuranceJobs** at http://www.4insurancejobs.com/ or **The Insurance Job Bank**, housed at http://www.iiin.com/.

AOL Free Résumés—*AOL, one of the most popular destination sites on the Internet, has direct links to their members' pages where you can find specific résumés, communities, and more.*

One of the most important things to remember about recruiting on the Internet is often, *you'll have to actively search for resources you can use.* Advertising on the Super Bowl or in bus terminals or on sandy beaches during Spring Break costs quite a lot of money, yet that's where many of today's society get their ideas about what job sites really are. You've heard of Monster.com, you've heard of Hotjobs.com ... chances are, you probably haven't heard of **Engineering Central** at http://www.engcen.com/, or the Oracle site **Orafans** at http://www.orafans.com/, or the steam professional site **Boiler Room** at http://www.boilerroom.com/ shown in Figure 1.6. Yet these sites are niche areas where you could definitely find professionals in that industry who are actively looking for new employment. There are literally thousands of such Web sites available on the Internet if you learn how to uncover them.

Another key fact to keep in mind is that many things are negotiable. Thus, if you come across any job site that looks like it might be useful, but costs money, you should always be able to ask for and receive a trial run. You might run into a salesperson who tries to convince you to buy more than what you require—always be certain to ask pertinent questions to determine if it would be money well spent.

Figure 1.6: Many industry niche sites have free career centers.

When You Shouldn't Recruit on the Internet

Yes, there are times you shouldn't recruit on the Internet. Not everyone is comfortable with this new environment—some people shun computers in general because of their, well, newfangledness. And that's okay. I'm a big fan about being comfortable with all aspects of one's business. If you view anything electronic with a large dose of negativity and disapproval, you probably won't see the kinds of successes you deserve with Internet recruiting.

Perhaps your business is still done in a paper and pencil mode. Remember, effective recruiting on the Internet requires the use of a computer at the very least—you need to become comfortable sending and receiving e-mail, downloading résumés, posting jobs, trying different searching techniques, and more. If this is simply not your nature, don't waste time trying to do the recruiting yourself—you can probably find more productive uses of your time dealing with the day-to-day aspects of your business. Hire a recruiter instead, or assign a computer-friendly person the task of finding your employees.

Finding people online, of course, is only one step. Other steps include:

- Defining who you need
- Creating a killer job post

- Assigning someone to receive résumés
- Broadcasting your needs to a targeted audience
- Reviewing the received résumés
- Ensuring star candidates don't fall through the cracks

Some individuals, quite simply, find the above tedious. And that's fine. Even people who are computer-phobic can call a local newspaper and put in a classifieds job post—quite often, those ads will find their way online at the newspaper's Web site. That's a great example of Internet recruiting without involving the computer at all!

No matter what you choose in regard to your online recruiting efforts, you can always custom-tailor a solution that meets your needs specifically. Not everyone has to jump on the Internet bandwagon. Those who do, however, will discover an incredible resource that's just waiting to help you out.

Ready to see what now awaits you?

Is It a Bird, a Plane?

Picture the following. A sporting event. A commercial. A topic. What is being advertised? Is it the ab-roller? Luxury cruises? Pokémon?

No. It's one of the first dot-com commercials that appeared on the Super Bowl, that for **Monster.com** at http://www.monster.com/.

Monster.com? I beg your pardon?

Unless you've been living in your 4×4 in the desolate snows of the Alaskan interior plains, you've somehow been exposed via commercials, radio ads, magazine reports, or Internet articles to the biggest career site of them all. Monster.com.

Big Business—*Internet recruiting nowadays is one of the fastest-growing industries. Corporations will spend millions of dollars simply to get your attention.*

When you think about the premise, it's quite swimming, actually. Thousands of job seekers will submit their résumé (for free, of course), and thousands of employers (like you) can pay a fee to access them.

And then it hits you like Godzilla kick-boxing. Hey! Your company needs to hire folks! Maybe you've just received a more substantial budget for your department's operations. Perhaps your last bank teller chose to quit after winning big on the stock market. It could be that your project is floundering, and your boss is desperately in need of fresh new talent to blast energy into your team (a healthy team environment is one of your most precious business strengths).

Because your idea of nirvana most likely does *not* include learning about recruiting sites, you instead mosey on over to several of the large job boards (what do you have to lose?) to see if that's a solution. And if you have an extremely large budget set aside for recruiting, it certainly could be.

In a word, it's expensive. Really expensive.

Now, keep in mind that there are dozens and dozens of well-marketed, extremely popular job board sites, each of them proclaiming "thou shalt find thine employees here first," as well as literally hundreds of smaller sites, all clamoring for your business. But some of them can cost more than a vacation at Disney World. So what do you do?

You Never Have to Overpay—*You should never have to overpay when looking to recruit on the Internet. You should always be able to find low-cost or free alternatives for posting jobs and hiring where your candidate population is residing.*

Elevating Your Bottom Line

Remember, the more time you endure minus a talented employee, *the more money you will lose.* Sad, but true. Why? Consider—every day you'll have to deal with:

Employee morale. If you're minus a person, the rest of your employees will feel the pinch of additional work. Unhappy employees lead to decreased productivity.

Increased management responsibilities. Not enough people means having to verify even more closely that work is being accomplished and projects are on schedule.

Decreased customer satisfaction. Lose key support or members of your team, and that's one less person available to deal with customer interaction (customers, of course, can be your fellow supervisors from different departments as well).

Thus, ideally you want to find and hire your new employee as fast as possible to boost your bottom line. The question now becomes, do you have to declare bankruptcy to achieve this?

Does the World Wrestling Federation have to dress up in ballet tights to attract viewers?

Speeding Up Your Success

Of course not! Because you can be (drum roll please) Powered! By! The! Internet! Ooooooooooooooooh! By now, you've probably heard of Internet hype. Make friends! Conduct business! Find a life partner! Trade stocks! Buy Beany Babies! Chat! Wait a second! Was that "Conduct business"?

Indeed. The Internet has enabled businesses to increase their profitability dramatically. By providing an easy-to-use medium such as point-and-click (I came, I saw, I clicked!), customers and businesses are processing more and more transactions every day. *Customers and businesses.* What about business to business?

Consider one of the tried-and-true ways of finding employees—that of posting ads in your local newspaper. Did you know that the majority of newspapers have an online presence, and your paper ad can also be displayed on the Internet? And that depending upon the industry, a single ad now has orders of magnitude more visibility in this fashion?

Think about it. The best way to find your employees fast is to get the word out as rapidly as possible, to as many interested (read: targeted) professionals as possible. And as the Internet operates almost instantaneously (post a message to a forum, and boom! it's there for the world to see), you can take advantage of this speed and reach out to your desired audience at a rate much faster than traditional "put an ad in the classifieds and see what happens" mode.

Faster Than a Speeding Bullet—When you advertise on the Internet, your ad is broadcast out to the world incredibly fast.

This is rather awesome. What other benefits can you derive from using the Internet to attract employees?

Advantages of Internet Recruiting

Who knows your company best? Who has the best handle on the needs of your own department? You guessed it—you do.

Think about it. If you are an accounts payable professional, and you need to hire another accounts payable professional, chances are you have a pretty decent understanding of the particular characteristics your position entails. If your boss has told you to hire an in-house sales rep fast, you probably know the company's goals by heart, the territories involved, the perks your company offers to new hires, and the like.

Take advantage of that! Along with considering delegating hiring responsibilities, you can participate in industry forums (forums that benefit you personally and directly in your own career growth), develop a name and reputation for yourself (and that's not difficult at all to achieve), and encourage other professionals in the industry to contact you for job opportunities. Now *that* certainly would look fantastic on your *own* end-of-the-year employee review.

***Your Personal Benefits**—When you find and hire needed employees fast and save money in the process, you yourself look good for your future performance reviews.*

I cannot emphasize the following enough. Not only can you recruit on the Internet, but you can greatly increase your marketability as a savvy industry professional, simply by taking advantage of all the free resources and discounts that abound.

But before you jump onto the computer and zoom online, ask yourself: What exactly are the benefits and negatives involved with Internet recruiting?

Incredible Positives

Finding employees for your positions on the Internet will open the doors for possibilities you probably haven't considered.

Free

Would you believe you can recruit for free on the Internet? You don't need to pay thousands of dollars for expensive services, you don't need to shell out your vacation money to locate the talent you desperately require—you don't need to spend an arm and a leg and a left toenail to find your future employees online.

***Zero Cost**—Done well, you can recruit for free on the Internet. You don't have to pay money. You do, however, have to expend time to sow the seeds of your success.*

The Internet is in general a free medium. It doesn't cost you anything to send e-mail, participate in forums, answer questions from your community, and the like. Quite often, you'll discover many sites where your employee base gathers, such as user groups or industry niche sites, where it is free to post your open positions as shown in Figure 1.7. *Sometimes you can even peruse résumés for free too.* When you think about it, it makes perfect sense; millions of people are on the Internet; these individuals participate in online organizations and trade associations, put up their own free Web page that quite often includes their résumé, and the like. They certainly wouldn't be there if it cost money to participate!

Figure 1.7: FlipDog lets you search résumés and post jobs for free.

When I was actively recruiting years ago, the only money I ever spent was to belong to a recruiter's organization, **Recruiters Online** at http://www.recruitersonline.com/, which provided an excellent résumé database, splits opportunities (discussed in Chapter 21, "The Benefits of Recruiters", and free job posting. That's it! I didn't subscribe to fee-based services; I didn't pay out large lumps of cash to uncover résumés; I simply visited the sites where my candidates would be and proceeded from there. One of my biggest triumphs was locating an NT systems administrator mailing list, and seeing an ad of mine broadcast out for free to the entire membership database. That wonderful event resulted solely because of the relation-ships I had created; money had nothing to do with it.

Free Résumés—*Depending upon how you network, you can almost always either find résumés for free or post your jobs for free. Some sites even actively encourage that, because it increases their own traffic (and more traffic means they can charge more money for advertising).*

Remember our earlier discussions about why people surf the Internet, and how it can be related to recruiting? So many things are being offered for free nowadays, and you can uncover excellent resources like free job postings or discussion groups that will aid you in finding your future employees.

Profit

When you recruit effectively on the Internet, you're saving money. Instead of paying thousands of dollars for a job service, you'll be taking advantage of all the free and low-cost opportunities that are available. That's money saved that you can plow right back into your budget and business.

Think what you could do with it. You can:

- Put the money toward research and development.
- Add it to the salary of prospective employees to entice them to consider your career opportunity.
- Dedicate it towards advertising costs in the marketplace.
- Pay for researching of your customer base.
- Add more visitor-appealing functions to your Web site.

And possibly most important of all, you could add to your personal end-of-the-year review how you saved your company a sizeable amount of money. This would look wonderful when your time for promotion and review comes up.

Speed

Depending upon where you post a job description on the Internet, it can be picked up by many other services and travel the globe in an instant. Don't forget that the Internet is international; anyone with Internet connectivity can view country-specific sites with ease. Remember Tienamen Square back in 1989? That was one of the first instances of wars being fought with faxes and e-mails—events would happen and then be broadcast back almost immediately via the Internet.

Blink of an Eye—Your job posts can travel 'round the world within hours. And if you post a job to a jobs-related mailing list, it could be received within minutes. This means your visibility grows in leaps and bounds.

Perhaps you'll uncover a mailing list dedicated to professionals with an interest in your particular industry. Many of these career-specific lists exist—MBAs, technical programmers, advertising execs, heck, just about anyone can sign up to receive job broadcasts via e-mail. Just check out **Vault.com** at http://www.vault.com/—that's only one example of the resources that abound. And if you post to one of those lists, your job opportunity will be seen immediately (well, as immediately as the recipient opens the e-mail) by the people who count—professionals with the skills you need.

One way to increase the benefits of this speed is to already have in place a network of people you can contact when you receive word to hire another professional. I know of a supervisor who, whenever he needs to hire, simply sends out word to the hundreds of colleagues and professionals he's gathered over the past decade in the industry. These people know him, they trust him—they love helping him. And help, in this case, is merely forwarding his e-mail to fellow professionals who might be interested in what he has to offer.

24x7

Does your business have a Web site? Are your career opportunities highlighted on that Web site? Do you provide opportunities for visitors to submit their e-mail for future contact, either by an electronic magazine or a broadcast of exciting new positions that are available? Do you showcase exactly why working for your company is the best option for a professional to consider? If not, you're missing out on a tremendous usage of your Internet space.

Think about it. Your Web site assures you of continuous, 24×7 visibility where people can learn all about your business, what you sell, and what services you offer. Potential employees at any hour can uncover all the compelling reasons why they should inquire about being employed by your company. Skillfully done, your career section will be a valuable tool in attracting the kinds of people you need to propel your business to the next level. And the effort required of you is nil—after the pages are up, that is! Not everyone works normal hours; some people are online during all hours of the night or the weekend and dedicate that time to searching for new positions. Obviously, you don't want to be at the phone 24 hours a day in hopes that a future employee comes knocking at your door. Your Web site can be an excellent resource that will do all the soft-selling of your career opportunities 'round the clock. It's all done in the background while you are concentrating upon managing your own career and building your business.

Always On—*Your Web site is available 24 hours a day to show visitors all of your offerings, ensuring that you have at least an hour or two to yourself to sleep at night.*

Reputation

If you decide to implement the epitome of Internet recruiting and become part of your customer's community (which isn't difficult at all), your reputation will develop faster than a desert blooms after the first rain shower. It's human nature to want to know and trust the folks with whom one is considering employment.

Let's say that you're looking for local financial professionals. Is there a town Web site? It's easy enough to find one—simply visit **USA City Link** at http://www.usacitylink.com/ to browse your specific state and town. Once you uncover such a site, you can check to see if there are:

- Forums available for the neighboring counties
- A section dedicated to employment classifieds
- Job fairs at your local colleges

If you become part of these communities and give advice or share your knowledge, your reputation naturally starts to grow via word of mouth. Your marketing is being done for you!

This is powerful stuff.

Perhaps instead you are familiar with technology and are looking for computer experts in your field. There is a plethora of newsgroups (special-interest groups) found at **Deja** at http://www.deja.com/ and online forums at **ForumOne** at http://www.forumone.com/ where you can actively participate and become known as a valued community member. Once you're perceived as a member, your overall reputation is enhanced.

Who Loves Ya?—*The Internet allows your reputation to spread like wildfire. And by participating in forums and discussions where your customers or employees are found, you are engaging in the free advertising of your services.*

Of course, it can go both ways. If one habitually cheats one's customers or otherwise engages in nonprofitable activities, that kind of reputation will expand faster than a four-alarm fire begun in a match factory. More on this under "Not-So-Incredible Negatives" below.

Ease of Use

One of the most valuable characteristics of Internet recruiting is the ease of use. No matter what your comfort level is, you can custom-tailor your own recruiting activities. If you sometimes find yourself just too busy to ferret out that new employee, you can find recruiters to do the work for you in many places, including **RecruitersOnline** at http://www.recruitersonline.com/, **TopEchelon** at http://www.topechelon.com/, or **NAPS** at http://ww.napsweb.org/, to name a few.

If you want to dabble in finding your employees online, you can whip up a compelling job post and advertise it for free in the employment newsgroups, your own company site, some niche sites, and the **Yahoo! Classifieds** at http://classifieds.yahoo.com/.

If you want to improve your overall sales and profit, you can become part of your business community by taking advantage of local and state organizations/associations, trade associations, user groups, newspaper sites, colleges and universities, e-mail lists, ISPs like AOL and CompuServe, town sites, forums and bulletin boards, personal sites, online magazines, and several other resources, all described throughout this book.

Tailored Comfort Level—*You can always find the perfect level of Internet usage that suits you personally. You want to derive benefits from Internet recruiting, not extreme pain and frustration.*

It's all up to you. What about the amount of money you can spend? It can range from thousands in job board fees to virtually zero if you post your jobs at free sites. Even better, the communications can be simple too. Applicants can e-mail their résumés to you. (Make sure, of course, to have a virus scanner like McAfee installed first!) You can simply store them on your computer and view them when necessary. If paper copies are required, merely print them when needed.

I'm a big proponent for individuals never to be pushed into doing more than they feel comfortable with. After all, *this is your own valuable time you are spending*—you don't want to feel pressured to keep up with the Joneses. Maximize your returns and benefits.

Community Riches

Finding employees online is not an esoteric art. It's simple. Consider the following: you've probably been online for reasons other than looking to hire people. Maybe you were checking your stocks at **DLJ Direct** at http://www.dljdirect.com/, buying books from Amazon.com, watching reruns of the Super Bowl commercials at **Adcentric** at http://www.adcentric.com/, or the like.

Don't you think your potential employees are doing the same thing? They're online at their interests, too. *So all you have to do* is discover where your brand of hires (i.e., your desired community) are congregating, and ensure your message is put forth in a netiquette-friendly, effective fashion. That's not complicated at all—financial professionals hang out at financial boards, industry professionals will find trade associations or magazine sites that deal with their specific needs, other potential employees are often located at social sites, and so forth.

Now more than ever, Internet recruiting is marketing and advertising. There are literally thousands of potential employees, thousands of open jobs, an astonishing number of career-related sites ... how can you convince the ideal professional that your job offering will deliver above and beyond what everyone else's will? In other words, how do you stand head and shoulders above the rest in desirability?

Networking with your community will achieve that and much more; not only will you be visible to your intended audience, but your future employees themselves will spread the word about your great services to their colleagues, too.

Recruiting Is Advertising*—Successful recruiting uses many popular advertising techniques including emotional "punch" words, evocative imagery, and more.*

Not-So-Incredible Negatives

Yes, it is possible to shoot yourself in the foot when recruiting on the Internet. Always be sure to avoid:

Spam

Unsolicited e-mail like "Earn 5 Million Dollars in Three Minutes!" and "Golf Ball Secrets" and the like are viewed extremely negatively on the Internet. Alas, there are no signs that such annoyances will disappear any time soon.

When you post your jobs online, you might receive offers of "highly targeted e-mail lists" of "people who really want to hear from you!" Run away, as fast as you can, whenever you receive such an offer. Unless you gather names yourself, you can never be assured from where e-mail addresses are harvested. Sending the wrong message to the wrong individual can result in your Internet account being closed down (yes, I am quite serious about this).

Never Bulk E-mail*—Unless you have gathered the names yourself via opt-in marketing methods, never ever send bulk e-mail. It can ruin your Internet endeavors, cause you to lose your Internet account, and contribute towards your name being smeared in a most unpleasant fashion.*

Reputation

Your reputation can be dragged through the mud if you treat your employees poorly. Check out **Vault.com** at http://www.vault.com/—you'll see unofficial message boards from both employees of companies and individuals who are considering careers there, as shown in Figure 1.8.

Always be aboveboard when searching for employees on the Internet. Recruiters encounter this problem often—boards like **RealRates** at http://www.realrates.com/ and **Contractor's Employment Daily** at http://www.cedaily.com/ encourage the discussion of both excellent headhunters and those who resemble The Creature from the Black Lagoon on a bad-hair day.

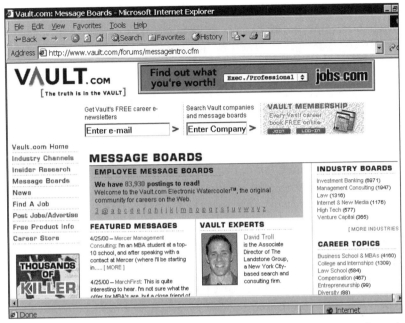

Figure 1.8: Vault.com has thousands of unofficial employee message boards.

Quick Fix vs. Long Term

The best way to achieve the maximum benefits from your Internet recruiting is to view it as a long-term proposition. Certainly, you can take the short-term steps such as creating and broadcasting dynamite job posts, exactly when you need new employees; I'll show you how to do that shortly. Permit me, though, to suggest another alternative. Wouldn't it be heaven on earth if, every time you required a new employee, you could choose from stacks of qualified professionals already at your fingertips? People already interested in what you have to offer?

Because your Web site is up 24×7, people can locate your business at any hour of the day (assuming they know where it is). What if you included a compelling career section about the benefits of working for you, one that led visitors to submit their résumé directly to you for employment consideration? Even if you aren't hiring at that particular time, you've taken the first step towards creating a database of interested professionals that will be available the *next time* an opening occurs.

Don't have a Web site? Not to despair. Is your business physically located within a building? If so, put up flyers in obvious areas that outline all of the benefits you have to offer. Remember, you can find corresponding activities offline to just about any method of Internet recruiting you'll uncover online. By making it easy for visitors to contact you about employment opportunities, you've simplified your own business life. And you can take that one step further—create a communities section on your Web site that is dedicated to your customers. Including an opt-in newsletter gives you an excellent method for emphasizing your name and brand in the minds of your customers and potential employees.

Career Section—*Putting up a career section on your Web site gives you a great opportunity to showcase how wonderful working for your company can be.*

Keeping your business healthy and on target requires a long-term growth plan. By starting your personal business/customer community now, you're laying the groundwork for healthy future achievements.

Future achievements. That reminds me:

What Is the Solution You Are Seeking?

Don't tell me, to hire someone. You don't just hire someone because of the undying thrill of actually, well, hiring someone. *You're looking for employees to create a solution.*

It could be that one of your sales folk quit, and you need to hire a person to round out your team. Perhaps you're preparing for the Christmas rush, and you have a temporary need for more peoplepower. Maybe you're an Internet entrepreneur or start-up, and you have decided to branch out your community reach. Possibly you realize you need another full-time programmer to allow you to meet your customer's schedule.

Reasons to Hire—*You don't hire just to hire or for the sheer pleasure of watching your business's hard-earned cash go bye-bye—you hire someone to solve pressing company problems and to meet business goals.*

What *is* the solution you are seeking? I'm serious here. It's so easy to become entangled in all the wonders you'll uncover on the Internet—focus is crucial! Are you looking for a long-term employee? A contractor? Someone who can program their way out of Houdini's castle? An MBA who is bilingual? A college graduate who isn't yet jaded by corporate politics? A CEO who can take a start-up from icicles to IPOs? Knowing the solution you are seeking is only one piece of the puzzle, of course; once you have that fully understood, you're in a better position to see how you can translate that need into something that benefits your future employees.

Everyone, you, me, the shoe salesperson down the street, everyone has a tendency to view opportunities with the WIIFM syndrome. What's in it for me! You *know* what is the solution *you* are seeking. How can you now take that concept and put it into terms that appeals to your future employees? *In other words, if they consider your position, what's in it for them?*

WIIFM—*Answering the What's In It For Me question simplifies your recruiting. All candidates want to know how a future employment position will benefit their own needs and goals. If you tailor your job advertisement to answer this question, you've already increased the probability of successful Internet recruiting.*

If you need a bigger sales force, you can offer future employees a great teamworking atmosphere and higher commissions. Do you believe in investing in your employee's future? Offering certification training for technical individuals is a very attractive feature. Want to retain your top executives? CEOs get offered the benefits of stock. Hiring for the Christmas rush season? Offer a discount for your employees. See where I'm going here? *Once you know what might turn on your future employees, you can include that information in your job posts online.* Again—a good portion of Internet recruiting is marketing. Marketing, marketing, marketing. Marketing! It's showing professionals how their life will be improved by accepting your open positions.

The great news is that's rather easy to do. Are you ready? Let's go!

Chapter Two

Know Your Goals

When you need to hire a new person for your company, generally the first goal you'll consider is just that: bringing a new person onboard. But consider the following: searching for that new individual takes time (sometimes a lot of time!). Thus, another goal might be hiring someone within a prescribed number of days. Or saving your company money by exploring alternatives to the big job boards. Or getting your production schedule back on track.

But to hire someone, you'll have to convince him or her to consider your opportunities. And given the thousands of competitors you probably have, you'll need to showcase just why your offer is so desirable. Before you jump onto the Internet to search to your heart's content, let's first go over some basic goals that will ramp up your success ratio admirably.

Maximizing Your Results

As a busy professional, one thing you certainly want to ensure is maximizing your returns from the time you spend online prospecting for future employees. After all, you don't want to dedicate hours and hours to this endeavor, only to give up in frustration because you didn't know all of the techniques to zoom directly to your targeted hires. Not only that; if you're a corporate Human Resources professional, much of your time is already devoured by putting out political fires, concentrating upon current employee retention, and other crucial business matters. Becoming focused is of paramount importance.

It is so easy to become lost when recruiting on the Internet. So many tempting resources might be unearthed, so many neat opportunities to pause and read entertaining information, so many places to discover why the stock market is crashing—searching on the Internet really *does* require discipline. You don't want to waste your precious time. I know I certainly don't—I'm a very busy professional myself. And alas, there's only 26 hours in a day (at least it certainly seems that way!).

One way that I've found to structure my time spent online is to break it down into manageable chunks. For example, every morning I wake up, roll out of bed, roll down the hall, and somehow manage to collide with my chair to start my day. After making that pot of all-blessed coffee with a double shot of caffeine, I'll methodically visit the sites upon which my business success depends. I participate in several forums to ensure my name is known by my customers; back when I was a recruiter, I'd use this time to scan incoming résumés, create new job posts, and actively search for new and better ways to network. When you create a schedule for yourself, it makes your online searching much, much easier.

Hocus Focus—*Always have a clear goal of your recruiting needs—it will save you time and assist you in finding the right resources fast.*

Your time management is not the only important aspect of finding employees on the Internet, however. The Internet allows for anyone, big or small, to compete for your precious attention. This could be the attention of buyers, sellers, mothers, children, boat racers, brokers, food fanciers, managers, CEOs—anyone. There's a cartoon about the Internet that features a doggie clicking on a mouse; the caption reads, "When you're on the Internet, nobody knows that you're a dog." This fact of life plays heavily in the online business world; you could be a one-person band yet possess a Web site that gives visitors the impression that they are dealing with a large corporation. It's a world without laws; initially, you never really know if people (and businesses) are who they say they are. Be that as it may, there are still excellent opportunities to home in on the people you'd like to hire in as efficient a manner as possible. To do so, however, requires that you take into account the following facts of life.

You're Only One Employer Out Of …

You only have to mosey on over to **Headhunter.net** at http://www.headhunter.net/, depicted in Figure 2.1, or any of the hundreds of career sites available, to see the incredible volume of companies vying to hire that one perfect candidate. Talk about competition! Future employees can pick and choose from thousands upon thousands of opportunities. How will you successfully compete against all of these other entities?

One of the most important exercises you can undertake is to understand *why* people should want to work in your business. The employment market is so tight that some companies unroll the red carpet in order to attract the best and the brightest.

Standing Out—*Thousands of other companies try to hire the same people you do. You need to figure out how to stand out from the rest of your industry.*

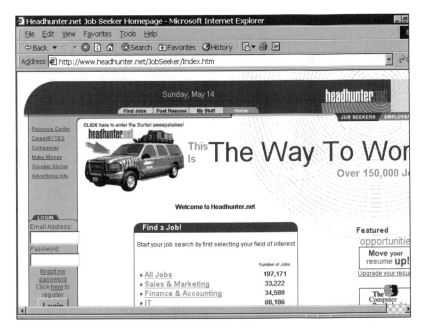

Figure 2.1: Thousands of employers can be found at hundreds of career sites, including Headhunter.net.

Some instances include:

Recreation. Some companies will close shop for an afternoon and take their employees out to the movies. Others will hold group lunches, offer certifications for employees to take their spouses out for dinner, or encourage participation in extracurricular activities. I once heard of a company that paid for all of its employees to attend several major sports events.

Material. Other companies will offer co\mputers for employees to take home— Ford Motor, for example, in February of 2000 offered free Hewlett-Packard computers and printers and cut-rate Internet access to its 350,000 employees worldwide. Some companies offer access to corporate vacation homes, and other material perks. One of the most interesting material perks I've heard of is Interwoven's offer of a two-year lease on a brand-new BMW Z3 sports car.

Environment. Work is only one-third of a person's life. Nowadays, the trend is moving towards providing as much comfort in the working environment as possible. Some companies are now including recreation rooms, onsite health and wellness centers, education and daycare reimbursement, ergonomic chairs and desks, free coffee, and other environmental ideas that showcase the benefits their employees enjoy.

Why is there such emphasis being placed upon work environments and enticing professionals to become employed at choice corporations? I think it's because the Internet is powering a feeding frenzy in many of the companies you see online. Sometimes it seems that everyone wants to be on the cutting edge of innovation, and there's only so much talent that wants to move around.

Unusual perks are all around us today in the work environment. Merely visit **Monster.com** at http://www.monster.com/ and search for `perks`. When I tried this search, I came up with jobs that offered:

- Free parking
- Paid lunches
- "Bring your pet into work" days
- Ping pong
- Air hockey
- Company car
- Health club membership
- Flex hours
- Great view of Manhattan
- Cool office space
- Employee happy hours
- Transportation allowance
- Rooftop deck

Keep in mind why such things would be included in job posts. Not only do companies want to ensure that potential employees have the skills needed, they want to capture their attention by showcasing the *benefits the job will offer them* as depicted in Figure 2.2. (No longer can companies pick and choose from legions of desperate job seekers; today's market is a candidate's market, and quite often, they are the ones who drive the process.) And one of the best ways to do that is to take advantage of several Internet marketing techniques when showcasing why your company and your job opportunities stand out from the rest of humanity's.

Perks—*Perks don't have to cost a bundle—sometimes showcasing appreciation is enough. You can find ways to include valuable perks in your employment offerings.*

We'll cover more reasons why someone would like to work for you later in this chapter. The thing to keep in mind, however, is no matter what your competition is, you can always uncover pertinent reasons why future employees should consider you.

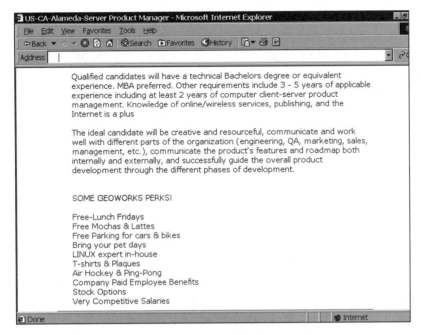

Figure 2.2: Sample of perks from an actual job advertisement.

You're Probably Not the Largest Software Company in the World

There's a very good probability that you are not the largest software company in the world, meaning you don't have billions and billions of dollars available to power up your hiring.

Maybe your company has less than ten people in total. Perhaps you're in a start-up mode, where you need to compensate future hires via the possibility of pre-IPO stock. How will you compete against the industry leaders? It is true—no matter how great your company might be, there will almost always be some company that seems bigger in size and scope. You needn't worry, however; not everyone is looking to work for the monoliths of the business world.

***TIP**—Not everyone yearns to work for corporate giants. Never be discouraged by the size of your competitors.*

Small companies might have the benefit of a more personal business atmosphere. Employees might find it easier and more inviting to drop on by the president's office to chat and say hello. Small companies also often don't have the level of bureaucratic quicksand that sucks out creativity and entrepreneurial tendencies as might their larger brethren. I can certainly vouch for that; long ago, back when wheels were square and I worked within a group from a large telecommunications firm, I had the unique experience of being a member of the Imanager team—a group of techies who had to keep the software build environment up, running, and ideally stable. Certainly, we were part of a larger corporate whole, but within our team we developed such a teamwork environment that nothing, even corporate politics, could disrupt our skills. Never before and never since did I ever have the honor and pleasure of being part of such a dynamic, nurturing team that simply made things happen; it was something indeed precious. That kind of atmosphere can be considered one of the greatest perks available.

Of course, the next position I had landed me in a group that made the movie *Kindergarten Cops* seem populated by PhDs in comparison. Ah well, these things happen.

When you showcase all of the compelling reasons for individuals to consider your company for employment, you don't have to worry about size, you don't have to worry about market share, you don't have to spend all of your revenue in advertisements emblazoned on the sides of jets. The world is so large that there should always be the kinds of professionals you want, looking for the types of opportunities and environment you offer.

Your Company Might Be Run by Idiots ...

It could be that frankly, you are a manager and your company is run by Dilbert's boss, yet you still need to find high-quality talent. Have you ever been in a situation where your boss couldn't manage his or her way out of a wet paper bag? And even worse—what if that was common knowledge? Idiot companies and idiot bosses are one of the most popular icons in today's culture; one only has to peruse **Dilbert** at http://www.dilbert.com/ or the **Lone Tyrant** at http://www.ddtmedia.com/lt/current.htm, shown in Figure 2.3, to see truly stunning displays of incompetence.

Be that as it may, still, you might need to find people fast. How will you compensate for unfounded (or even true) rumors? Before you start recruiting on the Internet, I want you to answer me one simple, tiny question.

Why *Should* People Want to Work for You?

I'm quite serious. What's so thrilling about that job you have to offer? Remember all of the points outlined; why *should* future employees want to give you their precious time and entrust their future to you? Think like a candidate; if you were actively searching for a position that your company offered, would you be compelled to explore it further? Or would you yawn, walk away, and look for greener pastures? Remember that the first introduction future employees have of you is generally your job advertisement or Web-site career section; you need to

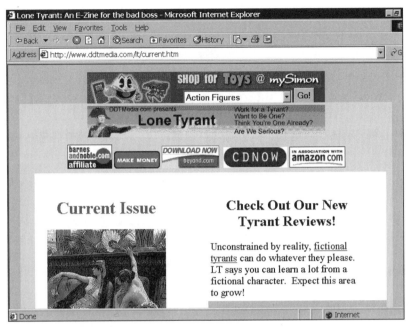

Figure 2.3: The Lone Tyrant is an e-zine dedicated to crummy bosses.

ensure that all the sterling reasons why people should work for you stand out more visible than a supernova.

It's something to think about, and something to crystallize *first in your mind* before you begin your online search. Once you have a firm grasp on what you have to offer, you are better prepared to deal with questions you might receive from professionals.

Quality of Life—*People can choose their work for reasons other than money, such as benefits, environment, location, and many more.*

Reasons why people would want to work for you might include

- Benefits
- Environment
- Family-friendly
- Training
- Location
- Diversity
- Dynamic environment
- Company reputation

These reasons are described as follows.

Benefits

Do you offer medical/dental? Vacation? A smashing 401K plan? Are your perks above and beyond the rest of the industry? If so, that's a powerful reason for someone to consider you. Perks go way beyond mere material offerings, however. Many companies are opening up to flexible work schedules, allowing employees to take off Friday afternoons or be home when their children arrive from school.

Focusing upon the family well-being can be a wonderful benefit. You don't have to be flush with cash, either, to incorporate benefits that will stop future employees dead in their tracks when they are picking and choosing from various employment offers. Is your business environment one in which "fun" is encouraged? Do you have a casual dress code? Does every department have a free coffee machine, complete with gourmet (or even instant) coffee? Now even more than ever, employees want companies to answer the WIIFM question—What's in it for me? Gone are the times when one could expect to work from cradle to grave at one specific corporation; professionals nowadays have to keep their skills sharpened constantly to meet new challenges. One only has to view daily layoff news at **Yahoo's Full Coverage** at http://fullcoverage.yahoo.com/Full_Coverage/Business/Downsizing_and_Layoffs/ to see how being able to turn on a dime is an attractive quality.

Environment

Does your place have a team environment that encourages interaction and fun? Fun, in this case, translates into "more productivity," as happy employees are inspired to ever higher levels. Pride is evident in your team. Because of the nature and stability of your environment, stress levels can be kept to a minimum. Make no mistake about it—a stable environment in which corporate politics is rarer than pink elephants can be a valuable health benefit as well (I've heard of several professionals having nervous breakdowns due to workplace stress). Consider your own business needs; don't you prefer to concentrate upon delivering a high-quality performance instead of putting out corporate fires every two or three days? When you're left to your own and can simply *make things happen*, that benefits not only the business but your own outlook. For the most part, I would imagine that employees would desire the same thing—excess stress only causes emotional pain and suffering. You wouldn't want to come into work in an office as cheery as tar melting on a roadway; neither do your future employees. If your office environment is healthy to begin with, you're ahead of the game; if not, you should work on ferreting out the problems and healing the internal strifes you'll uncover. Once fixed, your job position will have that much more appeal to it.

Environment can also be translated into the physical surroundings (track lighting, ergonomic chairs, muted colors), mental surroundings (classical music playing in the background), and emotional surroundings (open-door policy for employees to ask questions of their management). One of the best environments I came across in a corporation had an open cubicle format that encouraged free-flow conversation and work exchanges. Every person was able to personalize their space, yet wander down to whoever was required to assist in their next step of the process. It was open and airy and a pleasure to wander about.

Can you say the same thing about your company? If so, the above can be compelling reasons for individuals to check out your company.

Comfort—*Your workplace environment can make the difference between hiring a new employee or not. People often spend almost a third of their lives in the office—ensuring that is a welcoming environment can translate into quite the perk.*

Family-Friendly

This is a big issue. Do you hold family values highly? Do you encourage single parents to work some of the time at home when their children are sick, or offer a reimbursement of childcare tuition? What about events like "Take Our Children to Work" day? Such gatherings give employees the opportunity not only to show their offspring what they do for a living, but also to admire and show off their families. **Ms. Foundation** at http://www.takeourdaughterstowork.org/ has a site specifically for daughters, although many companies are now encouraging both genders to come.

Many professionals have families in which both parents work. Especially with mothers, but also becoming more prevalent with fathers, is the notion of balancing work and home; one wants to be a super parent, super employee, and super whatever, 100 percent of the time. Raising children requires an extra influx of energy and emotion. When companies support working parents, they're sending a direct message to potential employees—"We're concerned not only with our success but yours and your family's, too."

Training

This is an important quality for companies to have. Training enhances a person's own marketability, as well as giving them the skills they need to stay on the cutting edge of your industry.

Do you offer training or educational reimbursement? Many certification exams now exist that allow for professionals to showcase their learning. For example, developers in various and sundry Microsoft applications can become certified as a Microsoft Certified Systems Engineer, a Microsoft Certified Solution Developer, and more.

TIP—Offering training to your employees directly benefits you as well as them. This is another great reason for someone to consider working for you.

It's not only in the technical industries that certification opportunities abound. One can become certified as a financial planner, a geriatric pharmacist, or a crane operator, for example.

The times are certainly changing; I first realized this in 1992 when I was happily ensconced as a lead Unix systems administrator in a large telecommunications company. Our department members used solely SPARC stations (a computer on which Unix ran) for all of their computational needs; as that was my favorite type of hardware, life was joyous indeed. Alas, a few months later the PC (complete with 25 megs of RAM!) started infiltrating into our area, but I resisted being part of that migration. (It was—gasp!—Microsoft! Luckily, I've grown up since.) Soon, I was called in for a chat with my supervisor. I'll never forget what he said—it was along the lines of "Barbara, certainly you can elect to stay with Unix and stand still while the rest of the world (and your customers) move ahead. Or, you can choose to learn another new skill that can assist you in your future career goals and ultimately make you more marketable."

Wham! With all of the subtlety of a brick through a skylight, I realized just what being an IT professional meant—the times were continuously changing, and to stay ahead of the pack (and also to command a large salary), I had to keep my technical skills honed to whatever platform my customers would choose. My supervisor didn't consider, "Gee, if Barbara learns more skills, she'll start looking for another job;" he was more concerned with being able to provide the support his customers needed. Thus, both the corporation and I benefited from this train of thought. Never underestimate how valuable training can be for your future employees.

An easy way to locate what certifications will benefit your industry is to uncover industry niche sites or industry organizations whose best interests include keeping abreast of such things. If you're in business for the long haul, don't be afraid to invest in your employees' future training. It is literally impossible for another company to poach your employees from you if they feel they are receiving the best opportunities at your location.

Location

Location can be a compelling reason for a person to consider working for you. As well as meeting their career needs, offering a short commute gives professionals more quality time with their families.

Sometimes employees can commute ridiculous distances. A friend once relayed her daily commute—she lived in the shore area of central New Jersey, and had to drive up to White Plains, NY, every day to perform her job as a data analyst. This turned out to be an 88-mile commute each way; her car would consume a tank of gas every other day! Can you imagine the other costs one could factor in—the wear and tear on the car, the tolls, the two gallons of coffee she had to consume to stay awake, the speeding tickets presented from police as she'd leave her home at 4:30 A.M. to arrive at work by 6:30 A.M. while unsuccessfully gambling that no speed traps could possibly be operational before the sun dawned on the new morning?

***Proximity Perks**—The closer a workplace is to a candidate's home, the less time the candidate spends commuting. A shorter distance returns precious time that a candidate can spend with family.*

A business that is close by a future employee's home certainly can be a benefit and a perk. There are only 24 hours in every day; it's human nature to want to spend as much time as possible with one's family. The shorter the commute, the less time it should take to arrive at work (unless, of course, that mile commute is through gridlocked downtowns where the speed limit is three miles per hour). One thing you'll notice as you scan through received résumés is sometimes, individuals will include the phrase "will only consider the following locations ..." Generally, unless you're offering astounding benefits, you won't be able to convince such individuals to change their mind. It's pretty amazing the number of times companies will contact these people with offers that fall an hour outside of the requirements; I once received an offer from a company based in Seattle (my résumé stated in big bold letters that I would only consider places close to Warren, New Jersey). Making illogical offers only shows that you don't read résumés with care, which demonstrates to the candidates that you're ignoring their needs. That is not the way to impress professionals.

Another benefit to one's work being close to home is the ability to return home at a moment's notice. Some working parents like being able to pick up and drop off their children at the local preschool, while other individuals have elderly parents to take care of. And certainly, should you choose to improve your home, it's good to be able to drop on by during lunchtime to check out how work is progressing. When my family moved in 1998, we had to endure six months of **The Contractor**

From Hell (the story has been immortalized at http://www.contractorhell.com/). Having my husband only three miles away proved to be a lifesaver in more ways than one.

Proximity to home is not the only benefit to location, of course. Do your offices have excellent views of stunning cityscapes or scenery outside the windows? Are there plenty of different restaurants nearby, offering a broad selection of different cultural cuisines? Is your business situated downtown, where nighttime attractions for those working overtime are available within walking distance? I've seen job posts on the Internet that included a glorious four-color picture of a magnificent skyscraper, with an arrow pointing to a window below the caption of "Your new office is right here!" What a great way to grab someone visually and get them thinking, *"Hey! I could put my computer right by that corner, and by the door I'll hang up my family pictures, and … "*

Take a look at the surroundings of your office. What stands out in your mind? What can you extol? If you're located in the boondocks, you can speak of the countryside's calm serenity, the freedom from smog, smoke, and other undesirable atmospheric conditions, and the beauty of the natural wilderness close-by. If instead, your business is smack-dab in the heart of downtown New York City, you might speak of the cultural diversity, the nonstop continuous activity of the area, the 24-hour coffee shops, and the local theaters and museums.

What about cost of living? If your location is in a relatively inexpensive area (compared to buying a Mercedes Benz every couple of months), that could be an attraction to cash-strapped future employees. **Yahoo!** at http://verticals.yahoo.com/cities/salary.html has an excellent salary calculator to assist you in figuring out the numbers involved.

Diversity

Do you showcase your company's commitment to diversity? Do you have cultural-awareness months? Do you have internal employee organizations that focus not only on diversity-related issues, but also provide a network to learn about each other's cultures? Is your business wheelchair accessible? Do you provide rooms for mothers who are still nursing to pump milk? Do you have Braille signs on your elevators?

Diversity is a very important aspect in today's business dealings. Different cultures have different mores and norms when going about their daily life—fostering a sense of ethnic awareness can help build up the community and appreciation of the employees within your company. Consider the Chinese New Year—for many Americans, it means lots of firecrackers and Chinese food, and a lion dance where the lion tears up a head of lettuce. But what is the significance of the festivities? What is the background? What does it mean? Why lettuce? Why not a mango?

Effective Debates—*Every culture has its norms and mores for debating and conducting business. Teaching your employees appreciation for different business styles and how to work together while respecting one's personality can help your business tenfold.*

Another compelling reason to showcase diversity is it encourages a much more friendly environment. Some cultures generally prefer not to engage in direct verbal conflicts, while others revel in it. Members of the first culture would soon find their business future dampened considerably, as often the motto of "the squeaky wheel gets both the grease and the promotion" holds out. Do you hold diversity seminars in which effective means of debate are discussed? If someone is still loath to verbally challenge another, have you made it clear that your door is always open to discuss such matters in private?

Certainly, you can highlight commitments to diversity via trips to Ellis Island and the Vietnam Memorial. But it truly goes much deeper—it's an intuitive under-standing and appreciation for others' differences. When your company has an active diversity policy, you're making a direct statement that all races, all nationalities, all minorities will find equal opportunities for advancement. This is an attractive WIIFM (What's In It For Me) benefit, one that should greatly increase the qualified candidate pool from which you can hire. Of course, diversity, like anything else, can be abused; in one of my past jobs, I had the misfortune of seeing a female supervisor protect her incompetent female programmers while blaming the men for problems incurred. Then again, in another job, I witnessed a white male supervisor being twisted around the white male system administrator's little finger. Power can be always be abused; fortunately, that's not the norm regarding diversity. There are many resources on the Internet that showcase different aspects of diversity as seen in Figure 2.4.

The previous are only a few ways of highlighting diversity aspects. It is very important in today's business dealings.

Dynamic Environment

Is every day a dynamic adventure in your business? Perhaps you're a start-up or have a killer deadline to meet—some people thrive on these kinds of chaos.

Today's technology and business environments are constantly changing. Some individuals thrive on this kind of atmosphere—calling in for pizza or Chinese food

Figure 2.4: Diversity is important in today's business environment.

takeout at 11:00 P.M. is an everyday occurrence. When you have a dynamic organization or business, *exciting things simply happen*. It takes a certain breed of individual, however, to truly benefit from these conditions. People who are strict nine-to-five individuals might not see this as desirable, while folks who thrive on chaos would immediately want to learn more about what you have to offer. Obviously, this type of frantic work pace is not for everyone. You want to ensure whoever you hire revels in this kind of environment.

Start-ups and pre-IPO companies (heck, isn't every nonpublic company a pre-IPO company?) are especially representative of this atmosphere. And I was no less immune to the seductive siren song than any other wanna-be dot-com not-quite-yet-millionaire; back in 1996, May, in fact, I was asked to join a start-up company in New Jersey. Oh joy, shrieked I, of course I'll consider only two-thirds of my currently salary, so long as I obtain those heavenly stock options! I ended up with a low salary and a promise of 9,800 shares, and willingly worked ridiculous hours; one day ended at 4:30 the next morning as I worked with my colleagues to get our deliverables out on time. Like my mother says, however, if it's going to happen, it will always happen to my daughter—the company dreams went up like a rocket, came down like an asteroid, and I was out of a job six months later. The next year saw the company in chapter 11 and declaring bankruptcy. Everything does happen for the best, however; it was there that I learned how to typeset and write my own books. I've since learned my lesson. Millions of other dreamers have not.

Be that as it may, there are companies that simply make things happen and speed towards the stratosphere with their successes. If your business is one of them, you're making history—people who work for you will hang on for the ride.

Cutting-Edge—*Some individuals will sacrifice large salaries for the chance at striking it big at a start-up.*

Company Reputation

Are you or your business known as an industry or community leader? By working for you, will employees enjoy a reputation for quality? Additionally, perhaps your business already has the top names in science/marketing/finance/etc. that will allow your people to benefit from an environment of continued learning and challenges.

Never underestimate the power that is derived from pride of work. Consider Lucent Technologies—before it came into being it was Bell Labs. Now, Bell Labs has had in it's history some of the most brilliant scientists that have ever walked this planet; Dennis Ritchie, the inventor of Unix, David Korn, the inventor of Korn Shell, William Shockley, one of the inventors of the transistor, to name only a few. People employed at Bell Labs might have had the opportunity to work with these professionals; that's something money simply can't buy. I had the honor of being taught aspects of Korn Shell programming by David Korn, and security issues by Steve Bellovin and Bill Cheswick (authors of *Repelling the Wily Hacker*). Back then, no amount of perks could budge me from my position; the environment was one that just couldn't be duplicated elsewhere.

Do you see where I'm coming from here? Right from the get-go, you need to have a multitude of reasons why professionals should consider your job offer. If you don't, trust me, there's a gazillion other companies with money to burn who will pump up marketing and snap up the people you want.

Maybe, though, you'll be hit by the very first desire on a candidate's mind— compensation that you can't possibly equal. Maybe pre-IPO stock, perhaps a Mercedes Benz every two years, whatever. Oh, the dreams that exist! So how do you deal with that, especially in an era where everyone fantasizes about being in on the ground floor of the next Yahoo?

Overcoming Compensation Questions

Remember, the growth of the Internet allows all sorts of news and technology innovations to impact your future employee's ideals. It all hearkens back to the WIIFM concept—What's in it for me? And if you can't provide all the pre-IPO stock people can eat, what do you say?

The truth. When someone discusses a want or desire, it targets their emotional side. Never try to convince someone out of an emotion—instead, bring up points they might not have considered. For example, not all pre-IPO companies actually go IPO, and among those that do, not all are instant moneymakers (far from it!). **Garage.com** at http://www.garage.com/hellStories.shtml has some hair-raising horror stories of what can happen during the pursuit of an IPO.

FACT—*For every company that goes IPO, dozens never get half that far. And for every successful IPO company, dozens fail later. Everyone wants to go IPO—but saying it and doing it are two separate issues entirely.*

Then, see if you can fully understand what's the motivation behind the pre-IPO stock dreams. Is it a need to earn more money? Retire before the age of fourteen? Put in 96-hour workweeks for three years and then cash in and move out? Or are the reasons more personal? Is there a new baby on the way, and the employee needs to earn more money quickly? Is it a feeling of being left off the train to Millionairesville? Quite often, you'll uncover some key, underlying factors that are much closer to the employee's needs than a pipe dream in the sky.

Next, focus on the high points of the compensation you *do* offer that meet the needs. If a new child is on the way, do you offer comprehensive medical/dental/preschool benefits? If the employee's last car was totaled on the parkway, do you offer a company car? If family time is a high priority, do you offer three weeks' vacation? Family-friendly activities? Group lunches once a week? It's the wise employer who recognizes what *motivates* professionals to look for and accept jobs who will be the most successful in Internet recruiting. Nowadays more than ever, finding the kinds of candidates you deserve requires that you address all of their needs as well. Don't only ask yourself, gee, what can these people do for me and my business? Always factor in the need to address that question from the viewpoint of your future employees.

Don't zoom to your computer and start recruiting on the Internet just yet, however! There is one more critical (and I mean CRITICAL) aspect of the Internet community that you need to understand, embrace, and practice. And that is …

Netiquette

Ah, netiquette. The nirvana of the Internet. Netiquette (pronounced like *etiquette* proceeded by an *N*) is simply the practice of good manners on the Internet. There's a good reason why you should pay attention to netiquette. Let me briefly digress to explain why it's so important, and how to showcase yourself to your best advantage with it.

TIP—*Netiquette is the most important thing you can learn for recruiting on the Internet. It can propel your success to unbelievable limits.*

Introduction

Long ago, back before the earth's crust cooled, the Internet started to come into existence. Not in all the glory that it is now, of course—it simply provided ways for scientists and techies to communicate with one another in a text format via their computers. Back then, you needed to have a firm understanding about computers in general to participate. Bulletin boards and newsgroups were all the rage—I remember frequenting groups like soc.singles for recreation, creating comp. text.interleaf to assist me in my job, and asking help from the readers in comp.sys.sun.admin when networking questions arose. *The probability was that any communication was a wanted communication.* And because nerds built the Internet, the common culture was (for the most part, we're ignoring alt.flame here) built on respect.

Then came the mid-1990s. AOL started becoming popular. All of a sudden, millions of people could get online! Millions of people who saw the Internet as one great big mall in which to shop! Leaving behind, of course, millions of people who disagreed most strongly with that concept. This led to the beginning of spam, unsolicited commercial e-mail, which is a problem that continues to this day. If you offend someone with spam or just plain bad manners in general, the Internet allows the recipient to broadcast, far and wide, how undesirable a business entity you are.

Spam=Bad—*Spamming potential employees is one of the worst things you can do when recruiting on the Internet. It will cause you lots of grief later on.*

Definition of Netiquette

Netiquette can simply be defined, as earlier mentioned, as Internet good manners. It includes:

Never post inappropriately in newsgroups. One doesn't post a New Jersey job opening in the Arizona jobs newsgroup in hopes of finding that one Phoenix person dying to relocate. Trust me, they'll read the nj.jobs newsgroup first.

Never post commercial messages in the majority of newsgroups. Many newsgroups have their own special culture, which often doesn't include commercial messages. You would never post a job opening in comp.sys.sun.admin, for example, although other groups, like comp.lang.cobol allow you to post once a week provided you include the rate and responsibilities. If you do find a newsgroup in which your audience can be found, you can post an introductory e-mail that asks if job posts are allowed. I recently did that myself for an engineering firm when I questioned a newsgroup in the sci.engr category.

Never join a mailing list and start posting commercial messages. You should first become a member of the community (a great way to do this is to answer questions put out by other list members), and then ask permission from the list owner if a commercial post is allowed.

Never send out mass bulk commercial e-mail. Ever receive those messages that promise "over 1 million fresh addresses!"? Ignore them! The probability is that those addresses belong to untargeted individuals who would not hesitate to report you to your ISP.

The above are only some of the rules you should follow. As you can see, it's pretty simple; it focuses on the way you interact with other individuals online. The nature of the Internet is such that it's easy to be misinterpreted; written communications lack the tone of voice and facial expressions that real-world communications entail. Thus, you want to start off on the right foot from the very beginning.

Netiquette Is—Simply Internet good manners. The anonymity of the Internet offers individuals the ability to be quite obnoxious with little fear of retribution. Showcasing your politeness will assist your recruiting efforts admirably.

Benefits of Netiquette

The benefits you'll receive from following netiquette are huge. Because many professional headhunters and recruiters don't follow them (unless they've read my other book, *The Internet Recruiting Edge*), chances are their candidates (your potential employees) have been approached in a very commercial way (I have great jobs! Call me!).

It's human nature, really. People enjoy being treated with respect; they generally prefer dealing with professionals. The Internet today allows for incredible anonymity; people will e-mail or broadcast brazen challenges and insults in which they would never engage in real life. Some individuals feel so protected by the computer screen that they take on abusive, malicious personas in attempts to discredit others with whom they disagree.

This lawlessness that abounds on the Internet makes it doubly important that you embrace netiquette and all that it entails. You are probably only one of dozens of people with whom your future employees are communicating; being always polite and respectful will ensure that you and your message stands out even more. A friend once relayed to me a story about an employer who spammed a private e-mail directory of Ingres professionals—that person's name, contact number, and e-mail address were put up the next day on the Web site with the message, *Would you want someone with such ethics being responsible for your career? Why not call up this guy and tell him what you think?*

When you contact job applicants in a way that showcases what you have to offer and answers the What's In It For Me question, or first become a valued member in a community so other individuals would jump at the opportunity to become employed by you, you'll be perceived as a desirable individual with whom to do business. And that's something you just can't buy.

Mother's Always Right—*Netiquette shows you respect the communities in which you are finding your employees. Everyone in this world appreciates respect.*

Disadvantages of Not Using Netiquette

The main disadvantages of not using netiquette range from nasty e-mails to getting your account cancelled to having a lousy reputation spread about you.

Don't believe me? The **Blacklist of Internet Advertisers** at http://math-www.uni-paderborn.de/~axel/BL/blacklist.html, depicted in Figure 2.5, contains a list of folks who abused the newsgroups on the Internet (you certainly wouldn't want your name to appear there during a plain-vanilla AltaVista search). Additionally, there are dozens of antispam mailing lists and resources where your name will be smeared, big time, if you engage in spam.

You can experience far worse than that above, however. Militant antispammers have been known to shut down sites by complaining to the ISP's host, as well as send bills for unauthorized computer usages. Nowadays, many ISPs will include a zero-tolerance spamming policy—spam once and you're simply out of luck. Your account will be closed and no huffing and puffing from lawyers will bring it back. It's simply not worth it. You'll gain so many benefits by simply observing the rules, why take a chance that's almost bound to fail?

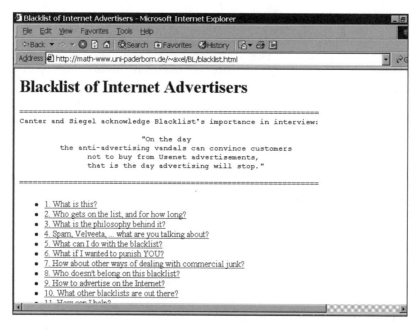

Figure 2.5: About.com lists excellent tools to defeat spam.

Blacklist—*If you annoy a powerful group of people often enough (or even once!) on the Internet, chances are your e-mail address and contact information will be shared as someone with whom professionals should not do business.*

Netiquette Resources

The Internet has plenty of excellent resources on netiquette and Internet good behavior. They include:

The Core Rules of Netiquette
http://www.albion.com/netiquette/corerules.html

Arlene Rinaldi's User Guidelines and Netiquette
http://www.fau.edu/netiquette/net/

Coalition Against Unsolicited Commercial Email
http://www.cauce.org/

SPAM Recycling Center
http://www.spamrecycle.com/

The Original David Rhodes Chain Letter
http://www.cs.rutgers.edu/~watrous/txt/David.Rhodes.chain.letter

Sometimes, of course, you'll run into situations that aren't discussed in general all-purpose netiquette guides. In this case, you simply can contact the people in question and ask. I remember when I was preparing a customized Internet recruiting seminar for the engineering firm RDS; I wanted to showcase all the different avenues for recruiting that were available. Because the firm specialized in design engineering, I decided to explore the engineering newsgroups that are currently available including sci.engr.mech, sci.engr.manufacturing and others. I posted an introductory note to these newsgroups and asked what the guidelines for job postings were—would they be accepted? The responses I received enabled me to present some rather valuable information to my clients. And because my question was phrased politely and was a request for help, I didn't receive any negative responses at all.

In closing, the more you learn and abide by netiquette, the better chances you'll have of finding and hiring the best professionals you can uncover on the Internet.

CHAPTER THREE

Tools You Need

Have you ever wondered what kinds of tools you'll need when recruiting on the Internet? If this is a new field for you, you might ask yourself: How are résumés submitted to me? Via e-mail? Fax? Can they be sorted? Stored? Where will I advertise my job inquiries? How do I actually enter them into the computer and then "see" my job posts online? This chapter presents a list of tools and requirements to make your online recruiting a comfort. They include:

- Your computer or WebTV
- Hardware connecting your computer to the Internet
- Internet connectivity itself
- A personal firewall
- A way to send and receive e-mail
- A browser
- Bookmarks or Favorites
- Company or personal Web site
- Post-It notes
- Patience
- Lots and lots of answers

Let's go over all of these one by one.

Technical

Computer or WebTV

To get the most benefits from recruiting on the Internet, you must connect to the Internet. Certainly, you can use your local library's or possibly a friend's computer, but the actual searching and correspondence makes having a computer or WebTV (i.e., a way to surf the Internet) desirable. What computer you should buy depends upon your needs. Two of the most important criteria you should consider are the amount of RAM (memory—the more RAM, the more applications you can use at one time), and the processor speed (the higher the number, the faster your computer operates). You can uncover many resources on the Internet to assist you in choosing what's right for your needs. **ZDNet** at http://www.zdnet.com/reviews/ provides many reviews on available systems, as does **C|Net** at http://www.cnet.com/.

Once you have a good idea about what to buy, you need to decide how to purchase it. Many price-comparison sites exist, such as **PriceWatch** at http://www.pricewatch.com/ and **PriceGrabber** at http://www.pricegrabber.com/; you should be able to find the best possible prices online. However, once you receive the equipment, you'll probably be on your own and have to configure it yourself. If you're comfortable with this idea, by all means go ahead; if you run into problems building your system, you could visit **MyHelpdesk** at http://www.myhelpdesk.com/, depicted in Figure 3.1, to help you troubleshoot. If you're unsure of such things, however, I recommend that you purchase your PC at a local store where personalized help is available.

WebTV at http://www.webtv.com/ is a technology alternative that offers you Internet connectivity without a conventional computer. This might be a logical choice if you are dead set against using computers, yet still want to benefit from the Internet.

Figure 3.1: MyHelpdesk.com is a free service that lets you troubleshoot PC problems.

Even if you're completely technology-phobic, don't despair! You can still contact your local newspaper and ask if their classifieds are available online. If so, you can simply phone or fax a standard newspaper ad, and be reassured that it will also be visible at the hopefully highly-trafficked site of the newspaper itself.

Hate Computers?—*If you're computer-phobic, start simply by using WebTV or perhaps an Internet appliance. You don't have to buy into the most powerful solution when you are just starting.*

Hardware to Connect Your Computer to the Internet

Should you choose to access the Internet from your own computer, you'll next need physical connectivity to actually get online. There are several ways to do this, including:

- A telephone modem
- A cable modem
- ISDN
- xDSL
- Satellite

Telephone modems are what many people use. It can be either external (a box next to your computer) or internal (a board in your computer). In both cases, a telephone line connects to the modem at one end and a phone jack at the other end. If you plan on being online for extended periods, consider installing a second phone line; you want to ensure your main business line is always free for incoming calls.

Cable modems allow you to connect directly to the Internet via your cable company. Because these are digital connections, the speed you'll attain can be blindingly fast; sites that used to take a minute to download appear within ten seconds or less. Alas, cable modems aren't available in all areas. However, if you can opt for this service, it certainly would behoove you to spend the extra 30 or 40 dollars a month to experience the benefits of such speed.

DSL, otherwise known as Digital Subscriber Line, comes in many flavors including HDSL (High-Rate DSL), VDSL (Very high data-rate DSL), and others. It is a technology that combines two-way voice and data transmissions at high speeds over normal phone lines; if you cannot opt for cable yet still want higher speeds, it could be an option to consider.

Satellite systems take advantage of wireless connectivity, but still require a modem. Instead of receiving Internet information via your modem, your satellite dish instead picks it up at a more rapid speed. **Hughes Network Systems** at http://www.direcpc.com/ is one satellite provider; their DirecPC system is one of the best-known. Like cable, you'll have to pay a monthly fee.

With every iteration of Internet evolution, more and more "things" are being packed onto Web sites, things that require time to download. That's one reason why we now have many options for high-speed connections to the Internet.

Internet Connectivity

Once you have a modem or alternate connection device and your computer configured, you're still lacking a crucial component to accessing the Internet—you need the connectivity itself (unless you're on a cable modem). This is achieved by buying a service from an ISP, otherwise known as an Internet Service Provider. Once you choose an ISP, you'll receive an access phone number to dial into the Internet. Your choices are many; they include local ISPs and great big mega-ISPs.

Local ISPs are companies that are based within your region. They generally have a focused customer base and will either provide you with e-mail and personal connectivity, business Web-site connectivity, or both. For example, I personally use Comcast@Home for my Internet connectivity but also have **Cybernex** at http://www.cybernex.net/ as a backup in case my cable modem goes down for any reason. Depending upon the company, local ISPs can also have more of a customer focus as they are smaller than the mega-ISPs that advertise all over the face of the planet. You can uncover local ISPs at **TheList** at http://thelist.internet.com/.

Mega-ISPs are large, powerful corporations that have access numbers in virtually all states and many cities. **America Online (AOL)** at http://www.aol.com/ is one such provider; **Microsoft Network** at http://www.msn.com/, **Earthlink** at http://www.earthlink.com/, and **AT&T Worldnet** at http://www.worldnet.com/ are others. For serious Internet users, I recommend against using AOL; it's basically a newbie's way to access the Internet. Sad but true, it doesn't get much respect online. When I'm traveling on the road giving seminars, I'll use **Earthlink** at http://www.earthlink.net/; I have yet to encounter a busy signal and always manage to find local phone numbers close by my hotel.

Personal Firewall

The next thing to consider prior to recruiting on the Internet is your computer's safety. No matter how you are connected to the Internet—cable, modem, DSL, what have you—you want to protect your computer from malicious hackers. A personal firewall merely prevents outside sources on the Internet from taking advantage of the many ways to access your system online. A tremendous resource to check your system's safety can be found at **ShieldsUP** at http://www.grc.com/, depicted in Figure 3.2, and an excellent free firewall is available from **ZoneAlarm** at http://www.zonelabs.com/zonealarm.htm.

Never think it can't happen to you! I was shocked when I realized how easy it is for one's computer system to become compromised. Were you aware that almost every unsecured computer has the ability to receive anonymous connections and share file directories? Many "script kiddies" will run software that automatically scans for unprotected computers and tries to break down the doors. For example, on one April Fools' Day, a new worm called 911 was announced by the FBI, and alas, it was no joke! This malicious bit of code would scan for unprotected computer shares. (A *share* is a portion of your computer's hard drive that is accessible by other users. It's very common in networks.) Upon finding one, it would install itself and potentially reformat the computer's hard drive. The insidious thing about this action is you're never aware of it until it's too late. Many thanks go to **Steve Gibson**, who was one of the first professionals to send out word of this hazard at http://grc.com/su-911.htm.

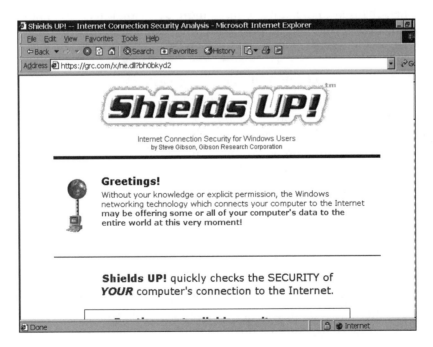

Figure 3.2: ShieldsUP is a superb application to test your PC's security.

I cannot emphasize enough the importance of not only a personal firewall, but also a general understanding of computer security. Many times, computer viruses are transmitted through e-mail by attachments; whenever you open such an attachment your computer will become infected. A good rule of thumb is never to open any e-mail attachment that is sent from an unknown individual; you might end up with a reformatted hard disk or worse.

Always Protect Yourself—*No matter what, when you are connected to the Internet, your computer can be vulnerable to script kiddies—teenagers who think breaking into systems is cool. You always want to protect your computer with a personal firewall.*

Sending and Receiving E-mail

You will rely upon your e-mail in many ways when recruiting on the Internet. Your e-mail address can be used to receive résumés, notifications about appropriate candidates, updates in job-posting statistics, and much more.

Be wise when choosing your e-mail address. You want to project a sense of professionalism and business stature; using an e-mail address like barbaraling@aol.com simply exudes an impression of "I'm here today but might disappear by tomorrow." Consider instead how the address btl@barbaraling.com appears—because the domain is personalized to me, it has a much more permanent feel. Having your own domain name as your address is akin to stating, "I'm here for the long run; *feel confident* in doing business with me."

If you're currently stuck with an AOL address, you can take advantage of free e-mail addresses offered by many of the large corporations on the Internet. For example, **Broadcast.net** at http://www.broadcast.net/ offers free e-mail forwarding as does **Women.com** at http://www.women.com/; these services will assign you a free address like barbaraling@broadcast.net—any e-mail sent there would be automatically forwarded to your AOL account. You can find lists of free e-mail forwarders at **EmailAddresses** at http://www.emailaddresses.com/.

Surfing the Internet With a Browser

A browser is how you surf the Internet. Popular browsers today include Internet Explorer, Communicator, and Opera. Normally, you will have a browser or two bundled with your operating system. Your browser, for the most part, is your actual lifeline to the Internet. With it, you can visit any site online, engage in e-commerce, participate in online chats, conduct business, and search for your future employees.

You might not be aware of all the goodies that your browser contains. Let's say that you visit a Web page that contains immense amounts of text. If you're searching for a particular keyword (perhaps a skill you're trying to ensure a résumé contains), instead of reading the whole blasted epic novel, you can invoke your browser's search function (in Internet Explorer, it's accessed via Edit|Find or Ctrl+F; in Netscape Communicator, it's Edit|Find or F3). This can dramatically cut down the time you spend scanning résumés or other information online. Another neat function you can exercise is changing the size of the text display; if you are having trouble reading the content on Web pages, you can simply alter your preferences and increase the font size. This is accomplished in Internet Explorer by using View|Text Size, and in Netscape via View|Increase Font Size.

Fast Find—*Use your browser's Find function to quickly zero in on keywords in long documents.*

Depending upon both the browser and the version you are using, you might not be able to see various components of Web pages. Ever visit a page and see a puzzle piece displayed instead of animated graphics? One reason might be because you haven't downloaded a plug-in called Flash or Shockwave. Not to fear, mind you—often you'll be able to get the gist of the site via the accompanying text (assuming that exists). If you're running extremely old versions of browsers, such as Netscape 2.0 or Internet Explorer 2.0, you certainly should consider upgrading to the latest and greatest (it's free, after all, to do so) and benefit from today's current technology.

Have you ever wondered exactly how you're going to go about recruiting on the Internet? One final usage you'll discover from your browser is being able to visit specific sites and enter your job orders. Read on to find out!

Exploiting Bookmarks or Favorites

How often do you uncover such an amazing site on the Internet that you immediately add a bookmark to it (if you're using Netscape), or create a Favorite link (if you're using Internet Explorer)? How often do you categorize your bookmarks? Hmmmm? Bookmarks are one of the most nifty tools of your browser. If you come across a job site targeted towards your kinds of professionals, or perhaps an industry Web site, or maybe a trade association that has a résumé databank, you could simplify your life greatly if you just added a bookmark. This way, crucial sites are now at your fingertips the next time you surf on the Internet. It really is a great time saver.

One of the most beneficial aspects of your bookmarks file is that you can customize it when you're recruiting online. In Netscape, this is accomplished by Bookmarks| Edit Bookmarks, and then choosing File|New Folder; in Internet Explorer, the process involves Favorites|Organizing Favorites.

You can create a powerful, customized business tool by manipulating and organizing your bookmarks. For example, perhaps you specialize in providing corporate training in the IT industries. You could organize sites that are important to you.

The above structure is something that you can modify and apply for your own business needs. When you come across sites that can provide you with long-term benefits, adding it to your bookmarks and then organizing them will assist you in the future, as shown in Figure 3.3

Company or Personal Web Site

Certainly you can recruit on the Internet without a company Web site, but you'll be shooting yourself in the foot. Consider the following: if you respond to a résumé online, one of the first things you'll do is direct them to your company Web site so they can learn all about the great benefits working for you will afford them. If your company Web site is as exciting as watching snow melt, you're already out of the game. If, however, you include a compelling career/employment section on your company's Web site, one that entices and compels professionals to learn more, you're quite ahead of your competitors. It's simply amazing how many companies will drop the ball on this; often, the main thrust for a corporation's Web site will be showcasing their products and services. While this is well and good, it adds zero benefit for your recruiting needs.

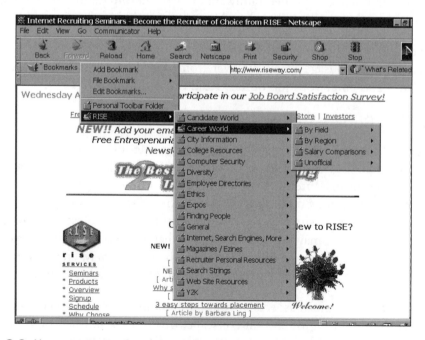

Figure 3.3: You can categorize thousands of links to assist your Internet recruiting.

Why waste this golden opportunity? As I had earlier mentioned, your business's Web site should be up and accessible 24 hours a day, seven days a week. You want it to become one of your killer business tools, one that assists you in convincing visitors that your company is the answer to their career dreams. One of the facts about Internet recruiting that you'll discover is quite often, your e-mail, followed by your Web site, will be your company's first introduction to potential employees. After all, your job posts will be broadcast out to the far reaches of the globe, where who knows who will be able to read it. If you've written your e-mail or job posts well, their next step will be to visit your company online to learn more about your opportunities. You'll have active interest! This is something you don't want to lose; you want to capitalize on a person's desire to learn more more more. And what's the best way to accomplish that? By including a well-crafted employment section on your Web site.

If you can't touch your company's Web site, however, do not fear! You can still create your own home page that focuses on you first, and discusses employment opportunities that you manage.

Can't Touch Your Company's Web Site?—*If you can't alter your company's Web site, you can always create your own site that showcases you as a business professional (and includes information for people to submit their résumé).*

Nontechnical

Post-It Notes and Atmosphere

Yes, I said "Post-It notes." When you are recruiting on the Internet, it's rather easy to become sidetracked. By writing down keywords that relate to your search on a Post-It note and sticking said note to your terminal, you're ensuring your goal is kept firmly in mind (as you'll be staring at it constantly). At first glance, this seems a tad silly. However, it really does make sense and can assist you in staying focused.

Everybody has a special brand of enhancing the working atmosphere. A few months ago, my husband, otherwise known as the "I can configure the Radio City Music Hall if I have enough cable" guy, offered to wire my office with piped-in, new-agey music from our local digital cable. Being an understanding wife, I agreed, and one hour (plus about sixty feet of cable) later, I could listen to that music. I was surprised to experience calmness and peace while I worked!

You, too, might have special ways to help you concentrate upon the work at hand. Some people like including fresh flowers in their office for the scent; others go straight for aromatherapy and dispense lavender, pine, and other fragrances nearby their computer. If it helps you accomplish your goals at hand, by all means, continue to do so and ignore any naysayers. They, after all, don't have your responsibilities.

Whatever Works—*Having your recruiting goals smack in front of your face is helpful when searching on the Internet. Post-It notes accomplish this admirably.*

Patience

One of the most important qualities you should be imbued with is that of patience. Alas, it's not too often that you'll uncover your superstar future employee with one simple search. More often, you'll find a resource that leads you to a link where professionals gather or maybe submit their résumés. From that, you have to initiate contact with the résumé owner, or submit a job post, or ask permission from a list moderator to join a relevant forum, etc. In other words, it's more than a one-step process.

This point is important and bears repeating. *Never start proactively recruiting on the Internet if you expect a quick fix!* Certainly, you might come across your star future employee quickly, but often it will require time. If you expect miracles during the first ten minutes, you are bound to become disappointed, and might even consider giving up on it. You'd truly be shortchanging both yourself and your company if this happened. Top-notch Internet recruiting takes time to seed the fields, but once they bloom, you'll uncover a multitude of resources.

There are two different kinds of Internet recruiting in which you can indulge: short term and long term.

Short-term Internet recruiting is a reactionary procedure. All of a sudden, you receive word that you need to hire a new employee, so you visit the popular job boards or post your available position in the local newspaper. In other words, this is the first time that future employees would see either you or your business on the Internet. It can have its benefits and be effective, but not nearly as effective as long-term Internet recruiting.

Long-term Internet recruiting involves much more effort, but gives you far and away, many more benefits over a longer period of time. It's a proactive action; instead of waiting for the call of "We need new people! Fast!", you instead actively search out places where your future employees might gather, take notes down about where you might be able to post potential jobs, and keep track of becoming an active, participating member of related communities. Certainly this does take more time than the short-term approach, but it helps you build up your network like nothing else can do. That in itself will be worth gold once your hiring needs do become apparent.

Lots and Lots of Answers

Finally, of course, to successfully find employees on the Internet, you'll need to have at your fingertips answers to all the possible questions your candidates might ask. Keep in mind that there are thousands of recruiters and corporate HR individuals who might be after the same professionals that you are. Not only that, but they are experienced employment professionals—they know how to present jobs and answer questions (at least, they should) in the best possible light.

What should you be able to answer? Questions such as "What's in it for me?", "What are the growth potentials?", "What kinds of continuing education do you offer?", and "What are the benefits and how do they compare to Joe down the street?", to name a few. Candidates want to feel that the people who hire them are individuals who can understand what it is they can accomplish. Certainly I am not suggesting that you memorize the entire corporate history of your company, but I am advising that you should understand at least the basic job requirements, the skills you desire, why a candidate should consider your company for employment, the growth potential, and other related topics. This holds true especially for the technical industries—if you're hiring a generic programmer, for example, you wouldn't approach a lead object-oriented programmer with a "wonderful opportunity to write C++ code." That would be akin to offering a master builder the opportunity to build a doghouse; sure, it has similar elements, but the skill levels required are starkly different.

After the time you'll spend actually finding individuals or posting jobs, it would be a shame to lose the momentum by not having the right answers at your fingertips.

Always Be Able—*Always be prepared to answer any questions your future candidates might have. Not only that, but familiarize yourself with the requirements of your jobs first—professionals want to feel employers know what they are talking about.*

The Process You'll Undergo

Did you ever wonder what is exactly involved when you look for people to hire on the Internet? How do you find résumés? How do people contact you? What about viruses in attached résumés? How do you deal with them? These are legitimate questions, but they only concentrate upon the actual, physical process steps you'll take. Before we jump into that, let's first address the logic *behind* recruiting on the Internet.

Long, long ago, back when wheels were square, I studied mathematics at Rutgers University. One of the most valuable techniques I learned was how to break everything down into a series of steps that just made common sense; a concept that is applicable to any situation on the face of this planet. The fundamental questions you need to ask yourself are:

- Where am I now?
- Where do I want to be?
- How do I get there from here?

These steps are described below.

Where Am I Now?

Indeed, this does sound rather philosophical, but the question does make sense. Where *are* you in regard to hiring? So many times, employers feel that one simply goes out, finds people, and that's it. But many factors are involved, including:

Needs. What kind of people do you need to hire? If you were stopped on the street and offered a million dollars to describe *exactly* your ideal future employee in three sentences or less, could you do it? Or do you only have a vague feel for what's required in your open positions?

Constraints. There are many constraints that might limit your success in finding potential employees online. First of all, who will be designated to follow up on all Internet-related hiring procedures? Are they comfortable with using the computer? Do you have unlimited Internet access, or must you pay per hour? Next, how much budget do you have in place to lure future employees? I'm not talking about your budget for Internet recruiting; I'm concentrating upon the hard, cold facts of actual salary. It's amazing the number of employers I'll hear declare they need a senior e-commerce architect yet offer to pay perhaps one-half the going rate for such professionals.

Expectations. Always keep in mind not only your expectations but those of your boss as well. *You* might be aware that low-cost, effective Internet recruiting takes time; your management might not. Will they be pounding on your door every minute asking you if you've succeeded yet? Will you have the time necessary to find the qualified professionals you need? Or will you be micro-managed instead?

Of course, constraints will manifest themselves in other fashions, too. Often, you'll locate superb potential employees that live across the country. Unless you offer relocation, you most likely will not be able to convince these people of your benefits. Thus, you must factor into your recruiting plan the resources you can expend upon attracting candidates.

Where Do I Want to Be?

The answer to this isn't simply, "I want to hire more people." Remember, employers don't hire for the sheer thrill of being able to pay out more salary! You are hiring to solve a problem or increase your overall business success. For example, perhaps you've decided to bolster up your sales and marketing force. By hiring two new salespeople, you've now covered more open territory and ideally increased your organization's earning power. When you define where you want to be in terms of your business, you're solidifying in your mind the qualities you'd like your future employees to have.

What about yourself? Certainly, ensuring your business goals are met is of paramount importance. Often, you can also factor meeting Internet recruiting goals into your own performance review with your supervisors or colleagues. This can prove to be very beneficial, especially if your company values saving money when hiring new employees.

How Do I Get There from Here?

Ah. The most important part of the equation. Now that you've outlined to yourself some basic points regarding your Internet recruiting needs, you can redefine this question into a concrete goal such as:

- Hiring three software developers who are local to my business, don't expect pre-IPO stock as a perk, and have at least two years of experience
- Freeing up my executive assistant to oversee finding another salesperson for my furniture store
- Locating project managers skilled in retail growth who would welcome a company car but have to live within the territory described
- Preparing for the holiday rush and finding people willing to work overtime for seven days straight

Whenever you embark upon new business ventures, asking yourself where am I now, where do I want to be, and how do I get there from here will always assist you in fine-tuning your *real* needs. Once the theory is down pat, you must then flesh out the actual physical steps to make it into a reality. They are as follows:

- Defining your needs
- Determining who will process résumés
- Writing a killer job post
- Visiting logical sites and posting your jobs or looking at résumés
- Processing the incoming résumés

Let me now describe them in detail.

Defining Your Needs

One thing that Internet recruiting has in common with generic all-purpose recruiting is you must first define your needs. Normally, you wouldn't spend hundreds of dollars for a classified ad that doesn't exactly showcase the types of professionals you're looking for, right? The same thing should be marked indelibly on your forehead regarding Internet recruiting, too. You'll see it's tempting to be brief and pithy regarding your job requirements; the ease of creating and modifying files lends itself to that. You must resist this impulse whenever possible; you want to ensure your job advertisements grab viewers by the shoulders and shake them up and down with excitement.

Consider the wonderful world of abbreviations. Every industry has their own specific favorites, understood by professionals themselves. But when you're recruiting on the Internet, you want to speak to the emotions of the readers, not only to their logic. What sounds better to you?

- Optnty in sales; cmpy car, M/D more included
- Dynamic opportunity in the sales and marketing field; perks include a new company car, comprehensive medical and dental, as well as …

You can define your needs simply on a piece of paper by talking with the person who requires a new hire and taking down notes. No computer is required; however, if you're comfortable typing while listening, you can use a word processor like Microsoft Word to store your information. Once these needs are defined, you should consider how to present them so they answer the WIIFM (What's In It For Me) question of the viewers. Perhaps you need to raise your sales figures by 38 percent by the year's end; how can you describe that in an emotionally intriguing manner? *"Opportunity to personally lead corporation to its highest earning marks this year while enjoying sole ownership of the Midwest territory"* could be one way.

Determining Who Will Process Résumés

I will touch more upon this in Chapter 18, "Your Own Web Site." Suffice it to say, you must have buy-in from the person processing incoming résumés; it can become a tedious job. You'll receive résumés via:

E-mail. Interested applicants might e-mail to you their résumés in an attachment. When this happens, you'll receive in the applicant's e-mail to you a notice that there is a file attachment (in other words, a file produced by an application such as Microsoft Word). In this case, you must be very careful about having a good antivirus scanner on your computer; often attached Word documents can be infected without the sender realizing it. Once you can safely open an attached résumé, you can either print it out, process it via a résumé-tracking program, or detach it from your e-mail and store it in a directory on your computer.

Fax. Other times, you might receive incoming résumés via your fax machine. Products do exist that allow you to scan in the information and then save it to a résumé-tracking program, or you can opt to process it yourself.

Paper mail. As not every person lives and breathes computers and the Internet, you might actually receive résumés via your local paper mail! These you can treat like your faxed-in résumés.

Another question you must answer is how do you respond to people who e-mail their résumés to you? Sending off a nice thank-you note certainly is polite, with the tag line that contains "Should your qualities match our open positions, we will contact you shortly. In the meantime, thank you very much for your interest in our corporation." Remember, politeness counts.

Who Owns Résumés?—*One of the first things you'll notice when recruiting on the Internet is the influx of lots and lots of résumés (and not all of them usable, either). Determining ahead of time who has ownership of incoming résumés will assist you in processing them effectively, without letting quality professionals slip through the cracks. An easy way to do this is to obtain buy-in from your designated résumé receiver; offer incentives for a job well-done.*

Writing a Killer Job Advertisement

Have you ever stopped and thought about what would excite people looking for new positions? It certainly isn't the dry delivery of required skills! You will need to excite and entrance professionals who are looking at your opportunities online; you will want to invoke a "call to action" (in this case, submitting their résumé to you). Have you ever noticed how visual the Internet can be? I'm not only talking about graphics and icons and cool animations, but different fonts, styles, and text colors too. This is another aspect to consider when formatting your posts for specific job advertising; sometimes you can change the color of the title, bold the benefits, and other activities that will make your advertisement stand out from the rest of humanity. Think back to when you've scanned classified ads or auctions on eBay, or possibly browsed through the title of current chat groups online. Often, you'll see that the title of these entities are only three or four words long, so the authors have to include action words to get you to even click on the blasted thing. The same thing holds for your job advertisements.

In the recruiting industry, job advertisements are sometimes called job posts.

Visiting Logical Sites and Posting Your Jobs

Once you have a killer job post created, you next need to uncover logical places to advertise it on the Internet. Certainly you can use the paid sites such as Monster.com or Headhunter.net; you can also proactively search for niche sites in which your future employees gather as depicted in Figure 3.4, and post your jobs there. Quite often, you'll find that places like industry organizations or trade associations will charge you considerably less for this service.

One of the most important things you'll need to determine is how well proposed job sites are known by your candidate base. It would truly be a shame to waste your time, effort, and money to advertise your open direct sales positions, for example, at sites that are frequented only by industrial engineers or nuclear physicists. Some ways of verifying this include:

   Current old-media advertising. If you hear of a job site on the radio often enough, or see it advertised in an industry magazine, or come across it online

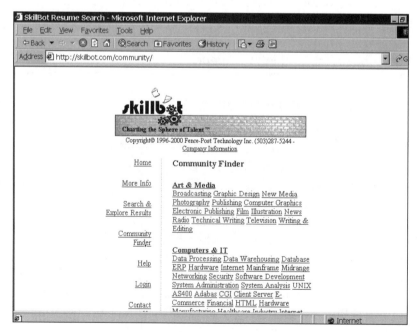

Figure 3.4: Skillbot has dozens of links to industry niche sites.

from niche sites, there's a good chance it's known by your future employees.

Number and age of jobs currently posted. When you consider using a job board, you can generally view the jobs currently posted. If the last one posted was from 1999, you're pretty well assured that your candidate population is not stampeding to that site. However, if the freshest job is within a few days, and is leading hundreds of jobs posted previously, you can feel quite certain that it's an active site.

Number of active discussions. Another way to determine how well a site is known is to monitor the active discussions (although this doesn't always hold true—some resource sites have a high concentration of traffic that consists of unusually mum individuals). The more active a board, the more visual confirmation you have of the vocal participants.

Number of active résumés. Some sites will allow people to post their résumés for free viewing, such as **Beverly Hills Software's NT** site at http://www.bhs.com/, **Unix Gurus Universe** at http://www.ugu.com/, and others. Like all of the above ideas, of course, this is not a hard and fast rule, but it should assist you in determining where to post.

Another key area in which to post your jobs is Netnews, the free virtual bulletin boards that abound on the Internet. Netnews (which was around before the World Wide Web came into existence) offers you free groups such as a general résumé board called misc.jobs.resumes, a New York City job board called nyc.jobs, and dozens of others. There are several techniques you can use to assist you in both posting jobs and uncovering résumés that will be discussed in Chapter 12, "Forums."

You can use either e-mail to post jobs (such as viewing Netnews—often called News—in your mailing program and submitting a job post to a newsgroup), your browser (many sites will offer you fill-in forms and fields to post your available positions), or a program itself (some fee-based systems will give you the opportunity to create all of your job posts and then upload them to specific sites). Because the Internet is so huge, however, you don't want to retype your job post every single time you advertise it online; you can also consider using one of the several job broadcasting systems like **eQuest** at http://www.equest.com/, **Ad-cast** at http://www.ad-cast.com/, and others. These will take your job post (generally through a browser) and shoot it out to dozens of other job-related sites; it can be a great timesaver.

You might want to consider formatting your own job posts and including them directly on your own site. One superb benefit you'll receive from this is that job advertisements, done well, are chock-full of the keywords that job seekers use when trying to find employment. If these pages are indexed in a search engine, you might receive higher visibility than before.

Saving Time—*Some sites let you post your job opportunity once and then broadcast it to many other sites—a great time saver.*

Processing Incoming Résumés

Finally, you will need to process all the incoming résumés. Make no mistake about that—it can take up quite a lot of your time. You might have to first scan incoming résumé attachments and clean them of viruses (your virus scanner should do this), print out a hard copy, distribute it, detach the résumé into a separate file, and store it on your computer. In this case, you want to make darned sure that star candidates don't fall through the cracks—it would be a shame if you didn't have in place a process for sorting through and evaluating incoming résumés.

You will increase your probabilities of Internet recruiting success if you are aware of all the subtle steps that can be required. A methodical, logical plan will provide the roadmap to finding your candidates quickly and effectively, without wasting your valuable time wandering about blindly on the Internet.

Chapter Four

Your Ideal Future Employee

If money, time, and stress were not a factor, who would be the ideal employee you would like to hire? Answering this is key; it will help you maximize the returns from your Internet recruiting. Consider the following exercise. You're responsible for selling accounting-based software for small- to medium-sized businesses. You realize that you now can hire a new professional to round out your team. Ask yourself:

Are you looking for a salesperson? Well, certainly. But maybe your company doesn't have the means to train freshly graduated students. So you need to refine your requirements a tad.

Are you looking for a salesperson with more than three years of experience? This question might be more in-line with your perception of your future employee. But your product also requires onsite installation, and you also pride yourself on your sales people being able to understand general computer problems that might be encountered during the software installation. Ah hah! Another criteria! Your requirements might now be:

Are you looking for a salesperson with more than three years of experience who can troubleshoot product problems on a client site? As you can tell, this is much more specific than merely "looking for a salesperson." What else might be ideal? Well, one of the qualities of superstar sales people is the ability to keep customers happy even when problems rise up unexpectedly. Such a requirement might be phrased as:

Are you looking for a salesperson with more than three years of experience who can troubleshoot product problems on a client site while not losing the sale? And so on, and so on.

When you look for future employees, you have in your mind *the ideal professional*. It will greatly help your recruiting if you can firmly state:

- The characteristics definitely needed

- The skills ideally needed
- The abilities that would be nice, but you can do without

Perfection—*It's always possible to define the "perfect" candidate. Such criteria include skills, background, location, personality, education, and more. Of course, finding that individual is another matter entirely.*

When you take your time to conceptualize the previous, it makes your Internet recruiting adventures much easier because you can weed out professionals who don't meet your needs. Following are some of the criteria you need to define when getting ready to search.

Professional

Some of the professional criteria you need to consider include the following:

- Skills
- Prior Experience
- Telecommuting

They are described more fully in the separate sections that follow.

Skills

What sort of skills are necessary to do the job? Are they intuitive skills (problem solving) or technical skills (knowing a particular computer language, being able to create a winning sales presentation, etc.)? What is the level of skills needed? Would a fresh college graduate with no real-world experience but a straight A average be a viable candidate? Are there exams professionals can take in these skills, such as the Microsoft Certified Systems Engineer (MCSE) or a Certified Residential Specialist (CRS)? If so, is having that certification a definite must?

There are many sites on the Internet that can describe the typical skills required of a particular position. They include:

Job Descriptions at http://www.jobdescriptions.com/. This site will provide you with complete, comprehensive job descriptions from a multitude of industries.

The Occupational Outlook Handbook at http://www.bls.gov/ocohome.htm. Put out by the Bureau of Labor Statistics, it contains good solid information about what is required in many jobs. See Figure 4.1.

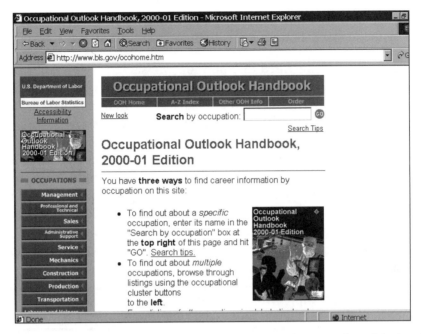

Figure 4.1: The Bureau of Labor Statistics has a useful site for learning about job descriptions.

Additionally, you can uncover needed skills by simply visiting large job boards such as **Monster.com** at http://www.monster.com/ or **Hotjobs.com** at http://www.hotjobs.com/ and searching for similar jobs. For example, perhaps you are a manager in a retail outfit, and you need to hire someone to mind the in-house computers (otherwise known as a systems administrator). Because retail skills are your strong point, you might not know what's currently required to be a candidate for such a position.

Perfecting Precision—*Saying you need "Web programming skills" isn't enough. Break it down further—what kinds of skills? Java? ASP? MySQL? DHTML? The more precise, the more keywords you're adding to your requirements, which generally improves your visibility.*

You have several choices—you can network with your peers and ask what skills their systems administrators have. You can visit some of the above job description sites and peruse the specific skills listed. You can visit **Hotjobs.com** at http://www.hotjobs.com/ and search for computer administrator retail. Additionally, you can visit specific niche-oriented computer sites and search for position descriptions. For example, **The Systems Administrator Guild** at http://www.usenix.org/sage/ has a good description of what systems administrators do at http://www.usenix.org/sage/jobs/jobs-descriptions.html. Reading information presented by the industry in question will often illuminate specific key skills.

Understanding the skills required in a position will serve you in good stead when discussing your employment opportunities with potential employees. For example, perhaps you're in charge of hiring a project manager for your national sales accounts team. If you don't appreciate what's required, how can you be certain you won't be bamboozled by a travelin' salesman and hire someone who lacks the critical qualities necessary to boost your team's productivity? Remember, every hiring decision ultimately reflects upon yourself! If a new hire turns out to be paradise contained within a human form, you'll be able to include on your own performance review a line like "Increased company's profitability by 245 percent by identifying and hiring star professional to manage the national sales account." Of course, if your new hire reveals himself or herself to be a black hole in disguise, that's difficult to ignore when discussions about your pay raise arise.

Need Help?—If you're not aware of what skills a job requires, you can find resources on the Internet to lay it out for you, step-by-step.

Prior Experience

Would you prefer hiring someone with previous experience in the industry, someone who has worked for your competitors? How much experience is necessary? Is more experience in one aspect of the job more critical than overall industry experience? Prior experience can be useful for several reasons; with today's industry becoming increasingly more competitive, some companies want to benefit from a future employee's previous employment with other corporations.

You have several ways to limit searches to these types of individuals. For example, perhaps you want to uncover résumés of professionals who worked at Microsoft Corporation. Adding the phrase `Microsoft Corporation` to specific search engine résumé queries will return only those people who have been employed by Microsoft and have that on their résumé. Indeed, finding employees with specific backgrounds and experience is becoming a fine art; recruiters are excellent in this aspect. If you want to take this to an extreme and delve into the field of competitive intelligence, you can benefit from resources available at the **Society of Competitive Intelligence** at http://www.scip.org/.

Another reason why prior experience might be of high value is your legacy systems and procedures. Perhaps your company is using outdated equipment and has no reason yet to upgrade; you certainly would want to ensure your future support hires, for example, are well versed in dealing with your current operating system, out-of-date though it may be. Think back to the flurry of Y2K (Year 2000) excitement; many companies were desperate to hire professionals skilled in COBOL, JCL, MVS, and other mainframe-related applications. There was a specific need for people who would bring these systems into the 20th century. I remember pitching in to assist a large corporation in the separation of two highly intertwined computer networks; because I had worked at the company in the past, I knew many of the hidden idiosyncrasies that existed in its computers, and how to reconfigure them to accept the new settings. While many telecommunications professionals can solve telephony networking problems, employees who have actively participated in the prior operation of said networking will often have an advantage over those who arrive at the situation cold.

What about non-skills-related prior experience? Perhaps you're beginning a new dot-com company. Along with specific business-oriented skills, you'd like to hire individuals who have had at least one *failed* start-up in their history. Why? Because entrepreneurs who have failed in one endeavor often learn key lessons that might make the next attempt a success. Benefiting from others' mistakes can help ensure you don't follow that road yourself.

Finally, consider prior experience with creativity. Not all creative leaps involve technical aptitude—the ability to think outside the box (after understanding exactly what *is* the box) will often provide leads for improving the business bottom line.

Telecommuting

Does the position for which you need to hire lend itself to telecommuting? For example, some research jobs can easily be done in the comfort of one's home. Your candidate population is much larger in this case—you can hire parents who work from home, the physically challenged who can't leave their homes, and stellar employees who deem telecommuting to be a desirable perk. Telecommuting is becoming very popular, and many sites on the Internet are dedicated to providing comprehensive information. They include:

About.com's Telecommuting Center at http://telecommuting.about.com/. This includes a tremendous amount of resources including sites for locating telecommuting jobs and professionals.

Gil Gordon Associates at http://www.gilgordon.com/. Downloads, articles, organizations for telecommuters … you'll find them all here. See Figure 4.2.

Tjobs at http://www.tjobs.com/. This site provides a place to view résumés or post jobs for telecommuters.

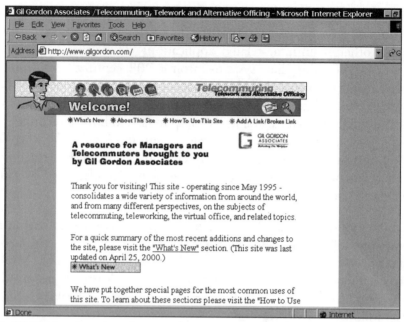

Figure 4.2: Gil Gordon Associates has excellent resources for all aspects of telecommuting.

If you're considering offering telecommuting positions, you should research all that's involved. *Inc.* **magazine** at http://www.inc.com/ has articles that discuss the legal issues, personal issues, and more (simply visit their site and search on `telecommuting`).

It takes a special breed of manager to successfully oversee telecommuting employees. Some managers can't bear to give up their micromanaging abilities, and will call constantly the employees at home to verify that they are indeed working and not consuming bonbons on the exercise bike while watching the latest edition of CNN's Financial News. This obviously is a distraction that will cause resentment later on. Other employees might think that telecommuting is given as a favorite's status and become jealous of coworkers; this can lead towards overall group dysfunction, a state that is the kiss of death for many organizations. Still another problem you might encounter are those employees who take advantage of the system.

How can you ensure you receive the best possible returns on telecommuting employees? You have to have in place a series of rules and measurable goals that are agreed upon by the telecommuting employee. You can find a **Frequently Asked Questions** list about telecommuting at http://www.gilgordon.com/telecommuting/faq.htm.

Personal

Personal criteria as well come into play when determining who is your perfect future employee. Two to consider are:

- Personality
- Local/Relocation

They are described below in the separate sections that follow.

Personality

What kind of personality fits best within your organization? If you're on the cutting edge of technology and industry, meeting killer schedules is the norm—do you want someone who thrives on that kind of pressure? Make no mistake about it—personalities can make or break an organization. Perhaps your business involves programming-intensive work. Some programmers might operate best if they are simply left alone to do their job—their personality might be very hands-off. What if your business is sales-intensive? You probably wouldn't want a social hermit being in charge of your latest perfume line—you would want an energetic, outgoing, people person.

You can always teach future employees needed skills if they are lacking in specific areas. Modifying one's personality, however, is far more difficult to do; you need to understand what personalities will bring in *the most benefit to your organization*. One way to do this is to consider a person's past employment history; if they've been fired from four direct marketing positions for poor customer interaction skills, most likely you wouldn't want to hire them for their fifth.

How can you figure out what types of personality meet your business needs best? One way is to consider your customers. Will your customers interact directly with your hires? If so, people skills are crucial for this scenario. If you're a supervisor within a large organization, are your customers your peers, the ones to whom you must submit timely deliverables? If so, you can probably shield personal contact if necessary.

Some Things Never Change—*You can teach skills, but you really can't modify someone's base personality. Never try to fit someone into a position in which that person's personality conflicts with your business goals.*

Finally, if you currently are supervising a close-knit group, it might help to poll your team members about what kinds of individuals work best. Nothing is more deadly to your business needs than when your group rejects working with new employees. Yes, it's true that such things are generally below people's dignity and maturity, but real life has shown that not everyone will always buy into management decisions. If these individuals contribute towards a dysfunctional atmosphere, it will only cause you grief and your business to lose time, profit, and money. I've seen so-called professionals declare, "We're paid to work together, not to like one another, so finish your work now!" and "Can you believe how he dresses; I wouldn't be caught dead in the same room with him!" Yes, such statements are completely irrelevant to work itself, but they have a habit of always reaching the outcast professional. Employees have emotions and feelings; you should always work on providing an emotionally supportive environment.

Local/Relocation

Will you offer relocation? Or are you only searching for those employees who live close enough to commute? Long ago, back when I was in the corporate world (I'm now independent and running my own company), I would only consider employment from those companies within a ten-mile radius of my home. Location, for me, was a critical factor. Luckily, the Internet affords you wonderful opportunities to search for local résumés or jobs. Consider newspapers—just about every major newspaper will have an online presence that includes job offerings or Situations Wanted.

Additionally, many job sites are popping up that are regional in nature. **Jobs-InMaine** at http://www.jobsinme.com/ target specifically the state of Maine, **Valley-Jobs** at http://www.valleyjobs.com/ deals with Silicon Valley, and **Butte Montana** has a comprehensive site at http://www.buttemontana.org/ that showcases how wonderful it is to work there.

Local Job Sites—*Hundreds of local jobs sites are scattered about the Internet. You are never restricted to national career sites! Not only can you find job-only sites, but newspaper sites have local job offerings, as might community directories.*

Perhaps your company would be open to relocating skilled candidates. If so, obviously, your future employee pool is much larger. Not only can you post your positions in the local job boards, but you can take advantage of all the industry niche boards as well. If you do consider offering relocation, you need to be able to answer cost-of-living questions from prospective employees. **Homefair.com** at http://www.homefair.com/ offers tools of this nature such as a salary calculator, a moving calculator, and a lifestyle optimizer that can be incorporated into your site (see Figure 4.3). **Yahoo!**, too, at http://verticals.yahoo.com/cities/salary.html offers a way to calculate salaries online. Relocation issues themselves can be addressed at **Virtual Relocation** at http://www.virtualrelocation.com/.

Figure 4.3: Homefair.com offers many relocation tools.

Relocation, however, doesn't just mean finding a new home in which to live. Many other factors are present in decisions of this nature including:

- Neighborhood schools
- Neighborhood demographics
- Elderly care
- Property tax
- Neighborhood personality and environment

If your future employees are considering relocation and have children, one question they'll ask is, "How are the public schools in the area?" The same thing goes with elderly care, too. This is where you can turn to your local realtor and create a business relationship—these professionals need to have the answers to such questions at their fingertips.

For information on local schools and elderly care visit

TheSchoolReport
http://theschoolreport.homefair.com/

SchoolMatch
http://www.schoolmatch.com/

Yahoo! School Reports
http://realestate.yahoo.com/realestate/schools/

SeniorGold
http://www.seniorgold.com/

Relocation expenses don't end there; you have to take into account moving expenses, the closing costs of the current home, and contracting expenses if the new home requires some work.

With the above in mind, sometimes it's much easier to try to locate new employees from a local pool of candidates. The money you save from relocation can then be applied to salaries, business growth, and other worthy ventures.

Hidden Relo Costs—Relocation can cost quite a lot of money. Not only might you be paying to move someone closer, but you might have to pay to help sell the home, live for several weeks in a hotel while a new home is found, etc.

Every job offering has its own ideal candidate. Be bold! Look with clear eyes and try to determine exactly the type of employee you want to find. O nce you have that concept firmly in your mind, you'll be less likely to stray down unproductive paths and waste time while recruiting on the Internet.

In What Industry?

When thinking about Internet recruiting, many business professionals immediately associate it with the technical industry. It makes sense; techies built the Internet, techies would rather watch the Teletubbies for six weeks straight than lose their connectivity—techies are what made the Internet into what it is today. Ah, but today's Internet embraces a whole range of subjects and interests, many of them most-definitely not technical in focus! **Garden.com** at http://www.garden.com/ provides a user-friendly way for individuals to satisfy their most demanding gardening needs. **Salon.com** at http://www.salon.com/ brings together an eclectic mix of timely, thought-provoking articles relating to all industries. **DLJ Direct** at http://www.dljdirect.com/ allows users to buy, sell, and trade stocks, while **The Motley Fool** at http://www.fool.com/ provides a tremendous resource for discussing all aspects of financial management.

And the chats at AOL! The **Hollywood gossip** at http://www.gossip.com/! The Captain Kirk of **Priceline.com** at http://www.priceline.com/! In a word, the Internet has moved into the mainstream with the speed of a cheetah on steroids.

The abundance of special niche sites for virtually any interest means that no matter to what industry you belong, you can probably find sites specifically created for professionals just like you. And quite often, said targeted sites will include job boards at which you can advertise your employment openings.

How to Target Your Needs

You no longer have to go to a one-shop-fits-all job site when hiring on the Internet. Think about it. If you were shopping for the soundtrack of the movie *Raiders of the Lost Ark*, you probably wouldn't go to a big department store first. Right? You'd probably either shop online or visit a (gasp!) music store, where the selection and quantity boggles the mind. And if you then realized you needed a fishing rod to go with your future vacation in which you'd be playing that new CD, you'd most likely hightail it to a specialized store that carried only quality fishing supplies.

Why might you do this? A large department store carries both music and fishing supplies too, you know. Buying from specialists, however, gives one a warm and fuzzy feeling that they're getting the best deal possible. Specialists (usually) have the largest selection, both of popular items (like the soundtrack to the latest Spice Girls album) and hard-to-find items (such as movie titles from decades-old blockbusters). *In other words, you'll have a better chance at fulfilling your needs when you shop at a specialty store.*

The same thing can be applied when recruiting on the Internet.

Save Time—Never only think, "I need to hire someone—I'll go to the national, generalist career sites on the Internet." Think specific—if you're hiring engineers, visit engineering career sites. If you need banking professionals, visit financial career sites. You can always target the industry in which you need to hire.

Let's say that you're looking for an engineer. True, you can plunk down thousands of dollars for a membership at one of the big job boards. You can also investigate posting your job at the **IEEE job board** at http://jobs.ieeeusa.org/jobs/ (see Figure 4.4). Boom! You're advertising at a site your candidates frequent, and where *your visibility to your targeted audience will be the highest.* The best thing about the above scenario is that it makes such perfect common sense—you're merely placing your job opportunities right in front of your future employees. They don't have to search Monster.com or CareerPath.com to find niche, exciting jobs—cutting-edge opportunities are already on their doorstep.

This trend carries over to just about every industry you can imagine. Marketing professionals might belong to:

The American Marketing Association
http://www.ama.org/

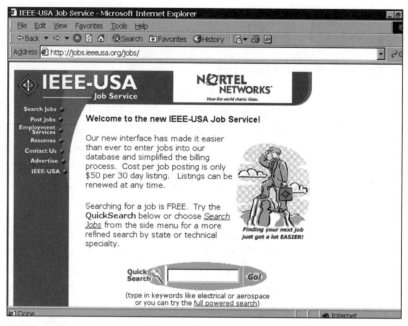

Figure 4.4: Engineers can go straight to their organization's Web site for targeted career opportunities.

The Direct Marketing Association
http://www.the-dma.org/

The Strategic Management Society
http://www.smsweb.org/

The Academy of Marketing Science
http://www.ams-web.org/

Manufacturing professionals might belong to:

The American Brush Manufacturers Association
http://www.abma.org/

The American Pipe Fitters Association
http://www.apfa.com/

The American Gear Manufacturers Association
http://www.agma.org/

The Association for Manufacturing Technology
http://www.mfgtech.org/

The International Oxygen Manufacturers Association, Inc.
http://www.iomaweb.org/

The National Association of Manufacturers
http://www.nam.org/

As you can see from the above examples, professionals can belong not only to generic organizations but also to trade-specific niche associations. Your quest is to locate these sites and see how best you can get your name and job advertisements noticed by the organization's members and visitors. But how do you go about finding the specific employees you require the most rapidly?

The process is quite easy; you need to define:

- Your needed skills
- The level of skills you require
- The location of your job
- Whether the job can be done onsite or not

The following four sections of this chapter provide the answer.

Step One: Define Your Needed Skills

When recruiting on the Internet, what skills are the most important to find? Before you respond, "that's obvious," consider the following. Let's say that you need to hire a manager for a retail store. One skill required (obviously) is successful management experience. But is that it? What *kind* of retail store is it? If you're selling retail women's clothing, would any old managerial experience fill the bill, or would you want someone who knows the fashion industry *as well as* can manage at the speed of light? In this case, you could target your Internet recruiting to focus on management sites, retail sites, and fashion sites, as well as the large general job boards.

Let's explore a second example. Maybe you are trying to find someone skilled in Java and e-commerce. These skills can be defined as Information Technology, so places like **Computer Jobs** at http://www.computerjobs.com/, **DICE** at http://www.dice.com/, and others are a viable option. Additionally, Java-specific sites might yield tremendous results at a fraction of the price—**The Los Angeles Java Group** at http://www.lajug.org/ allows free job posting, as does **The Java Supersite** at http://java.superexpert.com/. **JustJavaJobs** at http://www.justjavajobs.com/ offers a test run for free.

So what *are* the skills you need? Can you break them down into separate components? If you can achieve this, you've greatly broadened the number of logical

places you can search on the Internet. Sometimes you'll run into difficulty understanding the skills required, especially if they're not in your field of expertise;
consider our earlier example of finding an individual skilled in e-commerce and
Java. If your main business responsibility is running the e-commerce aspect of your
company's Web site, you might have a far better appreciation for the marketing
aspects, as opposed to the technical requirements, such a position would entail. In
situations like this, you can visit several sites on the Internet that should provide you
with usable definitions, including:

WhatIs
http://www.whatis.com/

Webopedia
http://www.webopedia.com/

AcronymFinder
http://www.AcronymFinder.com/

One thing you should keep in mind is that in almost all cases, you'll be able to
uncover answers online. Always be certain to take advantage of that.

More is Better—*The more required skills you can define, the more possibilities
open up when you search for employees on the Internet, because each individual
skill in your job is one more opportunity to appeal to a larger audience*

Step Two: What Level of Skills Do You Require?

Many Internet sites specifically target the entry-level or freshly graduated population. **CollegeRecruiter** at http://www.collegerecruiter.com/ is geared toward the
graduated student, and **Engineering Central** at http://www.engcen.com/ has a
direct link for discounted entry-level job postings. Another popular characteristic of
job sites is built around graduate degrees. **MBA Jobs** at http://www.mbajob.com/
focuses solely upon the MBA set, while **PhD.org** at http://www.phds.org/ specializes
in the sciences.

Do you value bright-eyed eagerness? If so, posting your job at a college or entry-
level site might net you an individual not yet jaded by corporate politics and ready
to work for macadamia nuts. And what about student interns? Or programmers
skilled in Y2K who are probably out of a job by now? Are these people who might
prove to be excellent employees?

One important criteria that will be discussed thoroughly in Chapter 19,
"Certification and Telling the Truth," is certifying that people are who they say they
are. Alas, it's quite common for professionals to stretch the truth a wee bit if they're

bound, set, and determined to obtain a job offer from you. In the past, I've been guilty of this myself; I was once asked during a job interview if I knew C libraries (C is a programming language, a library is a programming component you use in building applications). I quickly thought to myself, well, I've been in *a* library. And, ummmm, yes, I've seen books *about* C programming on the shelves. *Of course* I know C libraries! To my credit, I quickly taught myself the ins and outs of the skills required over the next weekend and ended up creating quite a success from that position. Still, though, it could have been disastrous if I wasn't able to rise to the challenge.

Some methods of determining skills include checking what kinds of certification professionals have. Many separate branches of different industries will award certifications based upon exams passed. Microsoft tools, for example, have dozens of exams one can take to become a Microsoft Certified Professional, and they can be quite difficult to pass. There is even a Certified Internet Webmaster exam now available! And these programs aren't only for the technical industry; many nontechnical professionals can pick and choose from a wide array of certifications within their niche field.

Another way is to administer an online test; several sites on the Internet now offer these as employment resources.

Skills—*Don't always discount freshly graduated students. They generally have yet to be jaded by corporate politics and often can be quite eager to learn at an entry-level salary.*

Step Three: In What Location Is Your Job Offering?

Did you know that many job boards are region specific? There are boards for states like **NJ Careers** at http://www.njcareers.com/, boards for groups of states like **JobCircle** at http://www.jobcircle.com/, boards for cities like **Kansas City Careers** at http://www.kccareers.com/, and more. Mailing lists dedicated specifically to careers are starting to pop up everywhere. Perhaps you're recruiting solely in the San Francisco area; **Jobs4Women** at http://ww.jobs4women.com/ will allow very inexpensive posts that are broadcast directly to the technical women in the Bay Area.

Got News?—*Even if you can't find a specific job board for your city, it's almost guaranteed you can find a local newspaper online that has an employment section in which you can advertise.*

Always factor in your job location before finalizing where you will post your open positions. Remember your local newspaper? Many newspapers have online versions of their classifieds and job advertisements. This can be an excellent forum in which to post your local position, especially if it's in a nontechnical industry.

Step Four: Does Your Job Need to Be Done Onsite?

Not all jobs require a committed onsite presence. Perhaps you're looking for an Internet researcher for your business; this kind of position doesn't require a 100 percent onsite presence—far from it! Give a responsible individual a computer, a goal, and your expectations, and you could enjoy the benefits of an employee where you don't provide the office or furniture.

Many communities of individuals enjoy telecommuting. Disabled people, unable to get out of their house, can easily perform computer-based research. Parents who stay at home, taking care of their children, often are extremely willing to engage in adult interactions (i.e., work) after 12 hours of baby talk.

TIP—*People at home such as the disabled and work-at-home parents make excellent telecommuting candidates.*

Resources for the above are easy to find—**The Inclusion Network** at http://www.inclusion.org/ discusses including disabled individuals in the workplace, and the **Work-at-Home Moms** page at http://www.wahm.com/ as well as the **Home Based Working Moms** at http://www.hbwm.com/ are places that would greatly ease your search.

Precise Is Good, Honest Is Better

Do you ever get the insane desire to fudge either the responsibilities or the perks of your open positions "just a little"? In a word, don't. When you hire someone *just to fill a position*, and that person either doesn't meet your needs or is overqualified, you've only postponed inevitable disasters. Such problems include:

- Employee quits in disgust, once he or she realizes the job is not what was promised.
- You fire the employee because of poor performance.

Obviously, this is not a desirable way to retain employees! Think of the costs you'll incur: unemployment wages, all the time you spent finding that person, and the like. And even worse, this dishonest practice might be broadcast to other professionals within the industry. Remember, the Internet is an international resource—it's simple for people to share their comments about sterling employers and those whom others should avoid. Check out **Vault.com** at http://www.vault.com/; you'll see thousands upon thousands of unofficial employee messages, ranging from rumors to all-out attacks. Remember how I had discussed earlier the anonymity of the Internet? You simply cannot control what other individuals choose to write about you. Many sites openly encourage comments about employers and recruiters in the name of "saving other job seekers from the pain of being burned themselves."

Smile! You're on Internet Camera!—*Your company's internal behavior, good or bad, can be broadcast on the Internet. Always remember to watch your actions.*

A Most Radical Idea

You have many ways to embark upon the adventure of Internet recruiting. The common practice seems to be: wait until you need to hire, and then start scouring the resources available to uncover people you'd like to interview. Let me propose the following most radical idea.

- What if when you needed to hire, you already had a network of potential employees into which you could tap?
- What if your hiring process simply required broadcasting your needs to your network and seeing who emerged as available?
- What if you could not only position your company as a desirable place in which to work, but also develop a reputation among potential employees as an industry expert?
- What if visitors to your Web site liked it so much they referred *their* colleagues to it?
- What if you included a section on your Web site that described all the benefits you offer?

What then? Your hiring would be a weeeee bit easier, eh? Indeed. One of the great wonders of the Internet is the ability not only to share resources, but to also *participate in communities*. Let me explain.

Networking Rocks—*When you become known as a valued contributor to your industry community, your reputation spreads as someone with whom one wants to do business.*

As an employer in an industry, you can position yourself as an expert for particular skills. Are you hiring auto-body workers? If so, you most likely have an in-depth appreciation of the talents your employees need. If asked, you most likely could explain in a simple fashion what certifications bring the most money, what models require the most repair, and the like. Take this a step further; you could participate in community forums related to this industry, and share your knowledge when needed. This is a tremendous way to become known favorably among your future employees.

Let's examine another career. Perhaps your accounting firm needs to hire another CPA. Are there local chapters of the American Association of Accountants near your neck of the woods? If so, can you tap into their network? Frequent their Web site and participate in local forums?

Reach Out And—*Many organizations or associations will have local chapters with which you can network, either by joining, attending meetings, advertising in their newsletter or on their Web site, posting industry work ads, and the like.*

It all comes down to *networking*, something that can be productive in your free surfing time. After all, how much time do you spend participating in chats, looking up stock quotes, visiting Yahoo!, and more? Such activities are a great way to reduce stress, and a portion of this time *could also* be dedicated to simply monitoring forums and communities in your industry, and contributing your knowledge when appropriate. Because you can include links back to your own company, you're in effect subtly advertising when you are bestowing your wisdom!

Perhaps, though, your industry isn't one that many professionals seek on the Internet. Maybe you look for stockers, cashiers, hamburger flippers, and the like. In this case, you can participate in your regional community forums. **New Jersey**, for example, has many regional forums at http://forums.nj.com/. If that fails, you can use the Internet to find the local hangouts of your targeted workforce—clubs, bars, the library, and the like.

Do your children go to preschool? Are you a member of a local church or synagogue? Do you play bridge every week? What's *your* network? It might be most valuable.

Other Sites Include—*If your future employees simply don't post their résumés online, you can still take advantage of community directories to locate them.*

As you can see, fine-tuning your employment requirements will go light-years towards helping you structure your Internet recruiting efforts. When you have a comprehensive idea of whom you need and what you're willing to offer, you can better pick and choose from the many applicants who respond to your advertisements. That is, of course, assuming people actually do take the time to respond! Simply having a job post out there doesn't automatically imply people will start beating down your door, begging to be hired—you have to cause that reaction in the first place. And luckily, you can create dynamic job posts to speed that process up, as follows.

CHAPTER FIVE

Sing A Song of Job Posts

Picture, if you will, the following scenario: a restaurant painted in drab colors, no windows, and a sign outside that says, "Eat here—you'll need a mouth to do so."

That's it.

Next, picture said restaurant in vibrant, dazzling hues, encircled by full-length custom-designed windows through which you could see other patrons simply having the time of their lives. The energy is more evident than the smile on the winning Presidential candidate's face, the excitement appears to be nonstop, and the patrons' expressions communicate an incredibly fulfilling experience. The sign outside reads, "Partaking in a meal at this fine establishment will be the culinary adventure of your lifetime. Don't you owe it to yourself?"

Which scenario do you want *your* job advertisement to resemble? *Remember, recruiting now more than ever is a function of your sales and marketing ability.* You want not only to grab your future employees' attention but also maintain a momentum and compel them to submit their résumé to you ahead of any other employer. This is a skill you can easily develop, and one that will increase the success rate of your job advertisements by leaps and bounds. When people read your ads, you want them to:

- Yearn to learn more.
- Follow up with questions about your opportunities.
- Visit your business Web site and learn even more about your superb employment benefits.

In short, you want to sell them on considering your open vacancies. And what's one of the most effective methods of selling a product or service? By showcasing the incredible *benefits* that such a thing will deliver. Benefits! You can compare this to shopping for a car; while you might not buy a SUV that is described as "Guzzles more gas than a thirsty elephant," you certainly might be intrigued by a benefit that includes "Conquer all kinds of weather and terrain" (especially if you live in a mountainous, snowy area). Or while the description of "fits three people comfortably" for an economy car might be boring beyond belief, the benefit "gets 51 miles per gallon" might produce enough excitement to overlook the initial drawback. View your job advertisements the same way.

Zing It!—*Boring job posts are less productive than tap-dancing moose. You must have your job posts reverberate with excitement and benefits that compel the viewer to contact you.*

What Makes a Blah Job Post Rock

It never ceases to amaze me how many downright lousy job posts exist on the Internet. At its heart, a job post is an advertisement for your company. Yet many job descriptions simply reek of "We're boring. Really." They contain zero information about *why* someone would want to spend their career there, they focus only on the needs of the company and don't expend a peep about benefits, and the like. Don't *you* want your career to be fulfilling? Your future employees do too! And because they failed Mind Reading 101, it's up to you to communicate exactly why they should consider your opportunities.

Your Career—*You want your career to give you benefits. Your future employees do too! One of the best ways to communicate this is through effective job posts.*

Put this book down now and visit **Monster.com** at http://www.monster.com/. Search for your current open position. For example, if you're looking for a sales rep in the computer industry. Search on `computer sales`.

Note the way the jobs are returned—you'll see this in virtually every large board. The only visible clue as to what the jobs require is the *title*. Viewers see a long list of position titles available like the following:

24. Apr 8 US-CO-Colorado Springs Consumer Direct Telesales Rep.	Compaq
25. Apr 7 US-TX-Dallas ERP/ISV SALES REP	Sun Microsystems
26. Apr 7 US-NY-Buffalo Sales Account Representative	CS Business Systems, Inc.
27. Apr 7 US-CA-Cupertino ACCOUNTING CLERK	Accountemps
28. Apr 6 US-CA-Los Angeles Data Service Specialist I	Source One Staffing
29. Apr 5 US-MA-Hopkinton Client Representative/Manager	Berkshire Computer
30. Apr 5 US-NJ-Berkeley Heights Client Manager	Berkshire Computer
31. Apr 4 US-MA-Milford Operations Manager	RetroFit, Inc.
32. Apr 4 US-CA-RANCHO CORDOVA COMPUTER SALES	Appleone
33. Apr 4 US-TX-BEDFORD receptionist	Appleone

Look at the above. What titles really grab someone's attention? None, right? Now let's try a different search, this time for VP. Look at the following title selections:

1. Apr 12 US-MA-Boston VP, Economic Development Xavier Associates

2. Apr 12 US-CA-Silicon Valley Sales & Marketing High Tech MRI

3. Apr 12 US-CA-Silicon Valley Semiconductor Engineers MRI

4. Apr 12 US-CA-Silicon Valley E-Commerce Internet MRI

5. Apr 12 US-CA-Palo Alto Director of Website Development Hall Kinion

6. Apr 12 US-CA-statewide VP of Sales - B2B Internet - Pre-IPO SILCO Software

7. Apr 12 US-CA-San Bernardino/Palm Springs Sales Manager MRI

8. Apr 12 US-AL-Mobile IT Project Manager - e-commerce MRI

Notice number 6? The title to that job post contains a term that is near and dear to the hearts of every software professional over the age of six—"pre-IPO." This is something that would immediately cause a job seeker to explore the position further. You *have* to think of your job post as a marketing vehicle, designed to attract the best-qualified candidate possible. And you don't have to panic and start thinking, "Ohmigosh, I have to hire a PR firm to craft my job advertisements!" You can learn to write sterling job posts by internalizing the following facts.

Superb job posts have the characteristics that the following sections of this chapter discuss.

- Benefits—Instead of focusing on what candidates can do for you, showcase what your job will do for them.
- Catchy titles—Titles are quite often the only opportunity you'll have to catch a professional's attention.
- Separation of *wants* versus *needs* and inclusion of critical skills—Wants are *wishes*, needs are *must-haves*.
- Complete contact information—Ensure interested parties know how to contact you via phone, fax, or e-mail.
- Résumé submittal instructions—Make certain you receive résumés in a format that you can process.
- Use both upper- and lowercase letters—Posting a job with all caps is considered rude or shouting on the Internet.

These are described below.

They Talk Benefits, Not Just Features

Great job posts *focus* on the benefits the job offers the candidate. Not only the skills required—that doesn't answer at all the WIIFM (What's In It For Me) question. Instead, they reveal (or at least hint at) benefits like:

Benefits!—*Never just focus on the features of your available jobs. Those are cut-and-dried. Instead, highlight all the great benefits professionals will gain should they receive employment from you.*

Continued training. If an employee knows that by joining your company she'll receive additional training for her own career certification, that speaks to the candidate's own self-interests. As earlier mentioned, gone are the days when employees can consider working for one company from cradle to grave; professionals have to stay on their toes to be competitive in today's environment. And as your business grows, you certainly want to ensure that your people can handle any new situation that comes their way. Training in a multitude of disciplines will benefit you in the long run.

Medical/Dental/401K/Vacation. If your position offers medical, dental, a 401K plan, vacation, or the like, again, those are added goodies that translate into compelling value. One thing that's becoming popular is letting employees pick and choose their coverages. For example, perhaps a future employee's spouse already has health coverage for the entire family. He might not then want to pay additional money for something he already receives. In this case, you might want to allow him the option of retaining that money in his salary. And what about carryover vacation days; some corporations will allow employees to "cash in" those days they didn't take during the year, or carry them over to the next year.

Teamwork—*Never underestimate the value of a sense of camaraderie and teamwork within an organization. A lack of corporate politics can be a very desirable perk.*

Environment. Does the group environment simply exude calmness and stability? Does the office have Thursday lunches at local restaurants? Are there employee special-interest clubs like Toastmasters, Aerobics, Chinese Lion Dancing, and Singles, where future employees can feel they are part of the group? What about the teamwork environment? Remember, your employees will probably be spending one third of their life working for your company; showcasing how desirable a place it is in which to labor will greatly enhance your overall employment message.

Location. Is your job located within a busy metropolis with neighborhood attractions? Some employees find the hustle and bustle of a busy urban life to be a very desirable feature in a career. You can easily put together a line or two that reads, "Close to downtown Broadway theaters," or "Located right across from beautiful, serene countryside." What about a window office or skyline view? This, too, can be a visual cue that intrigues your future employees to examine your opportunities more closely.

Reputation. Is your company an industry or community leader? Do your employees enjoy the prestige of being part of a popular company? If you're known as being the best, take advantage of that and include such information in your job post. I remember seeing job posts that revealed the company was in the top ten of *Fortune* magazine's list of the best companies for which to work, or other posts that listed its numerous industry awards like the Malcolm Baldridge.

Salary. Yes, I know, I didn't mention that first. That's because not everyone is motivated by money to change careers! As a matter of fact, many reasons exist why someone might consider a new position—we'll get to that shortly. However, always include at least a salary range on your job posts—it will give candidates a basic idea about compensation. If the salary is unusually low, you could define your offered salary as the base plus all sorts of intangible perks.

As you can see, an excellent job post requires that you take some time to really understand why professionals would find your offer attractive. Certainly you want to ensure you'll benefit from the candidate's skills—simply make it obvious that your future employee will *receive just as exciting benefits from working for you*. This admirably answers the WIIFM question; refer to Figure 5.1 for an example.

They Have Catchy Titles

Yes indeed, they do. Remember when you visited Monster.com and looked through the available jobs? When you post your job on the Internet, be it a job board, the jobs newsgroups, forums, etc., you should ensure your title pulls its own weight in grabbing the reader's eye. I well remember when I explored several popular career boards and came across the job entitled Dream Job—Unix VAX Administrator. Now, in my past history I was a lead Unix/NT systems administrator, so of course I clicked it! And the description read something like:

You will be responsible for the maintenance of 6 VAX machines that operate 24 hours every day, seven days a week.

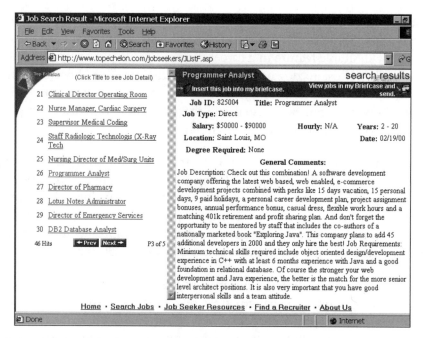

Figure 5.1: Note how the benefits described in this job post speak to the viewer's own self-interest.

That was it. *That's* a dream? Thus, the job title worked (I clicked on it!) but the description certainly didn't hold up to its promise. (I started laughing when I finished reading it, which probably wasn't the type of reaction the employer wanted.)

Get a Reaction—*Always make sure your job titles are filled with action words. "Dynamic," "Stock Options," "Dream," "Wow," "Zero Boredom," etc.—these will catch the eye of the casual scanner.*

You want to make sure you deliver on the title. Remember, you want to invoke that call to action, which in this case is simply to have the blasted thing read. Some job-related action words are benefits, challenging, company car, dream, dynamic, health club, ideal, leading-edge, new technology, opportunity, perfect, perks, pre-IPO, stock, top, training, vacation, window office, and wow. Of course, you can really go bananas with marketing copy and consider including the following too!

> absolutely, alternative, amazing, approved, attractive, authentic, bargain, beautiful, believe, benefits, better, big, bonus, colorful, colossal, comfortable, complete, confidential, convenient, crammed, delivered, dependable, direct, discount, discover, easily, easy, endorsed, enormous, exciting, exclusive, expert, famous, fascinating, fast, fortune, free, fresh, full, fun, gain, genuine, gift, gigantic, greatest, guaranteed, happy, healthy, helpful, highest, how, huge,

immediately, improved, informative, instructive, interesting, largest, latest, lavishly, learn, liberal, lifetime, limited, love, lowest, magic, mammoth, miracle, money, more, natural, new, noted, now, odd, original, outstanding, perfect, personalized, popular, powerful, practical, preview, professional, profitable, profusely, proven, pure, quality, quickly, rare, reduced, refundable, reliable, remarkable, results, revealing, revolutionary, right, safe, satisfying, save, scarce, secret, secrets, security, selected, sensational, simplified, sizable, solution, special, startling, strange, strong, sturdy, success, successful, superior, surprise, terrific, tested, tremendous, unconditional, unique, unlimited, unparalleled, unsurpassed, unusual, useful, valuable, value, wealth, weird, win, wonderful, yes, you

What if the job you're trying to fill is the most boring occupation on the face of this planet? In that case, you focus on the content and highlight the positives (salary, environment, stock options, free Friday lunches, etc.), for not all jobs will be as exciting as winning on the "Who wants to be a millionaire!" show. That doesn't mean you should make up qualities that don't exist, oh no. Remember, working for satisfaction is a primary goal, but millions of workers today view their jobs simply as a means to a paycheck. Even so, in jobs more boring than watching the earth rotate, you can still manage to find something (anything!) that will cause job seekers to explore your opportunity further.

They Break Out Needed Skills and Desired Skills

Along with discoursing most learnedly upon the perks and benefits that professionals will obtain, well-designed job posts will also specify (ideally without resorting to abbreviations) exactly what the required skills are, as well as what is desired. For example, you might have a position available for a Microsoft Certified Systems Engineer. Some of the needed skills might be experience with Sybase, running a heterogeneous NT network, and mastering the mail server. Additionally, because your environment has separate accounting packages that are tied into many of your business's operations, you would give more consideration to candidates who have knowledge of that software too.

One of the challenges you'll run into when considering the résumés is the level of skill these people have. I remember once being asked to quiz potential employees about how to run a Unix network for a large telecommunications company; I was astounded at the sheer idiocy of some of these so-called professionals. It was akin to a teenager getting their learner's permit and then declaring they can compete in the Indy 500! Still, when you structure your job post to include needed and desired skills, you're giving guidelines to individuals who can then make a more informed decision about your job opportunity.

They Contain Your Web Site and Contact Information

If you're expending the time and energy to post a job someplace on the Internet, make sure you derive 100 percent of the benefits possible. This means including in your advertisement the following information (space allowing, of course):

- Your Web-site address
- E-mail address to submit résumés
- Fax number to fax résumés
- Phone number to call for more information

It's astounding nowadays how many companies neglect to include their company's Internet information in job posts! As more and more people are swarming online every day, take advantage of this means of communication, and ensure you cover all of your bases. The easier it is to reach you, the higher the probability that you'll receive interest from the top candidates.

Contact Information—*Always make sure your Web site, e-mail, and telephone contact information is present in your job posts. You want to make it as easy as possible for interested parties to contact you.*

They Include Résumé Submittal Instructions

Envision the following. Your perfect candidate has stumbled across your beautifully crafted, highly informative job post. Intrigued by the tremendous benefits you offer, he decides to submit his résumé.

Ummm. In what format should he submit it? Text? Microsoft Word? Macintosh-based? HTML? Can you read all formats? What would you do if you received a format you couldn't decipher? Some employers prefer simple text résumés; they are very easy to read, unlike attachments, which require the firing-up of other applications (and might harbor a nasty virus to boot). Other managers already have a method in place to save attached résumés and store them for future reference. Deciding in advance the best possible ways of processing your résumés will save you headaches in the days to come; note how Figure 5.2 illustrates clarifying the process for applicants to submit their information.

Submitting Résumés—*Always make sure you specify in your job posts how interested professionals should submit their résumé. Can you handle Word documents? Text? Graphics? The more explicit you are, the easier a time you'll have processing incoming résumés.*

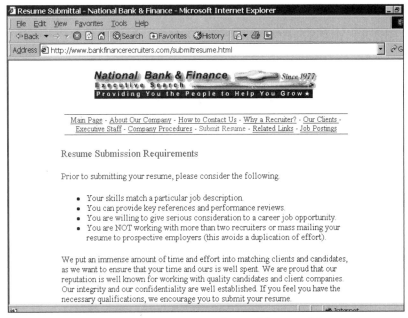

Figure 5.2: Résumé submittal instructions will simplify your life.

They Are Not All in Capital Letters

One of the easiest ways to cause viewers to lose interest in your job post is to write it in all capital letters. Not only does this make it more difficult to read on a computer screen, but all capital letters is regarded as shouting on the Internet. You should always use proper English (assuming you're writing in English, that is), with correct grammar and punctuation. Again, you want to appear classy and professional; ensuring you follow this particular rule will assist you in generating a healthy response on your job advertisements.

Additionally, They Can Include ...

The previous six topics are key components to your job posts. Additionally, you might want to consider adding the following information.

Job ID. This will enable you to track your jobs and allow interested parties to refer to your offerings via a unique identifier. Some common identifiers include using your company name as the first component, the date as the next batch of numbers, followed by ordinal number of the job you advertise. Thus, if my company Lingstar advertised three jobs on August 15th, 2000, I might use the job ID lingstar08150001, lingstar08150002, and lingstar08150003.

Job location. Many companies opt to use the format <state>-<town> for defining the location of the advertised jobs. Thus, a job that was based in Seattle, Washington, might have the location specified as "WA-Seattle." If the job were representative of a national opportunity, the location instead would be much more broad.

Education required. Sometimes your management will insist on including the level of education a potential employee must have. This can range from "must have finished high school" to "MBA" to "PhD."

Category. You'll discover as you use some of the free sites or other job-posting mechanisms that you'll need to fill in a category for the job. This usually is rather generic, such as Computers or Engineering or Sales etc.

Employee type. Some positions are permanent, while others (fondly known as the "sheddable workforce") are contractors—people who do not receive any benefits such as the 401K or health insurance and instead earn a higher salary. When money runs tight in a corporation, contractors are often the first ones to go.

Travel. Some job-posting places have a specific field for you to specify the amount of travel that's required. Sample entries could be 20 percent, 50 percent, every week, etc.

Questionnaire. If space permits, you might want to put together four or five questions or fields in your job posts, where applicants can highlight their skills further as seen in Figure 5.3.

Industry and company information. If your company is well known in your industry, and you can find links either about its accomplishments or press releases online, be sure to include one or two in your online job post. This will give your candidate third-party, dispassionate venues to learn more about what your company has to offer.

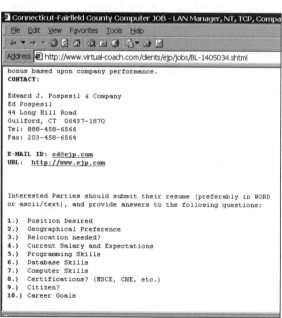

Figure 5.3: Simple questions at the end of job advertisements can assist you in weeding out applicants.

Put all of the points in the preceding list together, and you'll be able to create a job post that grabs the viewer's attention. But now a question arises! Getting the attention is one thing; what, *really*, is the action you'd then like your viewer to take?

Now That You've Got Their Attention

Trick question coming up. What do you want the viewers to do, once they're interested in your job offering? Submit their résumés? Stop right there! *What will you do with all the hundreds of résumés you could receive?* Have you designated someone yet who owns the responsibility of sorting and paging through the incoming résumés? Certainly you can delegate this responsibility to someone, or do it yourself. Just saying "Make it so," however, is no guarantee that you'll receive your résumés smoothly; you need to define a process and then get a buy-in from the person who will implement it.

Again, who receives them? Who determines if they are worth considering? Who responds to the applicants? How do you ensure your star future employees don't fall through the cracks?

Delegate This!—*Always ensure someone in your company not only is delegated to receive and review résumés, but also buys into that responsibility. It's all too easy to let things fall through the cracks if one hates shuffling paper.*

It's extremely critical to have a process in place for dealing with the résumés once they are received. If they're faxed in, someone should stack them neatly in a pile that can be organized. If they're e-mailed in, someone needs to either print them out or feed them into a résumé-tracking program.

Maybe, though, you *don't* want to see the résumé first. Hey, it happens! Perhaps your company prefers speaking with applicants prior to receiving their résumé. If this describes you, such a policy should be highlighted in your job post! This will eliminate frustration on the job seeker's part (why haven't they responded to my e-mail?) and yours (you get to follow your procedures). This is called *The Call To Action*. You've got your future employee's attention; now you want to focus it in the right direction. It's a simple detail that can save you time and aggravation.

Where Can Your Jobs Be Advertised?

Now that you know how to create job posts that attract star employees faster than a bull stock market attracts investors, what do you do with them (your job descriptions, not the investors)? Where do you advertise them? This section will explain in detail the following options:

- Before posting your jobs—What are the final checks you need?
- The lure of targeted advertising—Where are the best places to post your jobs?
- Free places to advertise jobs or scan résumés—Where are the free job and résumé banks?
- Low-cost places to advertise jobs or scan résumés—Where are the low-cost job and résumé banks?
- The most obvious place to post or advertise your jobs—Put your own company Web site to good use.

Before Posting Your Jobs ...

Before you even consider letting the waiting world view your killer job opportunities, ask yourself the following critical question.

Where will I increase the probability of my job being seen by the right candidate?

I cannot emphasize this enough! You should never ever ever! buy into a job-advertising service without knowing if your kind of future employee frequents it often. It's a logical supposition. Consider the local restaurant, down the street, the one that is known far and wide in your town for superb cuisine. Would it make sense for that outfit to expend thousands of dollars to advertise their specials three states over, a thousand miles away? I don't think so!

Let's take another example. Perhaps you are absolutely dying for the perfect scientist for your biotechnology research center. Do these people frequent general job boards, or will they be found instead at the niche biotech/medical sites like **Medzilla** at http://www.medzilla.com/ or **BioCareer** at http://www.biocareer.com/?

You always want to get the biggest bang for your buck. And that means making sure that your ad is being read by people who would be interested in it. In other words, *targeted advertising.*

The Lure of Targeted Advertising

Targeted advertising merely means advertising where your audience will be. You wouldn't want to advertise computer jobs to chemical engineers, or sing the praises of direct sales to Unix systems administrators. That would be a waste of your company's hard-earned money, and extremely ineffective to boot. Luckily, the broad reach of the Internet makes targeting your audience easier than spotting an infomercial on late-night TV.

In what industry are you trying to find employees? No matter what field, you can almost always find industry or association Web sites that are geared to this particular audience, such as seen in Figure 5.4. Looking for automotive engineers? The **Society of Automotive Engineers** at http://www.sae.org/ has a comprehensive Web site for their members and includes a career board. Trying to find professionals skilled in Oracle? **OracleProfessional** at http://www.oracleprofessional.com/ caters to this interest; **CplusPlusJobs** at http://www.cplusplusjobs.com/ targets those programmers who are looking for careers that require this skill.

Targeted Advertising Saves Money—*Targeted advertising will net you bigger results sooner than merely blasting your job willy-nilly. Taking the time to research where your future employees hang out will reap you benefits later on.*

You are never limited only to those incredibly humongous job boards that charge an arm, leg, and left earlobe! By searching on the Internet just a little, you'll be able to find sites that meet your needs admirably. Keep in mind the following warning, however: if you simply do not have the time to spend finding free or low-cost job sites on the Internet, you will have to consider the big-name, expensive sites instead. It's all up to you.

Figure 5.4: Medzilla is targeted specifically for the biotechnology, pharmaceutical, science, medicine, and health care industries.

Free Places to Advertise Jobs or Scan Résumés

There are several venues on the Internet that allow you to post your jobs for free; I'll be covering them in more detail later on in this book. They include:

Search engines. What's one of the first things people will put up about themselves, once they create their own home page? You got it—their résumé. Keep in mind that the majority of résumés you find on search engines are passive candidates, meaning they're not actively looking for a new position.

Free Résumés—*One of the most important pages people will put up on their personal Web site is their résumé. And if they index their pages with search engines, you can then find them rather quickly and for free.*

Newsgroups. Newsgroups are thousands upon thousands of special-interest groups that you can access directly from your ISP's news server. There are job-related newsgroups like misc.jobs.offered or misc.jobs.resumes, nj.jobs for New Jersey, dfw.jobs for Dallas/Fort Worth, az.jobs for Arizona, and more. It is free to post to all of these groups—you merely have to ensure you follow netiquette when doing so.

Megasites. A new trend is emerging that focuses on extremely large boards offering free job postings and résumé perusal. Such a site is **FlipDog** at http://www.flipdog.com/. This site boasts hundreds of thousands of jobs as well as a comprehensive résumé databank.

Niche or regional sites. Some special-interest sites will allow you to post your jobs for free. **BHS** at http://www.bhs.com/ has two forums for the free posting of NT jobs and résumés, and **ITToolBox** at http://www.ittoolbox.com/ has free job advertising for skills ranging from E-commerce to Oracle to SAP to BAAN to many others. You can find Boston résumés at **Boston Jobs** at http://www.bostonjobs.com/ and advertise your jobs there for free.

User groups. Sometimes a technical user group will allow job posts for free. **The Los Angeles Java Users Group** at http://www.lajug.org/ offers this benefit as does several others.

Special introductory offers. Many paid sites will offer a "test-drive" to see if the site meets your needs. If it does, of course, you then pay for the service.

Low-Cost Places to Advertise Jobs or Scan Résumés

Remember, sites don't have to be free to be good! The longer your position remains open, the more money it will cost you.

Low-cost places to advertise jobs include:

Association/organization sites. Looking for an accountant? **Accounting.com** at http://www.accounting.com/ charges less than $50 to post your job for a month. How about a mathematician? **The Association for Women in Mathematics** at http://www.awm-math.org/ charges less than $179 for a job post to stay on their site. Remember, organizations and associations want to bring more value to their members—providing a career section accomplishes that very goal.

Job compilation sites. Some enterprising individuals have created whole career networks and charge a fraction of the big-name fees. **CareerMarketPlace** at http://www.careermarketplace.com/ has over 40 different individual career/industry sites, from http://www.oracleprofessional.com/ to http://www.mechanicalengineer.com/ to http://www.BusinessAnalyst.com/. Of even more interest are the forums that the creator includes, which give job seekers more reasons to continuously visit the sites and see what's new. **LanJobs** at http://www.lanjobs.com/ is a member site of nine others, all of which offer extremely low-cost job advertising.

Make It Easy on Yourself—*When fishing, you generally search for places with the most, umm, fish. The same thing goes when you're looking to hire—search the professional organizations, associations, and other resources to uncover professionals in your industry actively searching for new positions.*

The Most Obvious Place to Advertise Your Jobs

While I certainly advocate finding effective methods to broadcast your jobs, your Internet recruiting solutions simply wouldn't be complete unless you took advantage of the obvious.

Your company's Web site. Think about it. Most likely, you already have a Web site that's dedicated to your business—your services or products that you sell. People who visit it are ideally already interested in what you are offering—why not carve out a prominent portion of your site that describes the wonderful career opportunities that you offer? Even better, why not include on that page a mailing list for which visitors can sign up to be notified when future positions open? This would benefit you and your company in more than one way; visitors to your site could now be job seekers as well as potential customers and clients. The more targeted traffic to your site, the more individuals learn of your offerings and perhaps tell their friends.

It's simply good business sense. And we'll discuss that in detail in Chapter 18, "Your Own Web Site."

Post Once, Populate a Gazillion Times

When looking to hire on the Internet, the more visibility you have, the better (especially if it's in front of your targeted audience!).

Let's say that you've crafted a job post that's worthy of an Emmy. Are you going to type it in, again and again, for every new job site in which you advertise? Of course not, that would be a stunning waste of your valuable time. Luckily, there are several services that will take a single job post and then broadcast it to multiple sites, such as seen in Figure 5.5. They include:

AllInOneSubmit
http://www.allinonesubmit.com/

Ad-Cast
http://www.ad-cast.com/

RecruitUSA
http://www.recruitusa.com/

eQuest
http://www.equest.com/

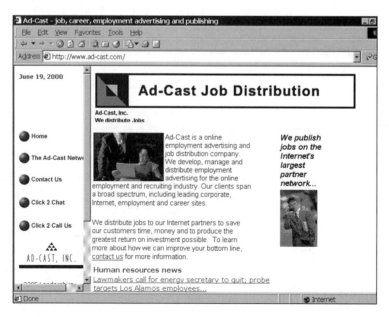

Figure 5.5: Ad-Cast is one post-once-populate service on the Internet.

When you create "the perfect job post," you can then use services to broadcast it to dozens of sites. This is an excellent benefit and will save you much time in the future; it broadens the exposure of your job opportunity many times.

Save Time—*You can invest in services that allow you to post a job once, and then see it broadcast all across the Internet with no extra effort on your part.*

You want to view creating your job advertisements to be as serious a project as designing your marketing and advertising campaign. After the time you spend finding free and low-cost sites to use, you don't want to waste all of that effort by providing a job post that is duller than limp dishrags. You want to find your employees fast; great job posts will improve that probability dramatically.

Going Beyond

The previous material explained in detail the components to quality job postings. But what do you do if weeks and weeks go by and your ideal professionals fail to contact you? This does happen, more often than one would think; depending upon the popularity of the field and geographic profusion (or lack of it) of available candidates, one might encounter difficulties in hiring in rapid fashion.

Should you experience this, do not panic. Revisit your job posting and ask yourself the following questions.

- Is the title compelling enough that people will click on it?
- Are the benefits the professionals will receive obvious at first glance?
- Is my contact information complete?
- Is the job advertised where my targeted candidate base will see it?
- Does my Web site encourage professionals to submit their résumé, even if they only intended to learn more about my company?

Remember, at its heart a job posting is an advertisement, not only for your company but also for how *future employees will better their careers*. Like all types of marketing, sometimes it has to be tweaked until it causes the reaction you desire (in this case, that "call to action" of submitting their résumé). It's not cast in stone, it's not etched in indelible ink; if it simply doesn't work, try different formats until you hit upon one that delivers. You can even create several job advertisements as tests, and see which one produces the most results. With practice, you'll soon discover what works best for you.

CHAPTER SIX

Internet Candidate Nirvana

So you're on the Internet, and you'd like to find qualified candidates to hire. What's the best way to go about it? High-quality Internet recruiting can be broken down into two main components—the short term (I need someone yesterday! or sooner!) and the long term (sowing the seeds for your reputation to grow online, so people are continuously beating a path to your door). Before I leap headfirst (most gracefully, I might add), let me first turn your concept of Internet recruiting on its ear.

The Internet Is More Than Careers

Ah, if only I could have half a million dollars for all of my obvious, profound statements! But let's look at this seriously. It's quite true—there is more to life on the Internet than just careers. It's communities. It's stock trading (and in my case, stock-losing!). It's movie reviews. It's personals. It's chats. It's sending cute little electronic greeting cards to 3,002 of your closest friends! In other words, *people are on the Internet for plenty of reasons other than simply finding a new job.*

Common Sense—*People are on the Internet for many reasons other than simply finding a new job. Your goal is to get your job advertisements in front of your targeted professionals; it doesn't have to be at a career-only site.*

I want you to internalize this concept. If people are online for reasons other than looking for a job, then *it makes sense you can find your employees at sites other than career locations.* People don't turn on and off their career desires depending upon the sites they visit—if they're in job-seeking mode, it will always be in the back of their minds. And if you can get your advertisement out in front of them in a netiquette-friendly fashion, you'll benefit from standing out from the crowd of other employers who only post at Monster.com or other large sites. Always remember this key fact, and you'll be far more alert to opportunities than your competitors.

Think on your own Internet usage. You probably don't go online with the express desire for changing your career, right? However, if by chance you participate in professional industry forums and see a compelling job advertisement that pushes all of your emotional hot buttons, you most likely would explore that further. This is a little known fact that the online job boards will not reveal; your future employees are literally all over the place online. When you advertise your message or job opportunities in front of their faces, you're in a category all your own.

Your Future Employees Can Be Found

One of the most important concepts to internalize is that the large job boards aren't the only places you'll uncover active job seekers; not by a long shot. You might think this because the *only* career Web sites you *do* hear about are the ones in which millions of dollars are spent to advertise their Internet presence; it simply is not true.

Consider the best-known, most expensive restaurant located in your community—the one everyone immediately thinks about whenever hearing of a wedding reception or a celebratory dinner. Every town has one; in West Orange, NJ, for example, one might think of The Manor on Prospect Avenue, while in New York City, one might consider Windows on the World. These places are known by continuous advertisements in all traditional media such as television, magazines, radio, and the like. Of course, other restaurants also exist that deliver a superb dining experience—they might not be as costly or as well known, but people can't deny the gastronomic delights of their own favorite choices. These restaurants start to become well known simply by word of mouth—satisfied customers tell friends and family, and their reputation starts to grow. A perfect example of this is Sammy's Ye Ole Ciderhouse Mill in Ralston, NJ—even though it never advertises its meals (twin lobsters, steak, shrimp, and the like), the place is almost always booked solid. The dinners one receives there are incredible; my family journeys there at least once a year to partake. But you don't see any active advertisements.

You can relate this concept to that of job-seeking on the Internet. There will always be the large megacareer sites that everyone talks about; they've spent millions of dollars to etch their brand indelibly into the minds of all the viewers. But there are also literally hundreds if not thousands of special-interest, niche career sites as seen in Figure 6.1, many of them well known by the professionals that frequent them. Their reputation grows on the Internet because of satisfied customers and creative Internet marketing. Remember, you don't necessarily want a site that has thousands of computer job seekers if you're looking for auto-body workers, or a Web site that contains a million candidates from all around the nation if you're only going to consider hiring in Dearborn, Michigan. You want to concentrate your expenditures on the job sites that will *return you, you personally*, the best results for your needs.

Consider your own Internet experiences. You probably have favorite sites that target your own interests, correct? For example, if you adore basset hounds, you most

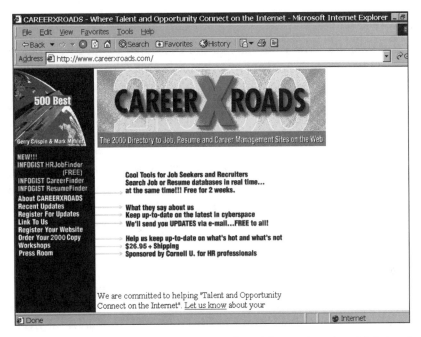

Figure 6.1: CareerXRoads is a great resource for niche and regional job banks.

likely know about **The Daily Drool** at http://www.dailydrool.com/; the rest of the world's population is probably unaware of it. If you live for Star Trek instead, you must have visited the official **Star Trek** site at http://www.startrek.com/.

This phenomenon holds for industry professionals and job seekers too; they are aware of sites that would interest them both professionally and personally. It is your challenge to locate these sites and benefit from them. No matter what your interest, passion, hobby, profession, philosophy, or anything else, you can find resources for it online; these wonders often will include links to individuals' résumés. When you start to search seriously on the Internet for your future employees, the resources you'll uncover include:

- Industry niche sites
- Professional organizations
- State and city job banks
- ISPs
- Search engines
- Colleges and universities
- Forums

- Mailing lists
- Community centers
- Newsgroups
- User groups
- Diversity organizations
- Internet classifieds

The following sections will describe these resources in more detail.

Industry Niche Sites

There are many sites on the Internet that are dedicated to specific industries. For example, **DataDetroit** at http://www.datadetroit.com/ focuses specifically on the automotive employment universe. **JavaLobby** at http://www.javalobby.org/ is targeted to those individuals who eat, live, and breathe Java. **WebSiteBuilder** at http://www.websitebuilder.com/ has a free forum where people in the industry can share ideas and debate issues.

Skillbot's Community Finder at http://www.skillbot.com/community/ will provide you with a great place to locate your targeted Web sites. When you look to hire new employees, ask yourself: Is there a specific industry site about which my type of professionals know? If so, can I post jobs or look for résumés there?

Professional Organizations

Do you need to hire engineers? The **IEEE** at http://www.ieee.org/ has a job bank specifically for these professionals. And the **Association for Mechanical Engineering** at http://www.asme.org/jobs/ allows you to post your entry-level jobs for free!

What about CPAs? **The American Institute of Certified Public Accountants** at http://www.aicpa.org/ lets you post jobs for a nominal fee. Keep in mind that these industry sites are viewed by the very audience you want to attract—your future employees. The same holds true for just about any industry. No matter in what field you are hiring, you can locate niche sites that service it. And these sites often have resource links (so you might contact them, showcase what you have to offer, and ask to exchange links), vendor lists (where you can establish business relationships), information about regional chapters, and more.

***Targeted Résumés**—Professional organization Web sites want to give the best value possible for their members. This can include career services as well as discounts for products, expos, and the like. Not only that, but you're virtually guaranteed a targeted audience if you advertise your job openings at such places.*

State and City Job Banks

America's Job Bank at http://www.ajb.org/ is a partnership between the US Department of Labor and the state-operated public employment service. It's free to both post jobs and search through résumés.

Many state- and city-specific job banks are surfacing too, as seen in Figure 6.2. **JobCircle** at http://www.jobcircle.com/ services the tri-state area of New York, New Jersey, and Pennsylvania, while **TampaJobNet** at http://www.tampajobnet.com/

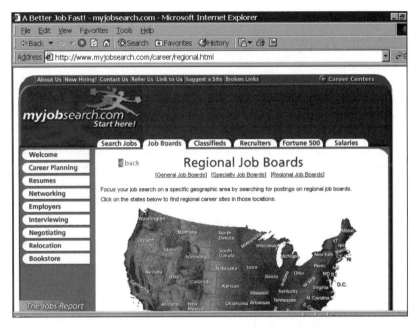

Figure 6.2: Myjobsearch.com provides a number of regional job bank links.

focuses on Tampa, Florida, **Craigslist** at http://www.craigslist.com/ is targeted towards the San Francisco area, and **Wisconsin Jobs** at http://www.wijobs.com/ specializes in the whole state of Wisconsin. If you are hiring locally, there's a good possibility that you can find your employees at job banks like the above. Not only that, but these sites are increasingly adding valued, local resources to assist job seekers in making their final decision. Considering a position in the Northwest? What would the relocation cost be? How can one determine the level of salary required to maintain the same lifestyle? Who are the employers? State and city job banks such as California's **Jobstar** at http://www.jobstar.org/ will often contain answers to these questions and many more.

ISPs

ISPs can be wonderful hunting grounds for Internet recruiting. Think about it. Literally millions of people are signed up to these services, and they all can create their own home page. And quite often, putting up their résumé is one of the first things newcomers to the Internet do! **AOL** even has a direct link to résumés from their members' page at http://hometown.aol.com/. Especially if you are hiring in the nontechnical arenas, you'll find these types of résumé pages very useful indeed.

Search Engines

Yes, you can find résumés, plenty and plenty of résumés, in search engines. After all, when people put up their own home page, quite often one of the first documents they'll upload is their résumé. And it's not difficult to track them down—just about everyone will name their résumé, well, `resume`, making it easy for you to target them via specific search engine queries.

The challenge you'll find with search engines is that the majority of professionals found are passive candidates (i.e., people not actively looking for a job). While this is wonderful for a recruiter (they specialize in this), you might not want to spend the time or energy to convince someone to try a different employer. Nevertheless, search engines are fantastic resources, not only for résumés, but also for uncovering locations where your future employees might visit. You only have to visit **AltaVista** at http://www.altavista.com/ and search on `MBA resume` or `java resume` to gain an appreciation for the number of résumés that search engine has indexed.

One little-known fact about Internet recruiting is you can take advantage of résumé resources in search engines as well. As earlier mentioned, many industry-specific sites such as professional organizations or user groups might have career resources too. Thus, as well as searching for résumés, one can also use search engines to uncover career sites, mailing lists, and similar places where your future employees might be gathering.

Free Résumés?—*You can find free résumés on the Internet via search engines merely by searching for the word* `resume` *in the title or URL of the document.*

Colleges and Universities

Colleges and universities have much more than seniors ready to graduate! They have alumni. And networks. And graduate or night students. And university magazines. And student organizations. And corporate research partners. This is very good indeed, and will prove to be extremely useful to you.

Consider the following. The majority of professionals are graduates of some type of higher learning such as colleges and universities; sometimes they'll have received advanced degrees like an MBA, PhD, or MS. Because many schools encourage continued support by alumni, there are often many resources available for these individuals, including career guidance, weekly magazines, on-campus meetings, and more. The Internet has made it quite easy to uncover any university that strikes your fancy; **ScholarStuff** at http://www.scholarstuff.com/ has a comprehensive directory of all of these institutes, making it easy to target those schools that are close to you.

Remember, one of the first questions students will have upon finishing their degree is, Where do I go from here to get a job? Sometimes students will even take it upon themselves to create mini résumé banks on their college Web server that you can access for free. Not only that, but if you're serious about getting great talent for entry-level costs, you can always offer to present a seminar about careers in your industry for niche student organizations like the Math Club or the Undergraduate Computer Science Club.

Never underestimate the wealth of information and resources you can uncover at college and university sites.

Forums

Forums are locations where people who share common interests can discuss their passion. For example, I often hang out at the following forums

Recruiter's Network
http://www.egroups.com/group/recruitersnetwork/

Inc. **magazine's forums**
http://www.inc.com/discussions/

The Electronic Recruiting Exchange
http://www.erexchange.com/

Recruiters Online
http://www.recruitersonline.com/

How can you use resources like the above for finding employees? If you become part of the community at which professionals who have the skills you need gather, you can share your wisdom and knowledge about your industry. Once you are accepted as a valued, contributing member (many online communities hate strangers popping onto the board to post a job opening and then disappearing), you can ask the forum moderator permission to post a request for the best ways to discover people skilled in a particular talent.

Free Publicity—*When you become well-known at a particular forum, people will often spread the good word about you. This can be very beneficial if you need to hire in a specialized area; well-networked companies merely have to let their network know about available positions to receive a number of qualified applicants.*

A great starting point for uncovering niche forums can be found at **ForumOne** at http://www.forumone.com/.

Mailing Lists

Like forums, mailing lists are for the discussion of specific topics. I'm on mailing lists for recruiter questions, computer book authors, gifted children, and moms who had children born in February of 1996. True, not all of them are business-related; I also use mailing lists for my social "fix."

Many industry and professional organization sites will have mailing lists where your future employees can be found. **Tile.net** at http://www.tile.net/ or **Liszt** at http://www.liszt.com/—are searchable directories for hundreds of thousands of mailing lists. Again, like forums, you must first become part of the community (unless of course it's a job-related mailing list like the **NT System Admin Résumés** mailing list, seen in Figure 6.3, at http://lyris.sunbelt-software.com/scripts/lyris.pl).

Another idea that I'll discuss in great detail in Chapter 18 under the section entitled "Your Opt-in E-zine" is creating your own opt-in mailing list or e-zine so you can keep your name out in front of not only customers but potential employees as well.

Town, Community, and Newspaper Sites

Many sites on the Internet focus specifically upon a particular town, region, or state. And many of these places will have forums to discuss community issues, classifieds for local employment, and business links where you can be listed. For ex-

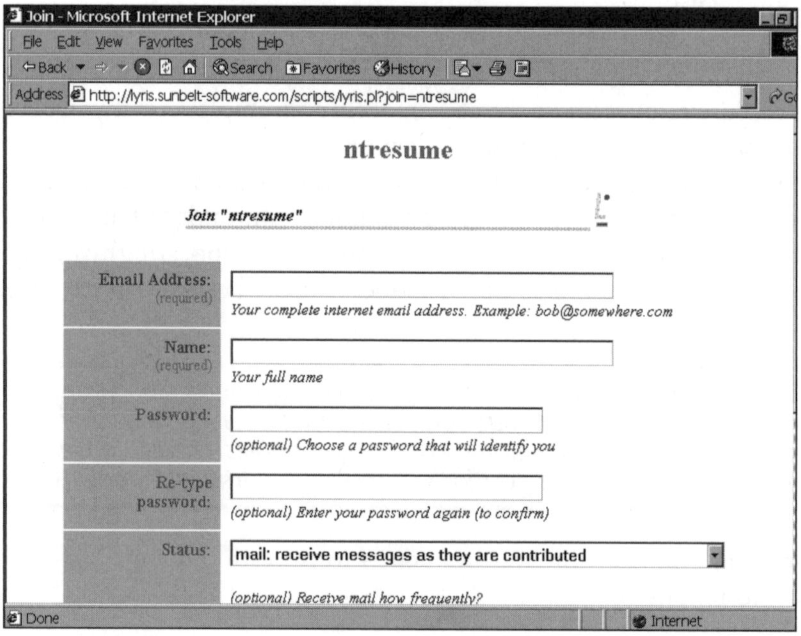

Figure 6.3: Sunbelt Software provides a free mailing list for NT professionals looking for jobs.

ample, **NJ.com** at http://www.nj.com/ has forums for all of New Jersey's regions, as well as direct links to state newspaper classified ads. *The Seattle Times* at http://www.seattletimes.com/ directs visitors to http://www.nwjobspace.com/ for career purposes, while the **DC Registry** at http://www.dcregistry.com/ contains both forums and chats (as well as a forum specifically for DC employment).

USA CityLink at http://www.usacitylink.com/ is a perfect starting point for locating region-specific resources.

Newspapers Have—*Just about every newspaper has an online site in which you can advertise in the classifieds. Additionally, you can probably uncover local forums and business directories in which you can participate, too.*

Newsgroups

Newsgroups were around before the Internet as we know it came into existence. Back before there was a World Wide Web, when you had to embrace computer technology joyfully to be able to take advantage of them, there were newsgroups, thousands upon thousands of bulletin boards that spanned every conceivable interest from parrots, like rec.pets.birds, to relationships, like soc.singles, to hobbies, like rec.skiing, to art, like rec.arts.books, to politics, like talk.politics, to … just about anything you can imagine.

This included jobs and careers too, to this day. Misc.jobs.resumes is a national newsgroup where tech-savvy folks can post their résumé. And there are state-specific career newsgroups like ba.jobs.resumes (résumés from the San Francisco Bay Area), nj.jobs (job offerings in NJ), dfw.jobs (job offerings from the Dallas/Ft. Worth area), and many, many more. It's free to post to these newsgroups, too. You can read these newsgroups from your Netscape or Internet Explorer browser. Like everything else in the Internet, however, you never want to post inappropriately or spam—there are rules of behavior (otherwise known as Netiquette) that will make your life much easier.

Deja at http://www.deja.com/ is an excellent interface to the online newsgroups.

User Groups

User groups are gatherings of people linked by a common interest. Usually technical in nature, they share ideas and suggestions about their passion. User group members are leery of unsolicited e-mail, so you have to first showcase why they would want to help you out.

One nice quality to user groups is sometimes they allow anyone to post jobs for free. **The Unix Gurus Universe** at http://www.ugu.com/ offers this feature, as does the **Los Angeles Java Users' Group** at http://www.lajog.org/.

CAUTION—*Never try to send mass e-mails to user group members. User groups, more than anyone else, are most touchy about unsolicited e-mail. Instead, use either their career forums or contact the board of directors directly.*

Diversity Organizations

Quite often, organizations will form that are based upon diversity characteristics like:

The Association for Women in Mathematics
http://www.awm-math.org/

Jobs4Women
http://www.jobs4women.com/

The National Society of Hispanic MBAs
http://www.nshmba.org/

BlackGeeks
http://www.blackgeeks.com/

As diversity should be a high priority in your employment, utilizing these resources can greatly assist you when you are looking for stellar professionals to hire.

Classifieds

Did you know that many popular classifieds sites like **Yahoo! Classifieds** at http://classifieds.yahoo.com/ or **Epage** at http://www.epage.com/ let you post free job ads? Not only that, but state or industry sites will often contain classifieds that are targeted towards their specific audience. Sometimes you'll uncover sites relevant to your industry that have no career links, but do include a section entitled Classifieds where Employment Wanted ads are allowed.

The above resources are only the start of your Internet recruiting adventures.

The Short Term

The short-term approach to finding employees on the Internet is to proactively post jobs where your candidates will most likely see them; these places can include career boards, industry sites, forums, and more. You normally invoke the short-term method when you don't have long-term processes put into place.

Short-term recruiting doesn't allow you the time to build up your reputation as the employer of choice. Your company's career benefits and job posts are visible *only* when you are actively hiring. Basically, it's advertising at any kind of job board you can find, *after* you've decided to hire, and is what the majority of employers do.

The short-term process can be boiled down to:

- Realize you need to hire someone.
- Write a brief job description and visit the popular boards that you've seen advertised on TV or in the train stations or heard about on the radio.
- Pay (generally without question) the fees involved and post your jobs online.

These steps are described in the three sections that follow.

Realize You Need to Hire Someone

Picture, if you will, the following. Your boss runs screaming into your office, waving his arms furiously, and declares in an excited voice, "We need to hire a new programmer! I'll expect her tomorrow! Go and find someone!" Or perhaps, you have just been allocated another $160,000 for a new headcount (at times corporations refer to permanent employees as *headcounts*) and decide to bring aboard another project manager for your district. You might even have experienced a current employee explaining to you in calm, lucid tones how another company has offered her 9,700 shares of pre-IPO stock, three months after you had hired her, and gee I'm really sorry about this but it's a once in a lifetime opportunity and I'll be sure to remember how you gave me this chance and oh, by the way, I'm starting tomorrow.

In other words, the mere idea of Internet recruiting has never even entered your mind before this crisis occurred. Like everyone else in your company, you were concentrating upon doing your own job, making sure your project's goals were achieved, worrying about keeping the new deliverable on schedule, and the like. It's not something you particularly care about; it's something you were thrown into and expected to make successful.

Write a Brief Job Description and Visit the Popular Boards

Your first reaction from the previous experience would be, "Hmmmm, what skills should my future employee have?" If the open position is in your particular area, you probably have a good feel for the skills required; perhaps the programmer needs to know C++ and e-commerce software, or the salesperson should have had at least a million dollars of revenue in the past three years, or the CPA must have been in the industry for at least five years and preferably have legal experience as well.

That takes care of skills. Additionally, you realize that applicants should know where the job is located, and perhaps add your phone number for immediate contact purposes. So you scribble down on a piece of paper, or perhaps create a file on your computer that has the basic information included.

Now that hiring someone is of prime importance, where do you go? If you're like the majority of individuals who are not aware of the wealth of employment resources on the Internet, you most likely cast about in your mind for the job boards you've heard advertised on TV. This could be Monster.com, Headhunter.net, Jobs.com, and Hotjobs.com, to name a few. Because of the superb marketing these companies do, you simply type the name of the company into your Web browser and visit the sites in question.

Pay the Fees Involved

The first thing you do when visiting these employment sites is to look around and see how to sign up and post your jobs or look at résumés. After all, these are big sites; you figure the sooner you get your job posts out on the Internet, the sooner active job seekers will find you. Additionally, the bonus of a résumé bank (this is a collection of résumés) makes you think this will take only a few minutes of your time; after all, these are résumés of people actually looking for new jobs.

So you explore the options available at the large job boards. What will you find? First of all, many will require a minimum commitment of more than one month. Hmmm, you think, that might be useful; after all, I might need to hire again in the future. You dig deeper, and find out that other money-devouring hidden costs pop up such as:

Location. If your job appears in more than one location, it might cost more.

Categories. Perhaps your job can fall under more than one category; for example, Sales and Marketing. You might incur more charges if you select more than one category.

Duration. Some boards will charge more for job posts to stay active for an extended period of time, or charge you again for reposting.

Résumés. Some boards will charge more for accessing their résumé bank as well as posting jobs to their site.

Let me digress for a second and spell out some things you might not realize about popular, large (and sometimes small) job boards in general. These are active businesses whose main goal generally is, quite correctly, the bottom line. The more packages/products/advertising they sell, the more profit they bring in. The more their salespeople sell, the more commissions they make, and the better performance review they receive. Thus, it's a pretty fair bet that when salespeople from these companies contact you, they will try to sell you on the package that not only meets your needs but also costs more than a single job post.

Selling as much as possible is a common trend in marketing. When you purchase anything from a company, you're identifying yourself as a potential customer for future products. If you invest in a single job post, for example, you've opened yourself up for salespeople to showcase how much more money you'll save in the long term should you buy a more comprehensive package! That's okay, of course; it's what good salespeople should do. *What you have to watch out for, however, is being sold more than you need.* I'll cover the questions you should ask of large career boards in Chapter 20, "Mastering Paid Job Boards."

Once you have the packaging and pricing in hand, you proceed to sign up, post your jobs, and view résumés. You're on your way to hiring. Life is joyous. Expensive, though.

The Long Term

The long-term approach is something you should implement as soon as possible. It merely means sowing the seeds of your quality where your future employees are most likely to be impressed and remember your name. Done right, this will enable you to always have either a candidate base at your fingertips, or dozens of loyal followers who will put the word out about your employment needs.

The long-term approach includes:

- Create a compelling career section on your Web site.
- Define the kinds of people you will hire sometime in the future.
- Uncover the best sites.
- Realize you need to hire someone.
- Write a comprehensive job description.
- Broadcast out to your personal network your hiring needs.
- Broadcast your jobs for free.

These steps are described in the seven sections that follow.

Create a Compelling Career Section on Your Web Site

First and foremost, a long-term Internet recruiting plan requires that you showcase how perfectly thrilling working at your company can be; think about it from your future employee's viewpoint. Your job advertisements will include facts about the requirements and benefits, as well as contact information that consists of your phone number, your e-mail address, and your Web site. It's human nature to want to explore further before committing to an action (in this case, submitting one's résumé). The Internet allows these people the opportunity to learn all about your company without requiring your assistance, simply by visiting your site.

Once you actually get them there, you need (you really do!) compelling information that hooks them even further. Probably you already have a business site; that's a perfect location for you to create a career section that details your benefits, your awards, happy employee testimonials, and more. You can liken this to your product section; in there, don't you showcase why your products or services are the ones people should choose? You want to apply this practice to convincing future hires that your company is the one in which they should work.

How can you achieve this? Well, think like your candidates do. What would impress *you* when learning about a new company? This important topic was covered in Chapter 5, "Sing a Song of Job Posts."

Define the Kinds of People You Will Hire in the Future

Successful long-term Internet recruiting means knowing ahead of crisis situations what kinds of people you will need to hire. This way, you'll be able to plan out an effective network to assist you in finding them. For example, perhaps your business is the local printing shop down by the corner. Ideally, you'd need sometime in the future to hire people to run the copiers, graphic artists, prepress specialists, and perhaps a manager or two. If instead, your business centers upon business-to-business networking and support, you might need to hire programmers skilled in cutting-edge technologies, administrative assistants to answer the phones, and project managers to take charge of offsite assignments and see them through from conception to deployment.

When you actually sit down and map out areas of business growth, you are crystallizing in your mind in what specialties you'll need to hire employees in the future. This information will aid you in creating a long-term recruiting plan. It's generally best to write this information down to help you create a plan of record.

Uncover the Best Sites

Now that you know the types of people you'll need to hire, your next step is to find out where they gather on the Internet. This means locating industry niche sites, professional organizations, regional sites, skill-specific sites, user groups, trade associations, mailing lists, forums, and other places where your future employees can be found.

When you research this information, you will almost certainly come up with relevant job banks where you can post your jobs or review specific résumés. But that's not the main purpose of long-term Internet recruiting; it's merely a side benefit. By actively finding where your candidates will be, you can then start becoming *part of their own community*. Remember the main purpose of the Internet; it's not to sell, it's not to engage in e-commerce; it's to provide resources and information so fellow professionals can learn and benefit. Your future employees are on the Internet for many other reasons besides that of job-seeking; they might want to check their favorite stock, research industry trends, chat with their peers about pressing business problems, and more.

When you start participating in community forums, mailing lists, and the like, your name will slowly but surely be built up in the minds of your audience. It's human nature to want to know and trust individuals with whom one does business; the more your future employees know of you, the better chances you'll have in attracting them to your site in the first place.

Realize You Need to Hire Someone

Let's say that you have taken the prior steps and are actively known in your professional community. It's taken some time; every few days or so you spend 15 minutes at specific forums or mailing lists participating with your peers, answering questions or simply lurking about. All of a sudden, your boss rushes in yet again with the news that you need to hire another programmer or another salesperson or another crane operator or another CEO or … you get the picture. One of the first things you'll notice is a lack of panic; the time you spent getting your word out has educated you a great deal about where the best candidates can be found. But not only that—because of the opt-in mailing list included in your career section on your business Web site, you already have hundreds of e-mail addresses of individuals who have asked you to keep them apprised of new career opportunities. Additionally, people know and trust you; if they're not interested in what you have to offer, chances are they will forward your opportunity to one of their friends who *is* actively searching for a new position.

In short, you don't have to panic, nor do you have to spend hours researching what job boards to use. You're already familiar with the regional and niche sites, as well as the professional organization boards and free résumé-posting places. You're knowledgeable about Yahoo's free job classifieds and the proper, free job-oriented newsgroups you can use. You can lay out a complete procedure for publicizing your new opportunity at a great discount and be confident that individuals will want to learn more.

Write a Comprehensive Job Description

The next step is to write a comprehensive job description. Because recruiting is nowadays more than ever based upon marketing and advertising, you aren't satisfied with including only the skills required. Instead, you not only write several paragraphs without abbreviations that detail the job itself, but also spend a fair amount of space describing all the benefits future employees will enjoy when working for you. These benefits can include salary, vacation, flextime, telecommuting, onsite free coffee, local parking, and of course, quirky perks that serve to spark more attention. Additionally, you make certain to include all the necessary contact information such as your company's Web-site address, your personal e-mail address, your phone number and a fax number, and you include space for future employees to answer qualifying questions such as career goals, number of certifications, availability date, and more. Finally, you make darned sure not to post the entire ad in capital letters; that's akin to shouting on the Internet, and makes reading an advertisement quite painful.

The more information present in a job post, the more keywords generally included, and this serves to increase visibility to the right audience. Not only that, however; when you demonstrate a thorough understanding of what the position requires, you're providing future employees with the data they might require to determine if the position would be of interest to them.

Broadcast Out to Your Personal Network Your Hiring Needs

Now that you have in your possession a quality job advertisement, you broadcast this information out to your personal network that you've been cultivating over the past few months. This could include an opt-in e-zine, a list of Web-site visitors who have indicated interest in being notified whenever a new position opens, or even mentioning it in a forum in which you're a leading contributor. This is one of the reasons why creating a network of peers and professionals is so valuable; while the majority of Internet communities frown on blind self-promotion, they are much more willing to let advertisements go through if you've already contributed extensively to the community in question. Give and take—that's what the Internet is all about.

Broadcast Your Jobs for Free

After your jobs have been advertised to your own private network, it's time to take advantage of all the free or low-cost places that abound on the Internet where your targeted candidates gather. For example, automotive engineers have a career section at the **Society of Automotive Engineers** at http://www.sae.org/, competitive professionals enjoy a career section called **The Society of Competitive Intelligence** at http://www.scip.org/, and project managers have a free career board at **AllPM** at http://www.allpm.com/ as seen in Figure 6.4. You also should benefit from some of the regional job boards that are dotting the Internet landscape. Advertising your opportunity to community Web sites or the online newspaper classifieds might generate more interest than blasting it out nationwide.

As you can see, the process isn't difficult at all; it's rather methodical. But it does take time and a commitment to developing your name and reputation.

FACT—*Long-term recruiting involves a commitment on your part to get your name and your company's name in front of the right audience in the right fashion for a long period of time. Luckily, this is rather easy to accomplish.*

Before You Dive In

It's most temping to zoom directly to all the goodies regarding recruiting on the Internet. But wait. One of the rather fascinating characteristics of the Internet is the speed at which it changes. What shows up today in a search engine query, for example, might be more invisible than oxygen on a clear summer's night tomorrow!

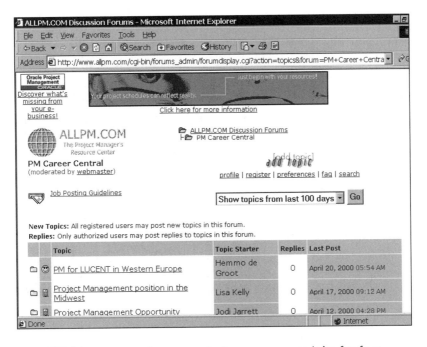

Figure 6.4: AllPM lets you post your project management jobs for free.

Thus it makes sense to first discuss the basics of searching techniques that you can apply for your own needs. Use the information contained here as a guide, but be certain to tailor it to your own queries during your own quests.

Faster Than the Speed of—*The Internet changes at the speed of, well, really fast things. What appears today might be toast by tomorrow. Always expect the unexpected when searching on the Internet—never become complacent.*

A Brief Description of Search Engines

Virtually all of the mysteries I reveal in this book have been uncovered by querying different search engines. You're probably familiar with search engines—there's **Yahoo!** at http://www.yahoo.com/, which really isn't a search engine (it's a directory) but everyone views it as such, **AltaVista** at http://www.altavista.com/ that last year underwent a metamorphosis to become a media portal, **Excite** at http://www.excite.com/, **Google** at http://www.google.com/, and many others. For the purpose of recruiting on the Internet, I'm going to focus only on the following search engines:

> **General all-purpose searching: Google** at http://www.google.com/ or **Yahoo!** at http://www.yahoo.com/. Google displays results based upon link popularity (the more other individuals link to a particular site, the higher relevancy it will have), and Yahoo! has a great metro/regional database.

> **Passive résumé finding: AltaVista** at http://www.altavista.com/ has an advanced search feature that allows you to string together queries like a logic puzzle. Other search engines have this ability too, but AltaVista's database is one of the largest available. For example, if you wanted to find résumés of individuals located in NJ, you could include the requirement that the area code contains 732 or 908 or 973 or any of the other NJ area codes, and that the title contains the word resume (an example appears in Figure 6.5). This allows you to directly target your query with extreme precision.

Maximizing Your Search Engine Results

Did you know that all the pages you see on the Internet via your browser consist of several components? They include the title, the address (otherwise known as the URL), and the domain (the machine on which the file is hosted). Search engines have been built to allow you to focus and target these specific criteria when searching. Put this book down now, and visit **Top Floor** at http://TopFloor.com/.

Now look at the top part of your browser. See the words "Top Floor Publishing Home"? That's the *title* of the document.

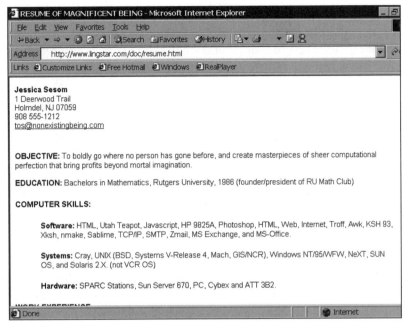

Figure 6.5: Note how the word `resume` appears at the top of the page.

Let me ask you. When people create a résumé, what will they most likely call it? You got it—`resume`! And quite often, that word will appear in the title of their Web résumé, too. You can target your search engine queries at AltaVista to focus on *words in the title.* This will greatly assist you in locating free résumés of people who have the skills you need. You can also query on the URL. (That's the address of any Web site. If you visit AOL, the URL there is http://www.aol.com/). Not only do people call their résumés `resume`, but often they'll store it in a file called `resume.html`. When you view that in your browser, you'll notice the word `resume` now appears in the URL, too.

Other tips that will maximize your search engine results are knowing when to use:

Quotes. Quotes are helpful when you want to uncover words next to one another, such as a phrase. For example, searching for "`new jersey`" should return sites that include that state's name, and not sentences like "New for the summer—Jersey cows!"

AND/OR. Some search engines will allow you to further define your search parameters by letting you use the words AND and OR. AND is used when you would like to specify pages to contain all terms, and OR is used when you want to ensure one or more of the terms is included in the results. For example, searching for `sales AND retail AND resume` should return pages that include résumés of professionals who list sales and retail; `sales OR retail` will instead return sites that deal with sales or retail or both. And `(sales OR retail) AND resume` will increase the probability of locating résumés with either one of those two skills.

Parentheses. Parentheses are used when grouping characteristics together. For example, you can use parentheses to specify that you'd like to find résumés of people that are in New York or New Jersey or Connecticut, and have Java or e-commerce experience, and that you want the word `resume` in either the title or the URL. Such a query might be written `("new york" or "new jersey" or connecticut) and (java or e-commerce) and (title:resume or url:resume)`.

Whenever you visit a search engine, always look for the Help link. This page will detail all the great ways to improve your searching. For example, **AltaVista's Help** can be found at http://doc.altavista.com/help/search/search_help.shtml.

***Help Is on the Way**—Whenever you use a service on the Internet, be it a search engine, a job site, an e-commerce site, etc., you can almost always find a link for "help" that will describe how to get the most out of your activities.*

Search engines can be very powerful tools for your Internet recruiting needs. You can use them for uncovering locations where your future employees gather.

The last thing to remember about search engines is that many of them now include directories in which you can browse. Quite often, you'll be able to uncover resources like niche career sites, industry links, community information, and much more, simply by looking around. But there is one more critical aspect to consider before you start searching for employees on the Internet. And that is managing your own and your business's expectations.

Managing Your Expectations

So often, people think that when they post jobs on the Internet, they will find, interview, and hire their dream future employee within a few days. If this is your idea, I beg you to read the following sections; there are many variables that will influence the time that transpires from searching to hiring.

What Do You Think Really Will Happen?

To listen to the hype that's surrounding all the large job boards and Internet recruiting in general, one would think that finding employees is as easy as fastening Velcro sneakers. Alas, this is not always the case.

Remember that you are not the only person looking for people to hire. You are competing against your fellow recruiters, corporations, retained search consultants, and the like. Sometimes you'll find the perfect résumé of the perfect employee, but she won't consider relocating to Nebraska. Other times, you'll find Java programmers, Oracle programmers, and Sybase programmers, but nobody skilled in your particular application who lives nearby.

Long Term—*Comprehensive Internet recruiting takes time. Generally, you will not find the perfect employee within ten minutes of searching on the Internet. It takes time. Factor that into your expectations.*

Not to fear! This is to be expected. If one avenue doesn't pan out, there are always 33 others to try. The best way to high-quality, low-cost Internet recruiting is to be *methodical*. There are dozens of ways of getting your message out in front of potential hires—you'll see a number of them in the upcoming chapters. When starting out, you might find dozens of résumés of people potentially dying to work for someone like you. Your job posts might start to bring in hundreds of e-mailed résumés every week; in short, you might all of a sudden find yourself on information overload. This can lead to panic, frustration, and a sense of "Oh gee, why even bother." Trust me, this is expected.

Let's take the simple action of posting a job. Perhaps you posted your position via a job-broadcasting service such as:

EQuest
http://www.equest.com/

Ad-Cast
http://www.ad-cast.com/

AllInOneSubmit
http://www.allinonesubmit.com/.

That one job post can end up being broadcast to numerous sites including newsgroups, job sites, classifieds, and more. From there, anyone on the Internet can view it; you might start receiving résumés from halfway across the planet. This increase in viewing will probably result in a flurry of résumés fluttering about you like monarch butterflies during their annual migration. How do you discover the diamonds without shoveling a lot of coal?

Halfway Across the World—*When your job is posted on the Internet, just about anyone, anywhere, can view it (unless it's been distributed solely to paid sites). This means that Bapu from India can see your New Jersey post and apply for the position.*

How Do You Define Success?

What is your definition for success when recruiting on the Internet? Generally, it's "when I find the person I want to hire, quickly and for little money." But is that your *real* definition? Sometimes management will want to see numbers as well. How many résumés did you uncover? How many jobs did you post? How many requests for future information did you receive?

It's always a good idea to finalize with your supervisor or colleagues what your definition of Internet recruiting success *is*. This will greatly decrease frustrations or misconceptions when beginning the exercise. Internet recruiting can be a speedy process; quite often, however, it will simply take time for:

- You to uncover what sites work the best for you
- Your visitors to spread the word about how beneficial your site is
- You to get the rhythm of Internet recruiting down to a fine art

A big problem you want to avoid is unproductive time management. When you begin searching for free places to post your ads, you want to utilize techniques that increase your success. If you find yourself doing the same thing, over and over, with no positive results, you might decide you're simply wasting your time. It's akin to running a marathon; you don't want to expend all of your energy at the very beginning and run up and down every alley that presents itself. You want instead to conserve your strength (in this case, interest) and follow a logical path towards uncovering the resources you need. If something doesn't work the first time, that's okay! You merely need to vary your searching techniques.

Managing Your Time

The amount of time you spend will decrease as your experience and familiarity increases. A good rule of thumb when searching on the Internet is to allocate a half hour every morning, preferably when you're enjoying your morning coffee, to looking for ways of hiring via the Internet.

When you create your own process, that which works best for you, you're *maximizing the returns of your valuable time.* Some people adore poring through search engines to find passive candidates (people not actively looking for a new position). Other individuals enjoy writing killer job posts and can spend hours fine-tuning their masterpiece, but only want to dedicate five minutes to locating job boards at which to place them. That can be okay too—one can learn dozens of excellent spots in which to post jobs and return there, again and again.

TIP—*Dedicate half an hour each morning, every morning, to looking for sites in which to find your future employees. This will help get you into a habit that fits best into your schedule, and ease the time demands you might encounter.*

Finally, you really need to be prepared for the unexpected. Never get your hopes up for zillions of résumés—for one thing, you might receive them, all from unhireable people, and for another, you might end up seeing only two. Wait until a week or two has gone by after you've begun recruiting on the Internet before making any judgments.

With that out of the way, let's begin! The next chapters will reveal to you many of the hidden tricks and techniques to take advantage of free or low-cost Internet recruiting; we'll start off with exploring the benefits contained within the numerous industry niche sites that abound on the Internet.

CHAPTER SEVEN

Industry Niche Sites

Do you stay on top of trends in your industry? For example, if your business deals with computers and the Internet, do you read magazines like *PC World* or *Network Computing*? If you're managing marketing and advertising, do you read trade newspapers like *Ad Week*? In other words, do you value keeping abreast of your industry trends so you can do a better job and advance in your own career?

Ten to one that your future employees are doing the same thing. Niche Web sites are a modern-day equivalent to niche magazines; these comprehensive sites provide one-stop shopping for all concerns within an industry. The more reasons professionals have to visit such sites, the larger a targeted audience the owner can claim, and the more money he or she can charge for advertising.

***Improve Your Career**—Professionals often turn to industry niche sites to stay abreast of cutting-edge developments in their field.*

The origins of industry niche sites began long before the World Wide Web: mailing lists, bulletin boards, and newsgroups were among the first resources to be used for these kinds of communications. Remember how the Internet first became popular via ARPANet? Diligent searching on AltaVista reveals that documents over 15 years old are still available online; for example, the archives for **Genetic Algorithms** (certainly a niche field of interest) date all the way back to 1985 at http://www.aic.nrl.navy.mil/galist/digests/v1n4.

As industry niche sites mature, they can become big business. But to increase, one has to provide compelling reasons for viewership to grow. Including timely resources from which visitors can benefit, such as community-building tools like forums and mailing lists, vendor discounts, and *career opportunities*, are some of the techniques currently being used. You can liken it to buying a new car for your family; right before purchasing, you want to find the make and model that delivers the most value for your money. Some car designs focus on safety, others focus on being a babe-mobile; still others are now being hailed as energy-efficient and long-lasting. What quality would first get you into the door (or online, as the case may be)? What extras would make you want to part with your hard-earned cash? What really would satisfy your desires? Industry niche sites such as CEonline.com, seen in Figure 7.1, face the same types of questions; not only do they want to provide quality information and benefits to the visitors, but they want to become number one as a *destination resource* for their community. The more visitors, the more visibility to the right audience, and the higher the probability the site owners have of making a substantial income from the site.

Everyone has lists of favorite sites to visit for specific reasons. I'll always browse **Yahoo! News** at http://dailynews.yahoo.com/ for current headlines, meander through **DLJ Direct** at http://www.dljdirect.com/ for financial information, and read the **Entrepreneurial Success Forum** postings at http://www.ablake.net/forum/ to stay abreast of current Internet marketing habits. These three places are a habitual stop for me; every single day I visit them to see what's new. Certainly there are other places I might meander by for the same kind of information; however, I find these three harmonize with my karma more than any others. I have no desire to uncover others; these meet my needs admirably. Industry niche sites want to evoke the same kind of loyalty from their visitors, too.

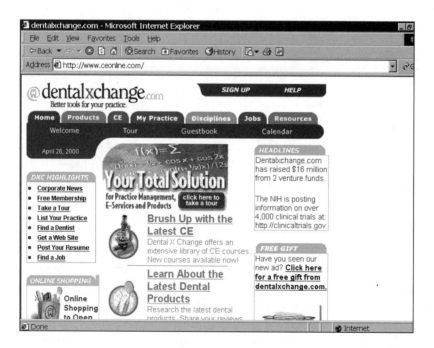

Figure 7.1: CEonline.com is a niche site for dentists. Notice the wealth of resources.

How Industry Niche Sites Differ from Job Boards

When you visit an industry niche site, you'll see much more than simply a career section (if a career section exists). Other resources that are bound to be available include:

Current news. Many times targeted headlines will appear on the main page of an industry niche site. This allows visitors to get their quick fix of what's happening in their professional field. Current news can include what companies are increasing their market share, what high-level executives are moving, new innovations in the industry, reports and polls about current employment statistics, bills that are being considered in Congress that would affect the industry, and the like.

Industry resources. Often you'll uncover industry resources—industry associations, trade show information, manufacturers and suppliers, to name a few. Remember the main goal of an industry niche site—provide as many useful resources as possible. Some very popular sites can charge businesses and suppliers to list their contact and product information; this is yet another revenue stream for the site itself. Other resources might include certification information (quite often, becoming certified is a guaranteed way of increasing one's salary), columns and essays about industry-related topics, and links to associations and organizations.

Vendor lists. Remember my point earlier about advertising dollars? Vendors bring revenue to the industry niche sites by advertising their wares in prominent positions. This can be very useful for business owners or managers that frequent the site; being able to call and compare vendors from a single list can be a great time-saver.

Community resources. Modern industry niche sites will include forums for professionals to discuss industry issues and mailing lists for different topics. Pay close attention to these kinds of resources—sometimes they will focus solely upon jobs offered and résumés posted. For example, **Orafans** at http://www.orafans.com/, a site dedicated to individuals skilled in Oracle, has two free career-related boards. And Donver Corporation's **Hotel Resource Center for the Hospitality Profession** at http://www.hotelresource.com/careercenter.htm allows you to post your jobs and view résumés for free.

Community resources are one of your most valuable tools for long-term recruiting. A forum on which nobody posts is as popular as a ghost town; visitors will almost always check out the discussions to see what's going on. If you can post quality information about your industry when other professionals ask, you'll be taking a large step towards becoming the job provider of choice.

Networking—*Many industry niche sites provide ample opportunities to network, including forums and mailing lists. Sometimes their job boards use actual forums instead of career-related software.*

Why do you want to be alert to all of the goodies offered by industry sites? Jobs and career opportunities are not the only thing you might find! Many Web sites today include a healthy dose of interactivity—forums, chats, questions and answers, and the like. Think about it. *These kinds of sites are attracting your kinds of employees!* On industry niche sites, you can build your brand and become a known, valued authority; this can go light-years towards encouraging professionals to look in your direction when job opportunities arise.

Other benefits can be uncovered. If you can't carve out some time every week or so to post in forums, you can take advantage of the targeted audience and merely advertise via links or banners at these sites. Just think, if you employ engineers, and you could score a banner advertisement in the job section of the IEEE ... what would the probability be that your job opportunity will be seen by your future employees?

How to Find Your Industry Niche Site

Locating industry niche sites specifically targeted towards your business is not difficult at all. It can be done via the following simple steps:

- Define your niche industry.
- Browse industry directories.
- Utilize search engines.
- Determine which sites to use.
- Post your jobs and monitor the results.

The following five sections describe these steps separately.

Step One: Define Your Niche Industry

Quite often, this will be rather simple to do. If you are the manager of a sales team, most likely you would want to uncover sales professional sites like **Sales.com** at http://www.sales.com/.

But think for a second. Can you narrow your focus even more? Selling computers, for example, can require radically different skills than selling cosmetics, which is different from selling insurance. And what if you're an office manager of real estate agents and need to hire a computer expert for the office network? Even though your personal industry is real estate, you probably wouldn't post a computer-based advertisement in a real estate–oriented site like **AgentNews** at http://www.agentnews.com/; you'd save that superb site for your Realtor posts.

Another way you can define leads for your targeted industry is to see where your competitors are congregating and what sites they are sponsoring. For example, perhaps you listen to the radio and catch an advertisement about a competitor's Web site. It's a pretty good bet that this company isn't pouring their money into that site unless they're receiving (or hope to receive) numerous benefits from having their name attached to the site. Ask yourself, if my competitor is supporting a particular industry niche site, would it make sense for me to mosey on by and discover the potential benefits for myself?

Step Two: Browse Industry Directories

Once you have your industry targeted, you then search for your quarry. This can be done by the following methods:

Visit several of the generic industry directories, such as **Skillbot** at http://www.skillbot.com/community/ and **IndustryLink** at http://www.industrylink.com/. There's a good chance you'll uncover some excellent resources at these places. **Skillbot**, for example, will provide you with direct links to specific resources; choosing **Technical Writing** at http://www.skillbot.com/community/technical_writing.htm reveals links to **Inkspot** at http://www.inkspot.com/, **The Society for Technical Communication** at http://www.stc.org/, and **The Write Jobs** at http://www.writerswrite.com/jobs/, among others. All of these places allow job posts.

Visit **Google** at http://www.google.com/ and search for `<industry>` jobs, `<industry>` careers, or `<industry>` employment. For example, if you were looking to hire banking professionals, searching on banking jobs might return sites like

BankJobs
http://www.bankjobs.com/

JobsInTheMoney
http://www.jobsinthemoney.com/

Fincareer.com
http://www.fincareer.com/ (as seen in Figure 7.2)

Figure 7.2: Fincareer.com targets financial careers.

The wealth of sites you'll uncover can stagger the imagination at times. Don't feel as though you have to wade through dozens and dozens of sites; quite often, you'll only need to uncover two or three excellent resources to meet your hiring needs. Of course, if other sites prove to be free as well, you definitely should maximize your visibility and post your positions there, too.

Visit **Google** at http://www.google.com/ and search for `<industry>` resources. For example, if you were looking to hire engineers, searching on `engineering resources` might return sites like

SciCentral
http://www.scicentral.com/

PhDs.org
http://www.phds.org/

EngineeringJobs.com
http://www.engineeringjobs.com/

Berkeley's Engineering Library
http://www.lib.berkeley.edu/ENGI/

As you can see, the process for actually locating niche sites is rather simple. Remember our earlier discussion about search engines; it's easy to become overwhelmed by information overload. Take it methodically and carefully; don't get flustered by all the possibilities that abound.

Perhaps after your browsing, you still will not have uncovered the resources you need. In that case, it's time to revisit your friendly neighborhood search engine. Before we go there, let's review search engine basics:

What am I looking for? Industry niche sites.

What are the keywords that I might use? Industry names, such as `sales`, `engineering`, `printing`, `distribution`, `metal`, `lumber`, `book publishing`, `computers`, or `finance`, combined with the keywords `jobs`, `careers`, `employment`, `links`, or `resources`.

Step Three: Utilize Search Engines

Let's say that you are looking for a technical sales professional. Searching on **Google** for `"technical sales"` `jobs` might return a link to **Denver's Computer Jobs** at http://www.denver.computerjobs.com/denver_html/Pub/salesmkt.htm. Visiting that link reveals a computer job site that has a section oriented towards technical sales as well as **Oya's Directory of Recruiters—Technical Sales** at http://www.i-recruit.com/oya/drecruiters_type_technical_sales.htm and **Career Central for Sales** at http://www.careercentral.com/Sales/. Did you notice the quotes I used in this example? Quotes are required when you want to search for phrases instead of individual keywords.

Search Engine Wisdom—*Sometimes adding quotes to your search phrases assists in narrowing down usable returned sites.*

Remember, the best way to search on the Internet for information is to boil down the requirements to the most basic possible. There is no need to flounder about online, trying hundreds of different word combinations! Another word you might be tempted to use is `free` when searching on the Internet. This can work but not as often as you'd think—many sites use "free" to mean "free for job seekers." Alas, this is a category that does not include employers. However, some industries are leaning more and more towards allowing free job posting as well as résumé searching. The IT space, for example, is becoming more and more crowded—you can start to see different marketing mechanisms being applied. Check out **IT Toolbox** at http://www.ittoolbox.com/—it's a portal site for ten related disciplines including **E-business** at http://ebiz.ittoolbox.com/, **Oracle** at http://www.oracleassist.com/, and **Peoplesoft** at http://www.peoplesoftassist.com/. All of these portals are notable for the wealth of resources they provide—forums, mailing lists, and job banks—all for free. **Superexpert** at http://www.superexpert.com/ is another gathering of complementary sites that provide free job posting and other resources.

At first, this might seem to be counterintuitive. With Internet recruiting becoming as popular as it is, why would specific career-related sites give such value away for free? What possible benefit could they achieve? Actually, depending upon the business goals, it can make a lot of sense. By allowing such value-added services to be available for free, traffic is bound to increase most favorably. More traffic enables the owners of such sites to charge more for advertising.

You can try to locate for yourself similar communities of sites. Let's say that you are looking to hire a marketing professional. What industries are related? Marketing interfaces closely with Sales—you could search for `sales jobs` to get leads on marketing jobs. It's rather straightforward to do. Visit **Google** at http://www.google.com/ and search for `"sales and marketing"` `jobs`. You might be returned a link to the **Riley Guide "Sales and Marketing Opportunities"** page at http://www.dbm.com/jobguide/sales.html. Now, this is not a sales job site! However, it does provide direct links and pointers to other sites on the Internet that do deal directly with sales and marketing jobs, such as

MarketingJobs
http://www.marketingjobs.com/

The American Marketing Association
http://www.ama.org/ (which has a career section on its site)

RetailJobNet
http://www.retailjobnet.com/

RetailSeek
http://www.retailseek.com/

If you want to become extremely proficient at sniffing out more opportunities for low-cost Internet recruiting, take a good long hard look at the original **Riley Guide "Sales"** page at http://www.dbm.com/jobguide/sales.html. Note that the URL includes the phrase sales.html. If there's a sales.html on a general-description site, there will probably be pages for other industries too! That's our first clue that this site is worth investigating.

The next clue appears at the bottom of the sales page. There's a link called **Job Page** that will bring you to http://www.dbm.com/jobguide/jobs.html. And on that page you'll find resources for Business and Finance job sites including

The American Association of Payroll Managers
http://www.aspm.org/

Bloomberg's CareerFinder
http://www.bloomberg.com/fun/jobs.html

Fincareer.com
http://www.fincareer.com/

Personal and Commercial job sites like

FuneralNet
http://www.funeralnet.com/

Equipment Leasing Association
http://www.elaonline.com/

CosmeticWorld
http://www.cosmeticworld.com/

Health Care job sites like

Health Care Job Store
http://www.healthcarejobstore.com/

Medzilla
http://www.medzilla.com/

HealthCareers Online
http://www.healthcareers-online.com/

Let's take a step back now and review the previous process. You've uncovered a multitude of excellent resources by examining one specific site. This is a key skill for Internet recruiting; quite often, places will suggest themselves for future exploration if you're alert to the hidden signs that beg, "Look further!" You'll experience a higher rate of success in ferreting out free or low-cost sites if you learn this skill well.

Step Four: Determine Which Sites to Use

The next task you must accomplish is to determine if a potential site has the kind of career resources for which you are looking. To do so, visit the site and ask yourself the following questions.

- Is there a section labeled Careers? If so, your search is over; that's where you'd go to post your jobs.
- If not, is there a section labeled Jobs, or Résumés?

- If not, is there a section labeled Classifieds? Sometimes job offers fall under this specific category.
- If not, are there forums or discussions in which career-related issues are present?
- If not, are there advertising or sponsoring opportunities available where your company can be showcased?
- If not, can you opt for paper or e-mail advertising in an industry newsletter?

Like just about everything else in Internet recruiting, you simply use a methodical process to uncover where you might be able to benefit by getting your message out to your future employees.

The previous steps describe how to evaluate a site visually. That's a good beginning; now you have to verify that your targeted audience can be found at the sites you choose. Of course, if it's free to advertise your jobs, go ahead and do so—the more visibility the better!

Otherwise, contact the site manager in question. It might be the owner, it might be the Webmaster—every Web site should have a contact page that reveals how to best get in touch with The Powers That Be. Ask them for their demographics—how many visitors do they get? It might be a wee bit impossible to verify the responses, however.

You could also ask your current coworkers what industry sites they frequent. And possibly most importantly, you can network with your colleagues in industry-related mailing lists. Think of it. Let's say that you're in the hospital industry and need to hire nurses. Wouldn't it be great if you could get ideas electronically from your peers regarding excellent locations to find employees? Mailing lists are so important to recruiting that I've dedicated all of Chapter 13 to them. For the purpose of this example, you could simply visit **Onelist** at http://www.onelist.com/ and search for nursing. You'll discover several resources that might prove to be quite valuable.

Peer Networking—*Asking colleagues for advice on what industry niche sites they use might prove beneficial in your own Internet recruiting plans.*

Step Five: Post Your Jobs and Monitor the Results

Finally, now that you've determined which job board to use, post your jobs and monitor the results. Remember to include all the points discussed in Chapter 5 about job posting! Are your ads chock-full of benefits? Is the contact information correct? Is there a catchy headline? Have you alerted the person who will be receiving the résumés that the job is now posted on the Internet, and be prepared to respond to inquiries?

There are several ways you'll be able to post your jobs. Some sites simply will provide you with one great big text box in which you can paste your entire job; others will insist you fill out specific forms and fields so the jobs are formatted in a specific fashion. In Chapter 5, we discussed how to create a stunning job post; you can save each job post in a file on your computer, and open it whenever needed. This will enable you to always have it at your fingertips when the opportunity to post it becomes available. Always remember, too, to factor in the cost; some industry niche sites will let you post for free, as seen in Figure 7.3, while others will require a fee.

Keeping track of your job-posting success will be one more way that you can streamline your company's operations in the future.

Examples

In this chapter, we learned how to find and network with job seekers who frequent the popular Web sites that relate to their industry. Let's put this information into practice and walk through the following two examples:

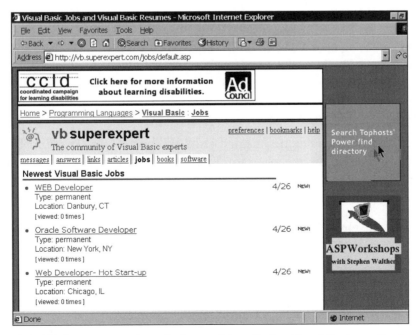

Figure 7.3: VB Superexpert is an industy niche site for Visual Basic professionals; it includes free job posting and résumé viewing.

- Locate California Java and e-commerce experts.
- Locate New Jersey architects.

These examples will show you how to utilize successfully the resources we covered in this chapter.

Locate California Java and E-commerce Experts

Jess is the owner of a Web-site developing company in California. One of his account managers informed him of a new client acquisition that will require individuals skilled in Java and the building of e-commerce sites. The nature of the business will allow him to consider candidates from across the country—developers don't have to be on the premises to deliver on their deadlines. Thus, his horizons are considerably wider than a local job search.

Whom does Jess need?

First Jess needs to define what kinds of individuals he needs. Certainly Java and e-commerce are requisite skills—additionally, Internet, design, and backend database design in languages such as Cold Fusion would certainly be desirable.

What does Jess need to find?

Ideally, Jess needs to locate industry niche forums where he can either post his jobs, review résumés, or participate in discussions where he can become part of the community. Thus, whenever he locates a specific site in his searches, he always tries to uncover links that deal with jobs, résumés, and forums.

Where does Jess look?

Before jumping to search engines, he first visits **Skillbot** at http://www.skillbot.com/community/ and sees that the page for Java includes a link to the **Cold Fusion Advisor** at http://www.cfadvisor.com/. Exploring further, he'll see a specific site for jobs that is free for both reviewing résumés and posting jobs.

Jess is successful! He now has one place to post positions and look for résumés.

Going back to Skillbot, he notices that Java is a category under Internet. Another keyword! There are links to **JavaWorld** at http://www.javaworld.com/ and **ITCareers** at http://www.itcareers.com/. Posting a position at ITCareers costs more than $100. Still, depending upon the traffic, it might be worthwhile.

Jess now has a second site at which to post his jobs.

It's time to consider targeting sites that are actively Java-job–oriented. He visits **Google** at http://www.google.com/ and searches for `java jobs`—sites that appear might include **AllJavaJobs** at http://www.all-java-jobs.com/, **JavaJobs** at http://www.javajobs.com/, **JavaJobsOnline** at http://www.javajobsonline.com/, **JustJavaJobs** at http://www.justjavajobs.com/ (all free), and **About.com's Java Jobs Resources** at http://java.about.com/education/java/msubjobs.htm, which contains even more links to Java-specific employment pages. There's a very good chance that at the above sites, he'll be able to either find a worthy programmer or post his own job.

Success again! Jess now has more areas in which to find targeted employees, all at a considerable discount compared to the major career job boards.

What about e-commerce? Searching on `e-commerce jobs` could return a link to **Ecommerce Times Job Bank** at http://www.ecommercetimes.com/jobs/ (paid) or **JustEcommerceJobs** at http://www.juste-commercejobs.com/ (free).

Next, Jess should consider the professionals themselves. Java or e-commerce developers probably have their own hangouts in which one might be able to post jobs or view résumés. Searching on `"java developer" jobs` might return the site **WebDeveloper.com** at http://jobs.webdeveloper.com/ or **Developers.net** at http://www.developers.net/. Perhaps he'll be able to find his Java professional there, too.

By searching for characteristics of his future employees (they're developers), Jess has uncovered more targeted sites.

Remember, Jess is in California, and Java is a technical skill. Searching on `california technical jobs` might return sites like **Computerwork's Bay Area** at http://bayarea.computerwork.com/ or **About.com's Technical California Jobs** at http://jobsearchtech.about.com/compute/jobsearchtech/msub20ca.htm (a list of over a dozen California-specific job sites including **California Jobs** at http://www.californiajobs.com/, the **California Online Job Network** at http://cajobs.com/, and the **Job Summit** at http://www.jobsummit.com/). These are all locations in which Jess can post his open positions. Some of them will have more activity than others, of course; he first needs to determine which site will return the most benefits from usages. He can do this by conversing with his peers (job posts almost always have e-mail contacts; he can send the poster e-mail asking if the job board has been a valuable resource), seeing how popular the site is, and asking his current employees their opinions.

Jess considered the locations where his jobs are available, and was able to find more job banks where he can post his open positions with success.

Finding sites for technical professionals is extraordinarily easy on the Internet. But what if you're looking in a nontechnical profession?

Locate New Jersey Architects

Theresa is the manager of an architectural firm headquartered in New Jersey, and has just been given the go-ahead to hire another architect. Her first task is to define the particular industry she needs to target.

Whom does Theresa need? Luckily, this time it's pretty obvious—she needs to hire an architect! So her next task is to uncover sites specifically dedicated to the field and see if any offer job-posting opportunities.

What does Theresa need to find?

Ideally, Theresa needs to locate local architectural resources in which she can post jobs or peruse résumés. Failing that, finding a network of architects (such as an architectural organization) might give her inroads into architecture-only job sites and career resources.

Where does Theresa look?

She visits **Skillbot** at http://www.skillbot.com/community/. While no link for Architect exists, there *is* a link for Construction. That site lists the **Building Exchange** at http://www.building.org/, where she'll find specific forums for architects and employment opportunities. It turns out there's a way to view résumés for free, too.

Success! Theresa has found an architectural resource that includes forums and job boards; this is an excellent opportunity for networking. It's now time to visit search engines.

Next, she visits **Google** at http://www.google.com/ and searches for `architect jobs`. One site that is returned is **ArchitectJobs** at http://www.architectjobs.com/. Looking at the site, she can tell that it's free to post jobs. A phone number and e-mail contact information is present on the site. Next, she has to call the site's owner and inquire: What is the traffic? How many résumés are present on the site? How many of the professionals live in New Jersey? Theresa's next step is to see what other sites have linked to ArchitectJobs, in hopes of uncovering other architect-specific Web sites.

Theresa now has another resource—one strictly for architects. Now she looks to see what similar sites exist.

Visiting **AltaVista** at http://www.altavista.com/ and searching for `link:www.architectjobs.com -url:www.architectjobs.com` reveals a complete directory of architect-related sites at **Netscape's Architects Directory** at http://directory.netscape.com/Business/Industries/Construction_and_Maintenance/ Design/Architects/. A directory! From there, she chooses to search on `architect jobs` within all categories and finds the industry niche for which she's looking: **Business > Jobs > Careers > Construction** at http://directory.netscape.com/Business/Jobs/Careers/Construction/. There, she'll uncover **The AEC Jobbank** with its free résumé search at http://aecjobbank.com/texis/script/findarésumé/.

Theresa has uncovered an industry niche site that allows for free job posting and résumé viewing.

Next, she visits Google again and searches now for `architect resources`. One site that comes up might be the **Texas Society of Architects Resource Page** at http://www.texasarchitect.org/arcres/. Visiting that site reveals a free resource to post jobs or look at résumés. Texas, of course, isn't New Jersey. But think; if a society for architects exists in Texas, perhaps one will exist in New Jersey. She revises her search and instead looks for `New Jersey Society of Architects` and comes up with their site, **AIA New Jersey** at http://www.aia-nj.org/. Alas, there doesn't seem to be a way to post jobs! She can either contact the Society and ask if such a section will be included in the future, or offer to advertise her positions via a banner or link. Poking around the site reveals a links page where she'll find a link to **The American Institute of Architects** at http://www.e-architect.com/, which contains an inexpensive way of posting jobs (and a free means of perusing résumés). Over a dozen New Jersey-specific résumés can be found.

Theresa has now found a New Jersey-based site for architects.

Remember how we came across this specific site. It was because we had uncovered a link to the Texas Society of Architects, and deduced that the same thing must exist for the state of New Jersey. All of the above sites might be quite viable for finding her future employees.

Some Final Comments

An excellent rule of thumb when searching on the Internet is to always be open to exploration, even if it might seem outlandish at first; you never know just what you'll uncover. As your experience with Internet recruiting increases, you'll develop a sense for effective and rapid searching. This will greatly decrease the amount of time you spend online looking for employees.

When searching for industry niche sites, you want to methodically uncover sites where your targeted audience resides. You can not only take advantage of job postings and résumé perusals, but also take part in community discussions, consider advertising or banner links, and otherwise network with your future employees. You are never limited to only posting your job advertisements.

CHAPTER EIGHT

Professional Organizations

Professional organizations or trade associations have probably been around as long as businesses have existed.

You're probably a member of one or two yourself. For example, if you're a banker, you might have joined the **American Bankers Association**. Did you know they have a Web site at http://www.aba.com/? And that their **Job Resume Bank** is housed at http://aba.careersite.com/? An excellent resource to locate bankers, I would say.

***Targeted Career Resources**—Professional organization sites often include targeted career resources specifically geared towards their members. Depending upon the industry, quite often you'll find your future employees at these sites.*

Maybe you're in the e-commerce industry, and need to hire software consultants. Did you know that the **Software Contractors' Guild** as seen in Figure 8.1 at http://www.scguild.com/ allows you to view résumés of independent consultants for free? Professional and trade organizations on the Internet are not limited to the current high-tech and business frenzy that this century is currently seeing, of course. Do you need to hire within the petroleum industry? The **National Petroleum Management Association** at http://www.fuelnet.org/ has a free job board in the shape of a forum to which you can post your openings. What about bakery technical needs? **The American Society of Bakers** at http://www.asbe.org/ has a guestbook/forum where you can ask for help to locate your targeted future employees.

In short, if you're in an industry, there's probably a society or association that is targeted towards your professional needs. Networking is an excellent benefit that members realize from joining these types of organizations; often local chapters will schedule regional meetings or dinners where members can mingle and form business relationships. This is a superb opportunity to get the word out about your future employment openings.

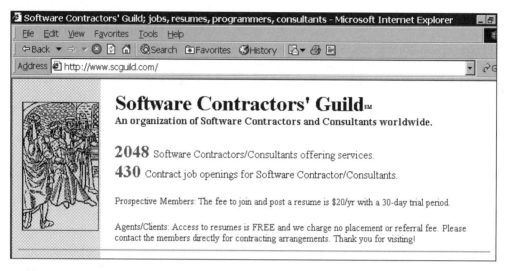

Figure 8.1: The Software Contractors' Guild offers free access to member's résumés.

Professional Organization Sites Consist of ...

Professional organization sites can run the gamut from a single page that has the contact information for the official bricks-and-mortar organization, to a comprehensive site brimming with information for the industry involved. As the power of Internet communications continues to grow, more and more professional/trade Web sites are beginning to add greater features. It makes sense, after all; one of the best ways for organizations to increase their membership is to provide valuable services that are easily accessible. This might include trade show information, message boards for members to discuss business issues, and career boards for targeted job searching. The more members, the more income, the more targeted eyeballs, the more Web-site owners can charge for advertising. Like industry niche sites, professional or trade association sites can include the following goodies for members.

Member benefits. Strength in numbers, I always say! Membership benefits might include discounts for business-related products or services such as phone rates, travel, insurance, a voice in political forums, monthly conferences, and the like. Another benefit might be a password-protected site within the main Web site that contains the member directory and private forums.

Certification/education. Many industries have opportunities for continuing education. Computer people can become certified in Microsoft and other products, home contractors can be certified by the National Association of Home Builders, and engineers can become a certified broadcast networking technician at the Society of Broadcast Engineers. Certification has the benefit of increasing the earning potential of professionals; it's becoming very popular in business today.

Industry resources. Often you'll uncover industry resources—associations, current headlines, trade show information, manufacturers and suppliers, and the like. Like industry niche sites, the goals here are to be a resource and ideally the definitive portal for professionals in the business.

Vendor lists. Remember my point earlier about advertising dollars? Vendors bring revenue to the professional organization sites by advertising their wares. This can be via a sponsor statement, a banner advertisement over a section of the Web site, or even a text ad inserted in the middle of an opt-in newsletter. And often, you'll uncover a comprehensive list of vendors and suppliers; sometimes their products will be offered at a discount—another benefit of membership.

Community resources. Comprehensive professional organization sites will include forums for professionals to discuss industry issues and mailing lists to subscribe for different topics. Consider the **Society for Automotive Engineers** as seen in Figure 8.2 at http://www.sae.org/—not only are there career sections, but you will also uncover forums that deal with all professional aspects of the automotive engineering universe.

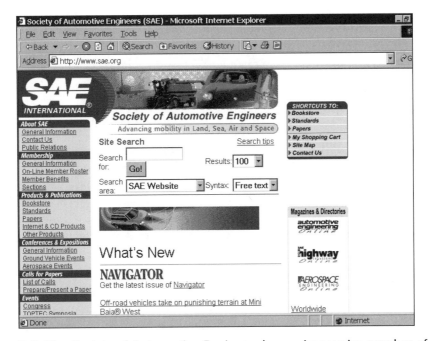

Figure 8.2: The Society of Automotive Engineers has an impressive number of professional resources—including careers!

It bears repeating. Community resources are not only for organization-to-person; sometimes the community uses forums and mailing lists to help each other out, business-to-business. For example, I am a member of a residential Realtor mailing list, in which realtors will often provide their comments, suggestions, and ideas to their peers so they don't make the same mistakes others have already made.

How to Find Professional Organizations

It's quite simple, as is almost all of Internet searching, to locate your professional organization sites. It can be done via the following easy steps:

- Define your professional organization.
- Browse professional organization directories.
- Utilize search engines.
- Determine which sites to use.
- Post your jobs and monitor the results.

The following five sections describe these steps separately.

Step One: Define Your Professional Organization or Trade Association

Ideally, you are already a member of a trade association or professional organization. In that case, you simply have to locate the corresponding Web site. Check all of your member materials! If they've created a Web site, chances are that Web site will be listed in their mailings.

If you need to figure it out from ground zero, just take the name of the industry in which the job will be offered. Are you looking to hire purchasing professionals? Your targeted organization might be called The Association for Purchasing Professionals. Interested instead in finding professionals in interior design? Perhaps the organization name would be The Association for Interior Designers.

What if you can't uncover a clue where to begin? Ask your colleagues what organizations they belong to. Visit sites on the Internet such as **MediaFinder** at http://www.mediafinder.com/ and search there for your particular industry. You'll uncover trade journals, reports, and magazines that should give you an excellent idea about what professional organizations exist. For example, perhaps your business deals with pizza and other fast foods. Searching for `pizza` at MediaFinder will result in the magazine *Pizza Today*. If there's an industry magazine, there's a good chance that you'll uncover an organization, too.

Step Two: Browse Professional Organization Directories

The nature of the Internet encourages individuals to create resources to share. Quite often, if you need to uncover a specific site on the Internet, someone else has already put together a comprehensive informational page about it! Take advantage of this phenomena whenever possible.

There are several generic, all-purpose professional organization directories available on the Internet. They include

American Society of Association Executives (as seen in Figure 8.3)
http://info.asaenet.org/gateway/OnlineAssocSlist.html

IndustryLink
http://www.industrylink.com/

Training Directory
http://www.trainingforum.com/Tools/directory/

Once there, actively search for the industry in question. Quite often, you'll uncover direct links to the sites you need.

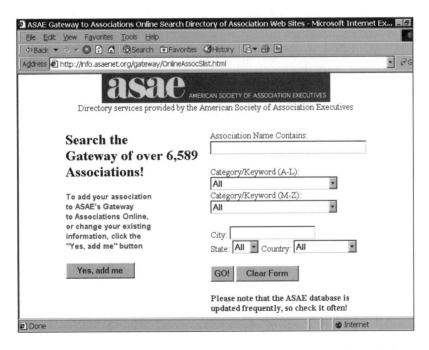

Figure 8.3: The American Society of Association Executives has direct links to thousands of professional organizations.

Perhaps you need to locate organizations that deal with the food industry. Visit the **American Society of Association Executives** and look through the menu choices—one category, appropriately enough, is called Food. Selecting that returns links to over 80 associations, including

> **The Association for Dressings and Sauces** at http://www.dressings-sauces.org/
>
> **Institute of Food Technologists** at http://www.ift.org/
>
> **International Food Service Executives Association** at http://www.ifsea.org/
>
> **North American Meat Processors Association** at http://www.namp.com/

Keep in mind your goals. You want to locate professional sites where your future employees might hang out. It could include forums, discussion boards, classifieds, job resources, and more. Always be open to exploration.

Sometimes, more specific searching will be required. In that case, it's time to revisit your friendly neighborhood search engine. Before we go there, let's review search engine basics and get them straight in your mind:

> **What am I looking for?** Professional organizations.
>
> **What keywords might I use?** Industry names, such as `sales`, `engineering`, `printing`, `distribution`, `metal`, `lumber`, `book publishing`, `computers`, or `finance`, combined with the keyword `association` or `organization`.

Step Three: Search for Professional Organization Sites

If you were not able to unearth your professional organization site from the previous lists, it's now time to locate it via a search engine. This can be done in either of the following ways.

> Visit **Google** at http://www.google.com/ and search for `association of <industry>` or `<industry> organization` or `<skill> professional`. For example, if you were looking to hire purchasing professionals, searching on `association of purchasing` might return sites like the **National Association of Purchasing Management** at http://www.napm.org/, the **National Association of Purchasing Management, Silicon Valley Inc.** at http://www.napmsv.com/home.htm, and the **Purchasing Management Association of Canada** at http://www.pmac.ca/.

Visit **Yahoo!** at http://www.yahoo.com/ and search for <industry> association or <industry> organization. Note how, for example, if you were looking to hire salespeople, searching on sales organization might return sites like the **National Association of Sales Professionals** at http://www.nasp.com/ and the **National Field Selling Association** at http://www.nfsa.com/.

Wasn't that simple? But don't stop there. Quite often you can uncover resources that list related industries. You can construct a specific search engine query on AltaVista to look for sites that list your known organizations to find more.

Visit **AltaVista** at http://www.altavista.com/ now. Let's take the earlier example of locating sales organizations. We had uncovered the **National Association of Sales Professionals** at http://www.nasp.com/. Try querying the following in AltaVista as seen in Figure 8.4: link:www.nasp.com -url:www.nasp.com

All the above does is request pages that include links to this site and that aren't in the same domain. (That's what the -url: construct does.)

You might be returned the **Marketing Career Page** at http://www.business.eku.edu/MGT/SIEGEL/careers.htm, which has links to the **Sales and Marketing Executives Association** at http://www.smei.org/, the **Outside Sales Support Network** at

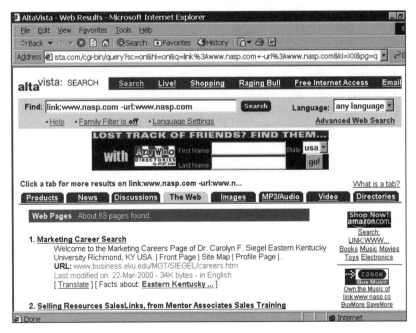

Figure 8.4: Searching for sites that refer to the National Association of Sales Professionals.

http://www.ossn.com/, and the **Direct Marketing Association** at http://www.the-dma.org/, among others.

This is an excellent technique to uncover needed resources! First you set your base association and then you merely look for pages that contain links to it. The Internet encourages those folks who keep resources up-to-date online to be as comprehensive as possible. Your goal is to take advantage of that (why reinvent the wheel?) and locate even more sites that will benefit your employment needs.

Step Four: Determine Which Sites to Use

Once you have a number of professional organization sites, what do you *do* with them? Like industry niche sites, you can follow these steps for uncovering needed resources. Ask yourself:

- Is there a section labeled Careers? If so, your search is over; that's where you'd go to post your jobs.
- If not, is there a section labeled Jobs, or Résumés?

If not, is there a section labeled Classifieds? Sometimes job offers fall under this specific category.

- If not, are there forums or discussions in which career-related issues are present?
- If not, are there advertising or sponsoring opportunities available where your company can be showcased?
- If not, can you opt for paper or e-mail advertising in an industry newsletter?

If a career section doesn't exist, you can contact the board of directors (generally such information is available on the site) and simply ask if one can be created. It doesn't have to be anything elaborate—it can even be a mailing list for professionals who would be interested. And vendors! What about vendors? Some professional organizations include detailed lists for which vendors will pay to be included. Vendors quite often have contacts within the industry in question—perhaps you can establish business relationships with local vendors and see how you can benefit one another. And of course, you can network with your colleagues in industry-related mailing lists.

Step Five: Post Your Jobs and Monitor the Results

Finally, now that you've determined which job board to use, post your jobs and monitor the results. You'll use the same method you did when posting to industry niche sites; you'll open up your already-created job post on your computer and cut and paste it into the site.

What if you decide to use a multitude of targeted job sites to advertise your position? You might want to review how you create your job ID for each open job; along with using your company name and date, also include abbreviations of the job sites themselves in the format *<company name>-<job-posting site>-<date>*. For example, if I were posting one of my Lingstar jobs to the IEEE, I might use something like "lingstar-ieee-081501" for an ID. Yes, the ID does appear to be a tad cumbersome, but you'll then learn what ads, where, are bringing you the most results.

Like everything else in business, you want to achieve the best possible results from the valuable time you expend recruiting on the Internet. By tracking how future employees find out about your opportunities, you can drop sites that deliver few benefits, add new ones, and keep those that provide the best returns.

Examples

In this chapter, we learned how to find and network with job seekers who are members of professional organizations. Let's put this information into practice and walk through the following three examples:

- Locate local pharmacists.
- Locate general computer professionals.
- Locate SAP and ERP professionals.

These examples will show you how to find local nontechnical professionals, nationwide computer industry job seekers, and those candidates who have specific skills needed for a particular position.

Locate Local Pharmacists

Mark, the manager for a drugstore in Wyoming, recently learned that one of his pharmacists will be leaving in two months. Instead of panicking, he decides to see what resources are available to help him hire a replacement.

Whom does Mark need?

A professional in the pharmacy industry who is board-certified (i.e., not a minimum-wage job). Preferably, this person would already have years of experience and be able to start work within two months.

What does Mark need to find?

Because Mark deals with a skilled industry, he needs to locate associations to which pharmacists belong, as well as pharmacy-specific sites where he can find forums, discussions, mailing lists, and other resources. These are areas in which any pharmacy-specific job posts would have a better probability of being seen by interested future employees.

Where does Mark look?

First, he visits the **American Society of Association Executives** at http://info.asaenet.org/gateway/OnlineAssocSlist.html/, selects the category Pharmacy/Pharmaceutical and clicks "Go." One of the resulting sites is the **American Society of Health-System Pharmacists** at http://www.ashp.org/, which provides a career section as seen in Figure 8.5 at http://www.ashp.org/public/pubs/ajhp/careerop/. Placing an advertisement here might result in a lead. There is a tremendous amount of resources at this site including current news, many practice resource areas, magazines, continuing education, internships, products, software, and journals.

Mark has uncovered the first industry niche site dedicated to pharmacists.

He now has the option of stopping, posting his jobs, and seeing what results occur. But that's only the first step in recruiting professionals via the Internet; now, he should investigate what other specific resources exist for him to get his job out in front of his audience as rapidly as possible. Because the last resource was a specific job bank targeted to pharmacists, it stands to reason that some enterprising

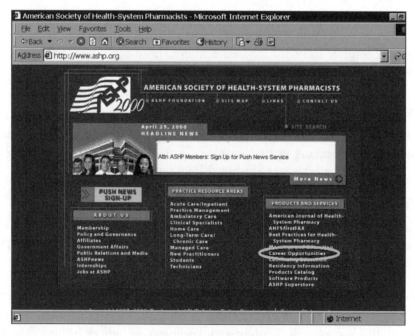

Figure 8.5: Note the link for Career Opportunities at the American Society of Health-System Pharmacists.

individual on the Internet would have included it in a general all-purpose "here's where to find pharmacy jobs" listing. Find such a list, and you'll probably uncover other pharmacy job banks as well.

Mark's next step is to visit **AltaVista** at http://www.altavista.com/ and search for all the pages that contain links to the site, yet aren't on the site itself. He searches on the following phrase, which yields up the page **Schools of Pharmacy** at http://users.erols.com/lpincock/schools.htm/ .

```
link:www.ashp.org/public/pubs/ajhp/careerop -
url:www.ashp.org/public/pubs/ajhp/careerop
```

This page includes links to **Pharmacy Week** at http://www.pweek.com/, which contains a jobs/résumé section and a link to **Jobs in Pharmacy Related Fields** at http://www.cpb.uokhsc.edu/pharmacy/jobs/jobs.html/. Not only are there additional links to other pharmaceutical employment sites like **The American College of Clinical Pharmacy Job Site** at http://www.accp.com/rec_search_pos.html, but there's also a **Situations Wanted** page at http://www.pharmacy.org/jobs/situation.html.

Mark has now found several sites where he can post jobs specifically for pharmacists.

Depending upon the popularity of the above sites, posting an ad for the open position might return some excellent results. Mark takes a closer look at the Schools of Pharmacy page. There's a link to a rather interesting association called **The National Association of Chain Drug Stores** at http://www.nacds.org/. As this association seems to be smack in the center of his field, joining it will give him increased networking opportunities. This will be excellent for his own career, if he plans on growing in the industry; it should give him an entryway to all aspects that will help him grow professionally.

Mark has now found resources for his own career.

The above are only the first steps for finding professional organization sites. Mark now visits **Yahoo!** at http://www.yahoo.com/ and searches for pharmacy organizations. The result, **Yahoo! Organizations** at http://dir.yahoo.com/Health/Pharmacy/Organizations/, contains links to the **American Association of Pharmacy Technicians** at http://www.pharmacytechnician.com/ and many *regional* associations. Regional associations? Depending upon the popularity of a regional site, it would be well worth Mark's while to check out regional associations and see if they offer job advertising, too.

Mark has just learned that a regional pharmacy association might exist.

Perhaps Mark's state, however, isn't listed in that directory. Not to fear—it might be created, but not yet indexed at Yahoo!

Mark visits **Google** at http://www.google.com/ and searches for wyoming pharmacy association. The resulting page leads to the **Wyoming Pharmacists Association** at http://www.wpha.net/. While there are no jobs available on the page, there is a newsletter to which one can apparently submit an ad. Remember, the goal here is to tap into the network of the professionals for which you are searching; ideally, you'll locate a much more targeted site in which to advertise your specific, niche positions. You don't always have to use Internet-only resources to assist you in recruiting efforts; sometimes you'll uncover print-only newsletters or magazines when searching. If that occurs, take advantage of it! Advertising via print might turn out to be just as effective as posting your jobs online, if your targeted audience diligently reads each issue.

Mark has found his state's pharmacy association.

Locate General Computer Professionals

Let's try another industry. Ed runs a software consulting company, one that provides customized solutions for the computer telecommunications industry.

Whom does Ed need?

Computer telecommunications can mean a number of different career fields, from project management (being able to take a project from conception to implementation, and oversee all that is involved with it) to specific skills (programming, hardware, diagnostics, and the like). Ed needs to determine where the employment needs will be, and target his search accordingly. Luckily, because telecommunications is such a broad field, chances are that all-purpose sites will contain links to the specific niches he'll require.

What does Ed need to find?

Ed needs to uncover managers, programmers, developers, testers, and the like in the computer side of telecommunications. Ideally, these people will already have years of experience in the specific fields. Ed's current experience in the field has educated him on several keywords he can use to further target his search.

Where does Ed look?

Like Mark, he first visits the **American Society of Association Executives** at http://info.asaenet.org/gateway/OnlineAssocSlist.html. He selects the category Computer and clicks "Go." Scanning through the resulting links, he immediately sees some associations that might be most beneficial, not only for finding employees, but also for his own career. If his company is a Certified Microsoft Solutions Provider, he can visit the **Association of Microsoft Solution Providers** at http://www.amsp.org/. Another site listed is the **Association of Internet Professionals** at http://www.association.org/. Over a dozen regional chapters are listed at this site, and some, like the **DC Chapter** at http://dc.us.association.org/, include job postings.

Ed has located computer job sites and niche boards.

Next, Ed visits **AltaVista** at http://www.altavista.com/ and looks for all the pages that include links to the Association of Internet Professionals, in hopes of uncovering other associations that could benefit him. Searching on `link:www.association.org -url:www.association.org` might return a link to a technical networking article from **Monster.com** at http://tech.monster.com/articles/networking/. There, Ed will see information about the **Association for Women in Computing** at http://www.awc-hq.org/, the **Association of Information Technology Professionals** at http://www.aitp.org/, which includes forums, and the **Association for Interactive Media** at http://www.interactivehq.org/, complete with a free job-posting service, and **AIM's Job Service** at http://www.interactivehq.org/html/jobs.htm.

Ed has found more sites for posting his jobs.

Certainly, Ed can now stop here and post his available positions. But he should also take some time to peruse what else the sites afford. The Association for Interactive Media has regional **Events** at http://www.interactivehq.org/html/events.htm, which he could attend to network, **Member Discounts** at http://www.interactivehq.org/html/member_discounts.htm, and the **Guide to Internet Organizations** at http://www.interactivehq.org/html/netgroups.htm. All of these links can benefit Ed.

Locate SAP and ERP Professionals

Can there be associations that target a specific skill instead of a whole career field? Jasmine's business requires individuals who are skilled in SAP and other related software.

Whom does Jasmine need?

Jasmine right now needs SAP (Systems, Applications, and Products in Data Processing) programmers. She can visit **Google** at http://www.google.com/ and search for `SAP software`; the results of this search might give her ideas of other keywords she can use when recruiting on the Internet. She'll find out that SAP falls under a category called ERP (Enterprise Resource Planning).

What does Jasmine need to find?

Like our previous managers, Jasmine needs to locate niche sites where her jobs would gain the most logical visibility. This will include career boards, industry forums, and possibly mailing lists.

Where does Jasmine look?

Being a techie kind of woman herself, Jasmine decides to start with search engines and visits **Google** at http://www.google.com/ to search for sap associations. She is returned a link to **MySap** at http://www.interactivehq.org/html/netgroups.htm; she'll uncover links to many **SAP user groups** at http://mysap.com/communities/sap/orga_sapuser_start.htm, most notably the **Americas' SAP Users' Group** at http://www.asug.com/.

Jasmine has uncovered user groups, a great resource for technical recruiting.

User groups? What are those? User groups are so important that all of Chapter 16 has been dedicated to them. Briefly, user groups are collections of individuals who are brought together by love of a particular technology, be it a programming language, an operating system, hardware, or software. Almost always, user groups focus on technical subjects; very rarely will you find a user group for, say, banking—unless, of course, it's a user group dedicated to enhancing the technical aspects of online banking! One of the great side benefits to recruiting on the Internet is often you'll uncover new resources of which you were not aware; you just have to be alert to them.

Associations contain professionals. Jasmine adds professional to her search strings.

What other words can Jasmine use? As she's looking for professionals, she changes her query to search for sap professional on Google. Success! The site **SAP Professional.org** at http://www.sap-professional.org/ is returned, where there are hundreds of resources (plus a free job board) she can explore to locate other SAP-related organizations.

Some Final Notes

Notice that the three previous examples dealt with different slices of specific industries. One concentrated upon the broad category of Pharmacy. Another was slightly more targeted by searching for Information Technology. And the last example zoomed directly to a specific skill. We were able to uncover professional organizations for all of them. Keep that fact in mind when you determine what organizations you want to target! You can certainly begin in a very broad sense, but quite often, you'll uncover splinter or super-niche organizations that will target your needs even more. Never be afraid to be proactive in your searching; you might be surprised with what you come up with. You can opt to advertise your positions in paper newsletters, attend local regional dinners or events, or even give a presentation to their members. You're only limited by your imagination.

CHAPTER NINE

State and City Job Banks

Not all employers need to hire nationally, of course. Why pay for national exposure if you're not open to shelling out thousands of relocation dollars? If you will consider only applicants that reside near the city of your job opening, you should definitely consider the regional and state job banks that dot the Internet's electronic landscape. More and more often, you'll uncover these resources popping up like fresh flowers in springtime; it only underscores how big a business Internet recruiting has become.

Depending upon the popularity, regional job banks can be very effective in helping you locate future employees. Remember, professionals who use these resources, if they are pleased with the results, will generally share that information with their peers. While it's true that this might be more for technical professionals than others (techies, after all, are glued to their computers and have a built-in radar for uncovering these types of resources), the popularity of finding employment via the Internet is growing so much that other industries are taking advantage of it, too. One doesn't have to rely only upon word-of-mouth to find regional job banks; cutting-edge sites will take the time and money to market themselves on the radio, in local cable TV commercials, and by other traditional means.

***Making Sense**—If you're only hiring locally and will not consider relocating future employees, popular regional job banks might reveal candidates sooner than the big job boards.*

Think about it from the candidate's point of view. If I were a C++ programmer based in San Francisco and not open to relocation, I would first concentrate my job-hunting on sites that were replete with career opportunities within a half hour's drive of my home. My time is valuable; I don't want to waste it perusing job offers that don't meet my own requirements. As well as using industry niche sites and searching for jobs within my location, I would also visit the popular regional sites as well. Depending upon my own networking, I might know of places like

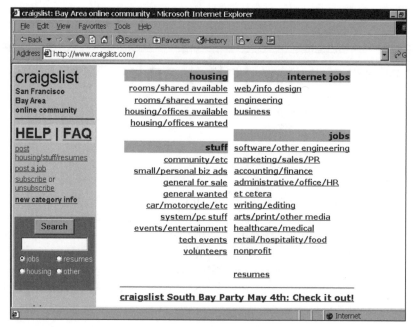

Figure 9.1: Craigslist has a jobs section specifically for the San Francisco area.

Craigslist as seen in Figure 9.1 at http://www.craigslist.org/, which is a San Francisco community resource (note: not only jobs), as well as **Jobs4Women** at http://www.jobs4women.com/, and the dozens of other San Francisco regional career sites. The large career sites are learning the value of regional job banks, too. **Computer-Jobs** at http://www.computerjobs.com/, **ComputerWork** at http://www.computerwork.com/, and **1-Jobs** at http://www.1-jobs.com/, for example, all have local job sites linked to their main Web site.

You might be surprised at the wealth of information you'll uncover at these types of sites. They now generally consist of much more than just "here are our jobs!" and "here are our featured employers!"—you'll now see career advice columns, relocation resources, simple, effective ways to submit résumés, and more. Recruiting is truly becoming a service market.

Benefits of Regional Job Banks

Regional job banks can bestow a number of excellent benefits that are not apparent at first glance. While many of them are simply job sites for specific cities and states, others have grown out of newspaper sites. This means that if you advertise your position in your local newspaper, you might find it also appearing on the Internet. Other benefits you might uncover include:

Local career information. Some job banks will feature specific employers, and also address the industries that are common within the state or region. Other information could be local colleges or universities and upcoming job fairs.

Career advice. In an effort to win more traffic, local job banks, like their large mega–Job Store counterparts, are including career experts who answer questions and give career advice. Such advice might be how to write a better résumé, how to dress for success, and how to evaluate your recruiter.

Local business links. Often regional job sites will include links to the local businesses and the Better Business Bureau. This can be most beneficial to you, especially if you are open to networking with your business peers. The more individuals who know you (for it's not companies you work with, it's the people who comprise them), the more your good name will spread.

Advertising opportunities. Many regional job banks (heck, many job sites as a whole!), will offer companies the opportunity to advertise themselves via a banner ad or preferred positioning.

Think about what advantages the above can offer to your company; it's always a good practice to consider *all* the options that an Internet site can offer. If there's a link for the Better Business Bureau, you can meet with your professional peers and build your own local, regional network. If you see a local business directory, you can often submit your own business's Web-site link for inclusion. If you determine that your types of future employees do visit the site regularly, you might be able to pay for a banner or sponsored link at the top of popular pages. This improves the probability that your message is seen by targeted individuals, even if they are not actively seeking a new position.

Of course, like other job-related sites, you must take into account the all-around popularity of the site before deciding to use their services (in other words, you want to ensure that your potential employees visit the site in great numbers). It takes less than $50 for someone to register a new state-related domain name, throw up a couple of compelling graphics, and declare themselves in business! You need to find out if your targeted audience is *there*.

Warning!—*Any entrepreneur can spend the money necessary to buy a great-sounding domain name like HolmdelJobs.com; you need to further investigate the popularity to see if it's worth your while to explore.*

Alas, there are no hard-and-fast rules for locating this information. You can certainly contact the owner of the site and ask for demographics. You can also see if the regional job bank in question is advertised via traditional means, appears in local newspapers, or appears to have a large number of jobs posted.

Regional Job Banks Consist of ...

As earlier mentioned, regional job banks can consist of much more than jobs, as seen in Figure 9.2. It all depends upon what kind of job site it is. Is it stand-alone? Is it part of a travel destination site? Is it the classifieds of an online newspaper?

Consider the newspaper site of the *Seattle Times* at http://www.seattletimes.com/. Along with the usual Arts and Entertainment, Local News, Nation and World, they include a link to **Classified Ads**, which leads the viewer directly to http://www.nwjobspace.com/, a service of the parent company. The job site stands alone, yet it springs from the classifieds of a major metropolitan newspaper.

Another example of the types of regional job banks you'll uncover is the state portal site like **NJ.com** at http://www.nj.com. Not only does this site have the requisite news information and **Career Classifieds** at http://www.nj.com/careers, but there's also a comprehensive **Forums** site available at http://www.nj.com/forums/ that includes discussion groups for all New Jersey regions as well as hobbies and lifestyles too. Interested in seeing what kinds of community associations are available? This particular site offers free Web pages for **NJ Communities** at

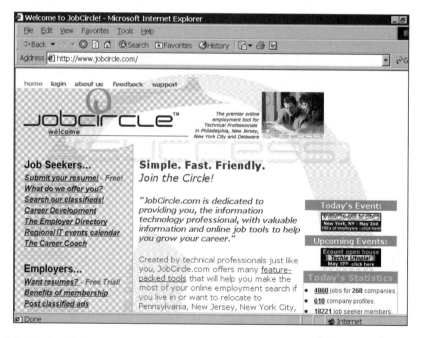

Figure 9.2: Notice all the resources besides simply jobs that JobCircle offers to attract visitors.

http://www.nj.com/njcommunities/, as well as pages for schools and associations such as **Seton Hall Prep** at http://school.nj.com/school/theprep/, **The Special Olympics** at http://sport.nj.com/sport/specialolympics/, and **Nancy's Parrot Sanctuary** at http://community.nj.com/cc/parrot/. In other words, if you're looking for local interests to support as a tax deduction in your business, quite often you'll be able to find links at these sites.

Still another type of state or regional job bank is the career-centric site; there are literally hundreds of them. Looking for an employee in Texas or Arizona? **TexasJobs** at http://www.texasjobs.com/, or **ArizonaJobs** at http://www.arizonajobs.com/ are two sites you might want to consider. If you visit these two sites, you'll notice a similarity in appearance—that's because they're owned by a parent company called **Local Careers** at http://www.localcareers.com/. One of the more popular trends nowadays is to create an umbrella site for jobs and then register lots of niche sites that fall under the category. If the marketing is efficient in the local community, you might discover some excellent returns on your job postings. **1-Jobs** at http://www.1-jobs.com/ is a similar site—their list of hundreds of distribution sites can be found at http://www.career-index.com/city-jobs.htm. Interestingly enough, the parent company is **1st Communications—Trade Shows and Exhibitions** at http://www.1st-communications.net/, a company that specializes in trade shows, exhibitions, and career fairs.

The components of regional job banks can vary from site to site. As well as local employment opportunities, they can also include community-related components like forums, mailing lists, and easy links to buy things at a discount.

How to Find Regional Job Banks

Locating regional job banks can be most beneficial for your recruiting. It can be done via the following simple steps:

- Define your region.
- Browse state directories.
- Utilize search engines.
- Use the sites effectively.
- Post your jobs and monitor the results.

These steps are discussed separately in the sections that follow.

Step One: Define Your Region

Okay, it sounds quite simple, but you can locate many more sites if you fully target where you want to post your jobs. Let's say that I want to find an employee in Tampa, Florida. The city, `tampa`, is one keyword and the state, `florida`, is another. And what about the whole southeastern United States? Sometimes an enterprising individual will create a job site that defines *region* to be *a collection of states*.

Another simple means of finding regional job banks is to consider the state (or state abbreviation) or city and then tack on the word `jobs` to it. For example, typing `http://www.ctjobs.com/` reveals a Connecticut-based job site. Typing `http://www.connecticutjobs.com/` is an entry point into the **MegaJobs** network, which is totally different from the first Connecticut site. Typing `http://www.floridajobs.com/` will take you directly to a Florida site, but `http://www.fljobs.com/` is not active yet. Remember, just because one Web site appears to meet our needs doesn't mean the others will too.

Your Region—*Your region can consist of only your town, or perhaps your community, or maybe your state, or even a collection of states. Always be bold when determining where to search for regional job banks.*

If `jobs` is one word to use, `careers` can be another. One popular New Hampshire site is entitled **NH Careers**, at http://www.nhcareers.com/. And **Career Path**, a major Internet job site, has a specific site for **Kansas City** at http://www.kccareers.com/. Don't forget your local newspaper, either; quite often, newspapers will have online career sections. This means if you take out an ad in the classifieds print edition, it will often appear in the Web site too. Newspaper sites can be beneficial; refer to Chapter 14, "Towns, Communities, and Newspapers," for more details.

Once you have a good feel for what kinds of sites would meet your needs, it's time to uncover them. The next section describes how to do so.

Step Two: Browse State Directories

The nature of the Internet encourages individuals to create resources to share. Quite often, if you need to uncover a specific site on the Internet, someone else has already put together a comprehensive informational page about it! Take advantage of this phenomena whenever possible.

There are several free directories located on the Internet that detail state and regional career sites. They include:

Quintessential Careers at http://www.quintcareers.com/geores.html. A career and resource job-hunting guide, it contains detailed information about specific state and region jobs. Browsing the resources contained will reveal **CareeRGuide** at http://www.careerguide.com/, a complete resource for Atlanta and the Southeast; **The Employment News** at http://www.theemploymentnews.com/, a site specifically for Colorado, Minnesota, and western Wisconsin; and **Town-Online** at http://www.townonline.com/working/, a Web site that targets New England.

Eagle's Résumé Service at http://www.richmond.infi.net/~leeann/state1.htm. Choosing Indiana will lead you to **Central Indiana's Job Source** at http://www.employmentweekly.com/, and selecting Nebraska will eventually bring you to the **Applied Management Institute's Nebraska Career Center** at http://www.careerlink.org/index.htm.

Job Resources by US Region at http://cdc.stuaff.duke.edu/stualum/employment/JobResources/jregion.html. Originally part of Catapult (now that's dating myself!), it contains some direct links to regional jobs such as **West New York Jobs** at http://www.wnyjobs.com/ and **California Bay Area Careers** at http://www.bayareacareers.com/.

About.com's Job Listings and Classifieds at http://jobsearch.about.com/jobs/jobsearch/msubmenuloc.htm. Broken down by both state and region, it has

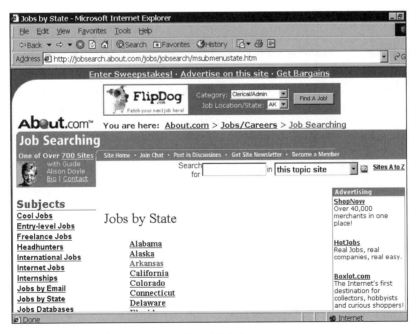

Figure 9.3: About.com lists many regional job banks.

links to a great number of sites, including **North Carolina** at http://www.coolbeachjobs.com/ and **Michigan** at http://pir2.com/.

Yahoo! Get Local at http://local.yahoo.com/. You can choose a state and browse down to Employment. For example, choosing Colorado and then Employment provides links to **CareersColorado** at http://www.careerscolorado.com/ and **Colorado Computer Jobs** at http://www.colorado-computerjobs.com/.

Of course, the Internet is always changing, and new sites are springing up left and right at a moment's notice. After you've browsed for your regional job sites, it's time to utilize a search engine and uncover more. Let's review search engine basics and get your goals laid out:

What am I looking for? State or region or city job sites.

What are the keywords that I might use? States or cities such as `california`, `texas`, `new york`, `seattle`, `triangle park`, combined with the keywords `jobs`, `careers`, `employment`, or `newspapers`.

Step Three: Utilize Search Engines

Remember in our last chapter how we searched for professional organization sites? We can take the same philosophy and just tailor it to our state searches.

This can be done any one of the following ways.

- Visit **Google** at http://www.google.com/ and search for `<region> jobs`, `<region> careers`, or `<region> resumes`. For example, if you were looking to hire individuals in Seattle, searching on `seattle jobs` might return sites like **Seattle Jobs** at http://www.seattlejobs.com/, or **Soba.net** at http://www.soba.net/. If you are trying to uncover sites for Philadelphia professionals, searching on `philadelphia jobs` might lead you to **PhillyTech** at http://jobhunter.phillynews.com/, or **Philadelphia Jobs** at http://www.philadelphia-jobs.com/. Figure 9.4 illustrates a complete index of city and state job banks.

- Visit **Yahoo!** at http://www.yahoo.com/ and search for `<region> employment` or `<region> resume`. Remember, Yahoo! is a directory and, as such, allows individuals to submit their own résumé there. Yahoo! also offers **Yahoo! Careers** at http://careers.yahoo.com/ and **Yahoo! Recruiter** at http://recruiter.yahoo.com/. Perhaps you are looking for professionals in Colorado. Searching on `colorado resume` will return **Colorado Online Job Connection** at http://www.jobsincolorado.com/ and

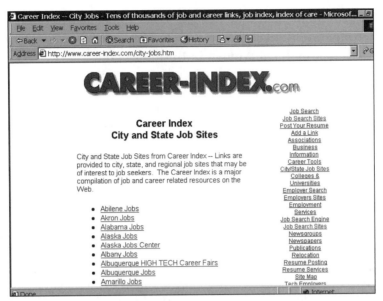

Figure 9.4: Career-Index includes hundreds of regional sites.

Denver's Preferred Jobs at http://denver.preferredjobs.com/, as well as specific individual résumés that hail from Colorado.

- Visit **Yahoo! Get Local** at http://local.yahoo.com/. Yahoo! makes it very easy to pinpoint regional and metro resources via this link. Need to hire Texans skilled in programming? From Yahoo! Get Local, choose Texas and then Employment. You'll uncover links to **Texas Computer Jobs** at http://www.texascomputerjobs.com/, **LockOn Jobs** at http://www.lockon.com/jobline/, and **Texas Jobs** at http://www.txjobs.com/.

In our last chapter we discussed locating similar resources by searching for other pages that included one uncovered resource. We can do the same thing here. Visit **AltaVista** at http://www.altavista.com/ now. Let's take the earlier example of locating Texans. We had uncovered **TexasJobs** at http://www.texasjobs.com/. Try querying on the following in AltaVista:

```
link:www.texasjobs.com -url:www.texasjobs.com
```

All the above does is request pages that include links to this site and that aren't in the same domain. (That's what the `-url:` construct does.)

You might be returned **Texas Employment & Links** at http://www.samford.edu/groups/cardev/webtexs.html, which contains links to the **Dallas Metroscope** at http://metroscope.com/dallas.html (lots of links to Dallas jobs there, including the

Dallas/Ft. Worth Employment News at http://www.employmentnewsonline.com/) and **Texas Information Links** at http://www.noplacebuttexas.com/texasinfo.htm (which contains a link to **Texas Women in Business** at http://www.twib.net/). This is an excellent technique to uncover needed resources; first you set your base regional job bank, and then you merely look for pages that contain links to it.

How else can you locate state or regional job banks? Advertising! I well remember driving along the shore with my husband from New Jersey to Boston. A movement above us caught our attention—it was an airplane dragging behind it a banner that contained simply: *Hotjobs.com*. The first thing I thought was, "My gosh, what size font did they use?" And the next thought that ran through my mind was, "How magnificent—instead of Broadway shows, one can see career sites now in the sky!" Think of the number of beachgoers who must have seen that particular ad. It was brief, it was pithy, it was to the point. It got the message across well.

***Advertising Pays**—If you start hearing a regional job bank advertised on the radio, or seeing ads for it in newspapers or billboards, it's a pretty sure bet that it's becoming well known and is worthy of future exploration.*

If you notice a job bank popping up more frequently on the radio, or perhaps see local cable advertising about it, or maybe spot banners regaling the site on buses, airport terminals, billboards, or the like, you can be assured that the site is spending respectable sums of money to attract visitors. This can only be a good thing. I remember driving home one day from visiting my current printer; the local Talk Radio station had advertised specific sites for New York employment. As a matter of fact, the site revealed was one I had never heard of and seems to be growing to this day.

Finally, another resource you might want to tap into is your local library. Libraries are repositories for all things of interest; more and more of them are getting online and learning how to maximize their patrons' Internet surfing experience. Your research librarian might be able to point you in the right direction concerning local job banks (and local job resources as well).

Step Four: Use the Sites Effectively

Once you've uncovered the state or regional job sites you'd like to use, how do you maximize the return on your investment? Certainly you should post your jobs. And make sure to include all of the local aspects that makes your job stand out! Close to home, easy commute, community leader, all of these qualities can entrance viewers and compel them to contact you for more information. Like professional organization sites, you can follow these steps for uncovering needed resources. Ask yourself:

- How popular is the site? Have I heard about it in advertising? How many jobs are currently posted there?
- Are there opportunities for me to gain more visibility for my jobs, such as preferred viewing (jobs in bold, perhaps)?
- If not, can I have a banner about my company installed on a logical page?
- If not, are there job-related community forums I can monitor or participate in?

If you can offer career advice (for example, what it's like to work in your industry), you can start to build your brand and become known as a knowledgeable individual. Many businesses and recruiters that use state or regional boards only see the obvious benefits; posting one's job to a local audience. However, if you take the time to really comb through relevant sites, you might come across ways of increasing your visibility without an extra cost.

Step Five: Post Your Jobs and Monitor the Results

Now that you know where to look, post your jobs and monitor the results. What kinds of people respond to your jobs? Are they targeted, quality individuals or just fly-by-nights?

Depending on the service, there are several ways you'll be able to post your jobs. Some sites simply will provide you with a single text box in which you can paste your entire job; others will recommend that you fill out specific forms and fields so the jobs are formatted in a specific fashion. In Chapter 5 we discussed how to create a effective job post; you can save each job post in a file on your computer and open it whenever needed. This will enable you to always have it at your fingertips when the opportunity to post it becomes available. Generally, state sites will charge a fee for job posting although there are exceptions; **BostonJobs** at http://www.bostonjobs.com/ currently allows you to look through résumés for free.

Remember to use a specific job ID. Keeping track of your job-posting success is one more way that you can streamline your company's operations in the future.

Examples

In this chapter, creative ways to ferret out local or state job banks were revealed. One can not only uncover these resources, but also take advantage of newspaper and community Web sites as well (a great benefit especially for the nontechnical positions, as nontechnical professionals will read the employment classifieds generally more than they'll search on the Internet). The following examples will walk you through actual searches for local employees:

- Find administrative assistants in San Francisco, California
- Find Realtors in Raleigh, North Carolina

These examples will show you how to narrow down your searching based upon job location when recruiting on the Internet.

Find Administrative Assistants in San Francisco, California

Andrea in San Francisco, California, would like to find an administrative assistant for her company.

Whom does Andrea need?

Andrea needs to locate people who are well versed in the role of administrative assistant. This would include familiarity with software, scheduling, dealing with harried executives, and the like. While she would prefer someone with many years of experience, Andrea can afford to consider fresh graduates from vocational schools.

What does Andrea need to find?

As it's quite rare for administrative assistants to be paid relocation fees from the get-go, Andrea would like to concentrate her searches within the regional, San Francisco area. Along with career-specific sites, she will also be alert to the online employment sections of newspapers.

Where does Andrea look?

She visits **Google** at http://www.google.com/ and searches for `california jobs`. One site that might be returned is **Jobstar** at http://jobstar.org/, a site that has a direct link to many **San Francisco** ad resources at http://jobstar.org/adjobs/, including **BayArea Careers** at http://www.bayareacareers.com/, **Craigslist** at http://www.craigslist.org/, and **The Silicon Valley Job Source** at http://valleyjobs.com/, as well as direct links to the *San Francisco Chronicle* and the *San Jose Mercury News* classifieds. Newspapers! These will certainly reach her targeted audience; all of them, as a matter of fact, are very viable places to post jobs or see if résumés are available.

Andrea has found niche career sites for her specific location.

Not only can she post her jobs, she can also see how much a banner or a prominent place for her site information would cost. Note that the search specified only the state and not the city; because San Francisco is so large, it's a sure bet that any site dedicated to California jobs in general would include links to San Francisco as well. Andrea could have searched on `san francisco jobs`; that might have returned **The San Francisco Job Bank** at http://www.sanfranciscojobbank.com/ as well as **San Francisco Jobs** at http://www.sanfranciscojobs.com/.

Andrea has now found even more targeted, San Francisco–specific career sites.

Andrea has uncovered some promising links that she will explore further. How many other sites pertain to the field of office administration? Are there other resources that would compel her future employees to submit their résumés there? Next, she should visit **AltaVista** at http://www.altavista.com/ and see who else links to the sites she's already uncovered. Searching on

```
link:www.bayareacareers.com -url:www.bayareacareers.com
```

might return Local U.S. Work Opportunities, Part 1 from **The Riley Guide** at http://www.dbm.com/jobguide/local.html; this comprehensive page includes links to many regional California sites such as **JobsJobsJobs** at http://www.jobsjobsjobs.com/.

Find Realtors in Raleigh, North Carolina

John in Raleigh, North Carolina, would like to locate Realtors to hire.

Whom does John need?

John needs to discover already-licensed Realtors, preferably within driving distance of his own office. Because of the nature of the job, John has no need to bring in out-of-state professionals.

What does John need to find?

He needs to uncover local job resources where his targeted future employees would visit. Because the field of real estate is nontechnical, John realizes that using the traditional source of employment ads, the newspaper classifieds, will be a good start.

Where does John look?

He visits **Google** at http://www.google.com/ and searches for raleigh jobs. One page that might be returned is **The News & Observer on the Web** at http://www.news-observer.com/—it turns out to be the site for a regional newspaper. Exploring it further, he finds that their career section is a completely different site called **TriangleJobs** at http://www.trianglejobs.com/. He can submit his position there.

John has now found two logical places in which to post his jobs.

John's next step is to see who else links to this particular site. He visits **AltaVista** at http://www.altavista.com/ and searches for

```
link:www.trianglejobs.com -url:www.trianglejobs.com.
```

One site that might pop up is **Employment Resource for Raleigh/RTP Area of North Carolina** at http://www.homesinraleigh.com/employment.htm. Note this page is from a Realtor! It contains a link to **The Research Triangle Park Directory** at http://www.rtp.org/.

From there, it's a simple matter of scanning the site and homing onto the **Jobs Resources Listing** at http://www.rtp.org/local/jobs/home.html. He'll find links to the *Herald-Sun* newspaper at http://www.herald-sun.com/, complete with **Classifieds** at http://www.herald-sun.com/adseek/, and **CitySearch's Triangle Park** site at http://triangle.citysearch.com/The_Triangle/Career_Center/.

John has now found both classifieds and specific Triangle Park career sites.

All of the prior searches have resulted in local, targeted sites. John could take it one step further—what about searching for local Realtor associations? He goes back to **Google** at http://www.google.com/ and searches for `raleigh realtor association`. He might come up with a link to the **National Association of Realtors Local Association** listing at http://www.realtor.com/ASPContent/NAR/StateLocal.asp, and discover that the **Raleigh Wake Board of Realtors** site is located at http://www.Triangle-REALTORS.com/. This would be an excellent site at which to network (not to poach, mind you, as that's against the **National Association of Realtor's Ethics** at http://nar.realtor.com/about/ethics.htm).

John has now uncovered a wealth of resources at the local Realtor board.

In Your Backyard

As the Internet continues to grow, more and more people are becoming well versed in using the resources that abound. This is one reason why regional and city job sites are becoming more prevalent; providing a one-stop-shopping Web site for local careers can fill a needed niche within a community. Remember, quality Internet recruiting encompasses far more than the typical high-visibility job boards; you always should take advantage of resources within your backyard (so to say).

CHAPTER TEN

Search Engines and Directories

One of the most practical ways of finding information on the Internet is to use a search engine or directory. Search engines are sites that index literally millions and millions of pages, allowing visitors to home in on specific topics of interest, while directories divide Web sites into orderly categories. These marvelous places can assist you in your Internet recruiting efforts admirably, should you learn how to use them well. This chapter will reveal how to optimize your results.

The Internet is growing at a tremendous rate. All you have to do is watch the media or read a few billboards to see all of the dot-com companies that are springing up like grade school children gathering around an ice cream truck. Not only that, but personal Web pages are offered for free to anyone using an ISP! This means that every AOL user, every Earthlink user, every person on the Internet might have a personal Web site as seen in Figure 10.1. And what's one of the first things people put up on their own Web site? You got it—their résumé. Millions and millions of Web sites, zillions of personal home pages—how do you blaze a path through all of this confusion and zoom directly to the resources you need? You do so via search engines, sites that automatically index a tremendous number of pages and directories, places where each individual site is categorized in an easy-to-browse format.

Search engines and directories are everywhere; have you ever heard the ad, Do You Yahoo? **Yahoo!** at http://www.yahoo.com/ is one of the most popular directory sites on the Internet (you can find a list of the most popular as measured by **PC Data Online** at http://www.pcdataonline.com/reports/).

Just about every time you look for something on the Internet, you are using some sort of search engine. Have you ever tried locating favorite forums within America Online? You can do that via their search function (which ties into the customized search engine at AOL). What about finding software or books at your favorite online vendor? That's also using a search engine (one tailored for the products that are available and being sold). Visit any large company's site on the Internet; almost always, you'll encounter a link to Search This Site. Again, it's a customized search engine.

Figure 10.1: Note AOL's direct link to member résumés.

When recruiting on the Internet, *search engine* generally means one of the megasites such as Yahoo!, Excite, AltaVista, Google, and the like. The problem you might encounter is the sheer amount of information that can be returned. Often, it seems that upon entering a query, you'll be returned either 3 million results…or three! Winnowing down that information to zero in on your precise needs can be, at times, most tiring. However, the resources and benefits you can uncover outweigh the negatives. Many sites are being indexed every day, which will assist you in uncovering the resources you need. Certainly, there might be a slight learning curve as there is for any useful application, but the time you'll save in the future makes it extremely worthwhile to become proficient at searching effectively.

The key for successful search engine usage is to view it as the guidebook it can be. Never go in expecting immediate success; sometimes it will take time to refine your queries (the way you ask search engines questions), while other times you'll discover that the page returned simply doesn't exist (quite often, Web-site owners will redesign their pages and neglect to resubmit them to search engines). Even if the page is no longer where it was flagged, that doesn't mean it's gone forever; sometimes a quick browse around a site will reveal the new location.

Not every site is indexed in search engines, alas. Consider the immense rate at which the Internet grows; every day sees a plethora of new sites become active. If the site designers aren't aware of how to register their pages in search engines, they generally will not be added. Thus, what you see in search engine responses might only be a small representation of what's really out there. Be that as it may, you can almost always uncover resources to help you out. You should be aware both of search engine limitations and how to maximize your results. Just don't go into searching with over-expectations, and you'll be surprised at what you will uncover.

Hunting for a Needle—*Alas, not every site is indexed in every search engine. This means that you'll probably receive different responses when using one search engine and then another.*

Benefits of Search Engines

When used wisely, you can benefit wonderfully from search engines. After all, millions upon millions of documents are indexed in these beasties—all you need to do is construct the *right query* to unearth your desired information.

One of the neat things about search engines is how they index Web pages. Ever take a moment to really look at a Web page in your Internet Explorer or Netscape Communicator? Look to the top of the window—you'll almost always see a descriptive title scrawled across it. Search engines will index this particular construct. Called the *title tag*, it's what Web-page designers use to describe their pages.

Let's apply this to your specific needs. When your future employees put up their résumé on the Internet, chances are, they are going to name that specific file `resume` (in other words, add that word to the title). And some search engines will allow you to specifically target words that appear not only in the title, but also in the URL. This is wonderful news; if you are looking to hire a programmer in New York City, all you have to do is set up a query that looks for the word `resume` in the title or URL, the proper area code, and the state abbreviation. This will be shown later in this chapter.

Other benefits of search engines are the communities they foster. **Lycos** at http://www.lycos.com/ not only has member pages, but you can also create your own personalized start pages that reflect your own current interests. Most of the big search engines have this functionality.

In Chapter 6, we mentioned some helpful tips for maximizing your search engine results. Let's go over them again in more detail. You have at your command:

Quotes. Quotes are helpful when you want to uncover words next to one another, such as a phrase. For example, searching for "`free resumes`" should return sites that allow individuals to either submit or view free résumés, and not pages that contain phrases like "Free trade résumés on the International border."

AND/OR. Some search engines will allow you to further define your search parameters by letting you use the words AND and OR. AND is used when you would like to specify pages to contain all terms, and OR is used when you want to ensure one or more of the terms is included in the results. For example, searching for engineering AND mechanical AND resume should return pages that include résumés of mechanical engineers; engineering OR mechanical will instead return sites that deal with engineering, or mechanical, or both. And (engineering OR mechanical) AND resume will increase the probability of locating résumés with either one of those two skills. Remember, *mechanical* doesn't always refer to *engineering*; one's résumé might include information about their mechanical skills in the garage.

Parentheses. Parentheses are used when grouping characteristics together. For example, you can use parentheses to specify that you'd like to find résumés of people that are in Florida or South Carolina or Georgia, and have accounting or accounts payable experience, and that you want the word resume in either the title or the URL. Such a query might be written (florida or "south carolina" or georgia) and (accounting or "accounts payable") and (title:resume or url:resume).

Wildcards. Some search engines will let you use a wildcard, denoted by *, in matching particular words. Consider the accounting example; we could have tried (florida or "south carolina" or georgia) and account* and (title:resume or url:resume). Wildcards are very useful if you want to match a whole slew of similar words.

Host. If you know of a specific site you'd like to explore, you can limit your searches to that domain by using the host: tag. For example, if you want to search only Microsoft's site, you could add the construct host:microsoft.com.

URL. The URL is what you see in the Address or Location field in your browser whenever you are surfing the Internet. For example, if you visit the resource page from **The zGates Project**, you'll see the URL is http://www.zgates.com/resources.html. Let's now apply that concept to finding future employees; you can use the url: construct to target pages that include the word resume in their name.

Title. Ah, the title tag, one of the most valuable resources you can use in search engines. Using the previous example, you'll see that the title of the zGates Project Resource Page is "The zGates Project|Certification Resources." Because the word certification appears in the title, it could potentially show up in searches when individuals target such resources. This is especially helpful when you are searching for résumés; using the construct `title:resume` will narrow down your results considerably.

Link. The link tag is very useful for competitive analysis. For example, if you want to see who is linking to **CareerBuilder**, you can search on `link:www.careerbuilder.com`.

Domain. Have you ever noticed that some Web sites end with .com and others with .edu? Using the `domain:` construct, you can fine-tune your searches to retrieve pages based upon their domain endings, as well.

Back when the Internet was first created, some of the domain endings were .com, .org, .net, .edu, and .gov; they are described in the following list.

.com. These sites are specifically commercial. If you have a business Web site, most likely it has a .com ending like **Amazon.com** at http://www.amazon.com/ or **eBay** at http://www.ebay.com/.

.org. These sites are tailored to organizations and associations. Such sites include the **Construction Industry Institute** at http://construction-institute.org/, the **Better Business Bureau** at http://www.bbb.org/, and the **Coin Laundry Association** at http://www.coinlaundry.org/.

.net. These were general networks such as Internet service providers, for example **Cybernex** at http://www.cybernex.net/ or **Superlink** at http://www.superlink.net/. Nowadays, however, companies are using these suffixes too, like **Headhunter.net** at http://www.headhunter.net/.

.edu. These are specifically for the educational universe; colleges and universities in America are almost always under the .edu domain, like **Princeton** at http://www.Princeton.edu/, **Rutgers** at http://www.Rutgers.edu/, or **MIT** at http://www.mit.edu/.

.gov. This suffix deals strictly with government entities like the **WhiteHouse** at http://www.whitehouse.gov/ or the **IRS** at http://www.irs.gov/.

Because the Internet is now an international phenomenon, there are literally hundreds of domain endings, reflecting the many countries that are online, such as the United Kingdom (.uk), China (.cn), Japan (.jp), the US (.us), and Vatican City (.va). You can find a complete list at the **Internet Assigned Numbers Authority** at http://www.iana.org/cctld.html.

Why is this important for your searching? Sometimes you might want to limit all the results to documents from colleges and universities in the United States (i.e., the domains all end in .edu). Other times you might want to focus on English universities (where the domains end in .ac.uk). Still other times, you might want to concentrate solely upon finding free places to post your jobs in organizations (where the domains end in .org).

Targeting Your Searches—*You can use search engines to restrict the sites you want to query. For example, if you're looking for résumés of college students, setting your search domain to* `.edu` *ensures you receive responses only from those kinds of sites.*

Whenever you visit a search engine, always look for the Help link. This page will detail all the great ways to improve your searching. For example, **AltaVista's Help** can be found at http://doc.altavista.com/help/search/search_help.shtml as seen in Figure 10.2. When you visit that page, you'll see all the possible variations on searching and how to use them best.

Because search engines are such a popular topic on the Internet, many sites have been created to assist you in determining what are the best to use for what purpose. They include:

   AllSearchEngines at http://www.allsearchengines.com/. Provides links to categories of search engines.

   SearchEngineCollossus at http://www.searchenginecolossus.com/. Includes an international directory.

   WebSearch at http://websearch.about.com/. Includes essays about maximizing your success via search engines.

   SearchEngineWatch at http://www.searchenginewatch.com/. One of the original sites that provides excellent resources about search engines and how they operate.

Should you like to brush up on effective search engine usage, definitely visit the above resources and benefit.

Search Engines and Directories Consist of ...

Search engines consist of much more than simply a means to uncover information on the Internet. Because the majority of search engines are owned by marketing media companies, you'll see portal information like stocks, travel, classifieds, and much more.

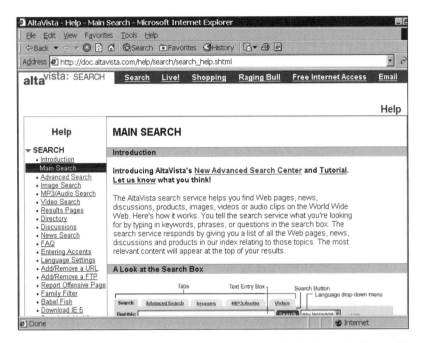

Figure 10.2: Every search engine should have a direct link for Help that will explain how to use it to its best advantage.

Wait a second! Classifieds? This is a great location to post your jobs (often for free). For example, check out **Yahoo! Classifieds** at http://classifieds.yahoo.com/; you'll see a direct link to add your job at no cost.

More Than Searching—*Search engines nowadays provide much more than simple searching; quite often you'll find a multitude of personal services such as news, classifieds, stocks, and Hollywood gossip.*

What else can you find, and what can you do with it? Consider the following:

Niche forums. Looking for information about stocks? Yahoo! has a complete **Message Center** at http://messages.yahoo.com. Want to find specific forums or boards about business? **Excite** has a similar site at http://boards.excite.com/. You might discover employment-related postings and also be able to answer industry questions.

Competitive information. Yahoo includes a neat feature called **Yahoo! Alerts** at http://alerts.yahoo.com/, where you can specifically configure news alerts such as `layoffs` to be e-mailed to you. This would give you a heads-up notice if future employees might all of a sudden become available.

People-finders. The **Yahoo! People** site at http://people.yahoo.com/ allows you to search for e-mail addresses, names, telephone numbers, and more. Some of these services will include a link for you to locate businesses geographically close to the individual or information.

Chats. Internet chat is a very popular activity. Sites like Yahoo!, Excite, AOL, and others have personalized, individual chat rooms. I'm not big on chats myself, but they can be an excellent means to network with colleagues, customers, and future employees.

Jobs. Yes, jobs. Not only jobs, mind you, but also general all-purpose classifieds. **AltaVista** has their own career section at http://careers.av.com/, as does **Excite** at http://www.excite.com/careers/. Keep in mind that often these sites result from partnering with job-opportunity Web sites.

Human interest. Stocks, current news, calendars, ways to send free cards, track down old friends, plan business trips… you name it, some search engine probably provides an interface to it. As a matter of fact, several popular search engines let you register to create your own member profile, encouraging you to use their services more.

As you can see, search engines are continually evolving to present more and more information to their users. You'll find search engines to be a wonderful addition to your Internet recruiting tools.

How to Choose Your Search Engine or Directory

It's pretty obvious search engines can be a wonderful resource to locate future employees. The thing is, though, with all of the choices you have, how do you determine the best one to use for your needs? The process will be quite simplified if you follow these steps:

- Review resources.
- Consider the most popular search sites.
- Search for résumés and resources.
- Print the résumés and proceed to contact.

These steps are described more fully in the four sections that follow.

Step One: Review Resources

Because search engines are such a popular topic on the Internet, there are several sites you can peruse to learn about which will meet your needs best. They include:

About.com's Websearch at http://websearch.about.com/. This site has a comprehensive library of not only how to use search engines effectively, but also a directory for niche search engines like career search engines, business search engines, MP3 search engines, and more as seen in Figure 10.3.

SearchEngineWatch at http://www.searchenginewatch.com/. One of the original sites dedicated to monitoring search engines, it has excellent tutorials about search engine usage at http://www.searchenginewatch.com/facts/.

Berkeley's Recommended Search Engines and Directories found at http://www.lib.berkeley.edu/TeachingLib/Guides/Internet/ToolsTables.html. Each search engine listed will have directions on how to best utilize it.

What are some of the qualities you'd like to experience with search engines? They could be:

Ease of use. Some search engines will provide you with a graphical way to execute search queries, such as **Hotbot** at http://www.hotbot.com/. Other sites will let you use parentheses and `and` and `or` to help you target your searching, while others offer directory browsing, such as **Yahoo!** at http://www.yahoo.com/. Different sites have their own particular style of using search engines; you should easily be able to locate one that you like.

Figure 10.3: About.com has comprehensive resources to learn about search engines.

Portal. Many search engines will provide you with direct, customizable links to human-interest material such as news, stocks, weather, and travel. This might be something you find to be beneficial.

Step Two: Consider the Most Popular Search Sites

Some search engines make finding employees much simpler. If you would like to find free résumés on the Internet, **AltaVista** at http://www.altavista.com/ is one of the best around. Containing more than 300 million pages, it makes looking for the word `resume` in titles much easier.

Yahoo! at http://www.yahoo.com/ is a tremendously large, popular directory. You can find many résumés there, but keep in mind for the most part that they are not "fresh" (fresh meaning active job seekers). Certainly, however, you should visit the site and search for `<skill>` `individual` `resume` to assist you in your recruiting (replace `<skill>` with the specific skill for which you are searching). Perhaps you are looking for Java developers; searching on `java` `individual` `resume` will return over 100 responses. Note for the first time we've included the word `individual` in our queries—that's because Yahoo! has dozens of specific categories that contain the phrase `individual` `resumes`.

AOL at http://hometown.aol.com/ is the entry into the AOL members' sites. It includes both a résumé and a community search. You might find more nontechnical résumés at this site than indexed in AltaVista. **Google** at http://www.google.com/ is one of the best all-purpose search engines around. While not as comprehensive as AltaVista (yet), it determines ratings by link popularity, which simply focuses on how popular the link is on the Internet in general (in other words, how many sites reference it as well). It's a great site for locating job banks, professional associations, and other specific needs.

Step Three: Search for Résumés and Resources

There are many ways you can use search engines to find employees—you could search for both résumés and résumé resources (e.g., professional user groups and organizations). Let's say that you need to find Web programmers in New York City. Ask yourself the following questions.

Area Codes!*—Knowing the area code of where you'd like to uncover future employees will allow you to target with great precision the available online résumés for free.*

What skills does my future employee need? Web programming? Okay, that's a start—would it also include Java? Oracle? E-commerce? If e-commerce, is that spelled with a hyphen or not? (Hint—people will spell it either way.) A good way to locate keywords would be to visit **Monster.com** at http://www.monster.com/ and simply search for similar jobs—you can then see what skills other companies or recruiters are looking for.

What area code is close by? You certainly wouldn't want to search for only new york city in résumés—people do live in New Jersey who are willing to commute. Thus, the best way to broaden your search yet keep it regional is to search for area codes. You can accomplish this objective in several ways; 555-1212.com's **Area Code Finder** at http://www.555-1212.com/area_codes.cfm has a Power Search that allows you to specify cites and states. I simply prefer to browse **NewsDirectory.com** at http://www.newsdirectory.com/ and choose my specific state—you'll find lists of online newspapers broken down by area codes.

What state am I looking for? Perhaps a silly comment, but consider the previous example—New York City's main area code is 212. You want to reduce the possibility of finding that number in the middle, like 732-212-5555. Adding the state abbreviation to your query helps that.

Now that you have all of the above information, you can search!

You're looking for a Web programmer in NYC. Visit Monster.com and search for web programmer; you'll see another word we could use is design or designer. Next, visit **NewsDirectory.com** at http://www.newsdirectory.com/ and browse the **NY** newspapers at http://www.newsdirectory.com/news/press/na/us/ny/. You'll see that 646 and 718 are near the area code 212. Armed with this information, visit **AltaVista** at http://www.altavista.com/ and click "Advanced Search." We want to look for all pages that contain the word resume or resumes in either the title or the URL, includes NYC area codes, and contains the state abbreviation. Your query will look like:

```
(title:resume  or  title:resumes  or  url:resume  or
url:resumes) and (212 or 646 or 718) and ny and ("web
designer" or "web developer")
```

Try it yourself (be sure to get the parentheses right)—you'll see how simple it is to uncover free résumés on the Internet, as seen in Figure 10.4. You can use the above ideas on other search engines, too.

If you're looking for nontechnical individuals, consider also trying out AOL's member search. Because AOL is the first way many nontechnical professionals get on the Internet, it's a fair bet to say a good number of those people will put up their résumé on that specific directory, too. Visit **AOL's Member Search** now at

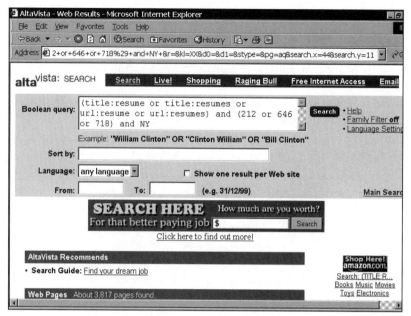

Figure 10.4: A sample advanced search on AltaVista that locates résumés near New York City.

http://hometown.aol.com/. Immediately, note two categories of importance, Résumés and Local. If you're looking for specific regional individuals, clicking "Local" will bring you a page that allows you to query in specific cities. Perhaps you're looking to hire sales professionals in Dallas; clicking "Dallas/Ft. Worth" first and then searching on `sales resume` will return several local responses.

There's a couple of things you should keep in mind regarding the résumés you find. For the most part, they probably will not be active job seekers. Thus, if you contact them, they might have already found employment. Still, it's nice to know such an option exists.

What else can you do with search engines? Locating résumés is only one factor—getting your position known (job posting) is also an important step. Sometimes search engines will include a free classifieds network like **Yahoo! Classifieds** at http://classifieds.yahoo.com/. Visit that site now and click on "Individual Submissions." You'll be brought to a log-in page (which is free), and then a site to submit as many free job postings as you'd like. Because Yahoo! is so highly trafficked, there's a good possibility that your future employees will see your ad.

As earlier mentioned, résumés are only one thing you can locate in search engines. Remember all of the other searches in the previous chapters? They were accomplished by querying upon different keywords in specific search engines. You can find professional organizations, user groups, trade associations, regional job banks, and many more resources by using a search engine.

Search Engines Aren't Only for Résumés—*Remember, you can also find professional organizations, trade associations, regional job banks, and more via search engines; you don't need to look only for résumés.*

Step Four: Print the Résumés and Proceed to Contact

After you've uncovered résumés that meet your needs, decide whom you'd like to contact. If the phone number is present, a simple call will suffice, but what do you do if you can only uncover their e-mail address?

Remember in this day and age, unsolicited e-mail is considered to be quite a pain. Thus, should you contact someone whose résumé you discovered on the Internet, be certain to mention where you found it, why you are contacting the individual, ask if they are interested, and then invite them to your site to discover more. I'll cover more about how to enhance your Web site and invoke the call to action in Chapter 18, "Your Own Web Site."

And remember, you can uncover much more than mere résumés via search engines! If you come across professional organizations or trade associations, visit those sites and see if they allow niche job postings. If you locate regional or local resources, see if there are any business networks in which you can participate. Truly, search engines can be one of the most valuable tools you can imagine for Internet recruiting.

Examples

In this chapter, we learned how to take advantage of the power of search engines, and fine-tune queries to target even local professionals. Let's put this information into practice and walk through the following three examples:

- Locate Microsoft Certified Systems Engineers in Chicago, IL.
- Locate entry-level techies.
- Locate MBA professionals in New York City, NY.

These examples will show you how to find local nontechnical professionals, nationwide computer industry job seekers, and those candidates who have specific skills needed for a particular position.

Locate Microsoft Certified Systems Engineers

David would like to find résumés of individuals who have passed the Microsoft Certified Systems Engineer exams, and who live near Chicago, Illinois.

Whom does David need?

A skilled computer professional who has passed six Microsoft exams (the criteria for a MCSE), and preferably lives in Chicago.

What does David need to find?

Because David's requirements are highly skilled, he needs to uncover specific résumés that highlight the keyword MCSE (general all-purpose computer résumés simply won't satisfy his needs). Additionally, he can locate NT (a Microsoft product) user groups as well.

Where does David look?

He first visits **NewsDirectory.com** at http://www.newsdirectory.com/ and browses to the state of Illinois. He sees that 312 is an area code listed along with 773. He then goes to **AltaVista** at http://www.altavista.com/, selects Advanced Search, and looks for all documents that have the word resume either in the title or URL, and include the keywords MCSE and MSCE (sometimes people misspell the acronym). The resulting query looks like

```
(title:resume or title:resumes or url:resume or url:resumes)
and (312 or 773) and (il or illinois) and (MCSE or MSCE)
```

Over a dozen résumés are returned. Keep in mind these people aren't necessarily actively looking, however. Still, they might know of colleagues who are.

David has found Chicago professionals he can contact.

Next, David decides to track down user groups located in his targeted area. Because Chicago is a large city, he visits **Google** at http://www.google.com/ and searches for chicago nt user group. One site that might pop up is the NT User Groups list from **NT*Pro** at http://www.ntpro.org/wantug/memberlist.asp; several links to NT sites are listed there.

David has discovered a wealth of user groups that contain MCSE members.

If one of the sites turns out to be outdated, David can try some of the other results from the original search, perhaps **About.com's Windows 2000** site at http://windows2000.about.com/blusergroups.htm. From there, David can query from the About.com search engine as well.

David has now uncovered several additional resources that enable him to find his candidates.

Locate Entry-Level Technical Professionals

Scott would like to locate the résumés of college graduates who are looking for their first entry-level job in the computer field.

Whom does Scott need?

As the positions available are entry-level, Scott decides to target both colleges and vocational schools. Prior experience is not necessary; however, the candidates should have a degree in computer science.

What does Scott need to find?

Scott needs to uncover college-specific sites such as university Web sites. Additionally, he can search for college-oriented sites as well.

Where does Scott look?

Figuring that such individuals would have Java experience as well as general all-purpose programming (Java is a very common skill for college grads in computer science), Scott looks for the word `resume` in the title or URL, the words `java` and `programming` in the page itself, and limits the searches to universities by specifying the domain `.edu`. The final search looks likes

```
(title:resume  or  title:resumes  or  url:resume  or
url:resumes) and java and programming and domain:edu
```

Over 12,000 résumés are returned. That's an awful lot of pages to peruse! Scott realizes he needs to be more specific in his query. Following our last example, Scott can add the area codes as well; if he lives near Arlington, Virginia, he can add `and 703 and (va or virginia)` to his search string; this will return a much more manageable number of résumés.

Scott now can find targeted résumés specifically for his needs.

Next, Scott would like to search for places to view résumés for free. He visits **Google** at http://www.google.com/, searches for "`entry level`" `jobs`, and comes up with **CollegeRecruiter** at http://www.adguide.com/. This site is geared towards the entry-level college job market.

Another search he tries is `college resume`. One site that might be returned is **Virtual Résumé's College Résumé Banks** at http://www.virtualrésumé.com/colresd.asp; there, he'll find direct links to university résumé sites such as the **University of**

Maine at http://www.umeais.maine.edu/~career/reslist.html and **Purdue University** at http://www3.mgmt.purdue.edu/mpo/. **JobTrack** at http://www.jobtrak.com/ is another site returned, which is dedicated strictly to the college job market.

Scott has now found free sites for college résumés as well.

Locate MBA Professionals in New York City, NY

Moses is a financial manager in New York City, and has learned he now has the budget to hire an MBA for his company.

Whom does Moses need?

A seasoned professional in the financial industry who ideally has had experience on Wall Street and has graduated with an MBA from a prestigious university.

What does Moses need to find?

He needs to locate the résumés of professionals within commuting distance of New York City. Because New York City has a very substantial subway and train system, other states can be considered for searching, such as New Jersey.

Where does Moses look?

Moses first visits **AltaVista** at http://www.altavista.com/ and creates the following targeted search engine query:

```
(title:resume or title:resumes or url:resume or url:resumes)
and (ny or nj) and (212 or 718 or 201 or 908) and MBA
```

Note the addition of the New Jersey criteria as well. Over a hundred résumés are returned.

Moses has found targeted résumés that might provide excellent results.

Because an MBA is not generally known as a technically oriented degree, his next task is to visit **AOL's Member site** at http://hometown.aol.com/ and search there. Visiting that page, he selects Resumes and searches for

```
(ny or nj) and MBA and (212 or 718 or 908 or 201)
```

Over a dozen more region-specific résumés are returned.

Moses now has more résumés to consider.

Moses realizes that MBA organizations based in NYC might also provide excellent resources. He next visits **Google** at http://www.google.com/ and searches for NYC

MBA organization; one site that might be returned is the **Urban Bankers Association Links List** at http://www.ubcny.org/org.html. This provides a link to the **NY Chapter of the National Black MBA Association** at http://www.nyblackmba.org/, **Black Data Processing Associates of NY** at http://www.bdpany.org/, and others.

Moses now has several MBA-specific organizations to explore.

Final Comments

The uses for search engines are many and varied. You can uncover résumés and other resources to ferret out your future employees. So far in this book we've seen how one can locate organizations, associations, and college-specific resources; in the next chapter, we'll explore more fully the benefits you'll discover when examining collegiate sites themselves.

CHAPTER ELEVEN

Colleges and Universities

Ahhhhh, colleges and universities! The very concept evokes grand ivory towers, fresh-faced students eager for a chance at proving themselves, a wonderful abundant opportunity for new talent, just ready for you to shape into the needed professional. Is that what you think when you mull over colleges? Or perhaps, do you consider that fresh graduates have zero real world experience (for the most part), and why even consider hiring them until they've been seasoned by a healthy dose of corporate politics?

Colleges Contain—*As well as graduating seniors, colleges contain alumni, network groups, career centers, job-posting opportunities, student organizations, tie-ins to professional organizations, and more.*

Have I got wonderful news for you! Colleges and universities are great locations for uncovering valued professionals. Typically, you'll find many different populations that can benefit your hiring opportunities, including:

Undergraduates. Undergrads are generally delightfully free of the corporate politics and disillusionment many seasoned professionals possess. And because they are new to the real world, salaries are often entry-level. Many corporations will engage in on-campus recruiting to pick the best, as well as set up shop during spring break (you can read about **IBM's venture** at http://www.businessweek.com/1999/99_14/c3623136.htm).

Alumni. Alumni, by virtue of being alumni, generally have real-world experience. And because alumni often contribute to their alma mater, you can generally find extensive alumni networks in place that include career resources.

Student organizations. Many of the academic departments in universities or colleges will have student organizations. I was founder and president of the RU Math Club when I was a student; every week I would scramble about to generate interest for student meetings. Sometimes companies would offer to provide a seminar on life in the real word; this was quite appreciated.

Search engines. Almost every university has present on its site a way to search all files on the Web server. Since students are often given space to create their own home page, you will often be able to uncover lots of undergraduate résumés.

Career centers. Because employment after graduation is a priority concern, universities and colleges have a "career development center" to assist students in their specific goals as seen in Figure 11.1. On specific occasions, these centers will invite companies and corporations to interview students on campus. These resources are generally located on university sites under either Careers or Student Services.

Résumé books. Different departments will often gather the résumés of their graduating seniors and Masters or PhD candidates and offer them either online or for purchase.

As you can see, there are many resources that colleges and universities can afford you when you are trying to locate employees to hire. You can network with the undergraduates to create a long-term relationship for when they graduate. You can elect to participate in on-campus recruiting. You can post your jobs to various and sundry collegiate networks. Remember, college students are often unjaded when it comes to the sheer hell of corporate politics. This would be a valuable benefit if you want to mold your employees to your own specifications.

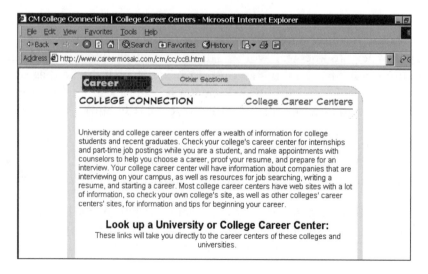

Figure 11.1: Career Mosaic lists direct links to specific university career centers.

One thing you never *ever* want to do, however, is to convince students to drop out of school and work for you. That is simply unethical. Yes, there are superstar kids who could probably program their way into the *Guinness Book of World Records*, but almost always, you are doing an extreme disservice to these students by hiring them prior to graduation. You don't know if the job will be long-term or if the student will work out; if you have to let the student go later on, he or she is now left without a college degree to include in a résumé.

Be Student Smart—*Never try to convince a student to leave school and work for you. You never know if said student will work out, and you've just robbed them of completing their education in a timely fashion.*

Other characteristics one should take into account when considering university students are their extracurricular activities. One can achieve a straight-A average in rote learning without demonstrating the creative leap so often required in today's dynamic business environments. Has your potential entry-level employee:

Started or run any local student organization? Such achievements show organizational ability as well as leadership traits. Presidents of such groups have to schedule weekly meetings, coordinate study sessions prior to exams, and otherwise enhance their members' university experience.

Volunteered for any community efforts? Community work demonstrates a commitment for activities that require effort but don't return monetary profit. This can give leads towards a person's willingness to expend extra effort for the good of an entity.

Won any awards? Many academic departments will offer various awards to students who solve incredibly complicated problems in a competitive environment. Depending upon the requirements, winning awards of this nature is indicative of a persons' ability to think and reason creatively and academically.

Not given up? Not every job opportunity requires the most brilliant person you can locate. Students who have demonstrated a dogged persistence in trying to achieve academic success, even those who fail, showcase a willingness to go beyond their perceived abilities. Someone who isn't afraid of failing can be invaluable in corporate projects.

There are many different ways to determine how well a potential hire from a university will fit in with your organization. Remember that colleges and universities are not the real world; freshly graduated students (unless they've interned) are often woefully ignorant of the cutthroat world of business in general. Keep that in mind when considering where to place such a hire.

Benefits of Colleges and Universities

Colleges and universities are great resources for networking. Not only will you uncover students eager for an internship, but you'll also unearth the many graduate networks including alumni networking, academic networking, and career networking. Additionally, local colleges and trade schools can provide you with a long-term potential for future employees. Help a gifted freshman or sophomore this year, and almost guaranteed she'll think of you come graduation.

Another benefit of colleges and universities is the direct links you'll find to professional organizations, hidden within students' home pages. Consider the IEEE, for example; they have a list of all **Student Branches** at http://sandbox.ieee.org/. When you uncover the student organizations, you'll find links to the professional organizations as well (and most likely their niche career-posting services too). Often these student branches will have local meetings about topics relating to their major; if you introduce yourself to the president of these organizations, you might be able to offer a free career seminar entitled "What Can I Do With a Math Degree?" (or whatever field in which your business is located). This will help you build a network in which your good name is spread not only to future graduates but also to the professionals already working in the industry. Not only that, but you can bypass this step by visiting the professional association's Web site directly and uncovering their links to all of their student organizations, such as seen in Figure 11.2.

Figure 11.2: Many professional organizations such as the Association for Computing Machinery will have student branches.

What about the students themselves? It is true that many students do not have real-world experience; however, do not let that dissuade you from considering them as future employees. Fresh students are generally quite motivated to make a difference and put in 110 percent when working. Of course, you should always designate another employee as a mentor and outline the required tasks as clearly as possible; mentors are quite useful to help guide new hires through the treacherous waters of corporate politics (unless the mentor is a sadistic dweeb who likes watching mentees take their falls). Remember, it's not only academics that colleges and universities teach; they should also instill a comprehensive methodology of solving the "What do I have, what do I need, how do I get there from here?" questions all businesses encounter.

How to Choose Which College to Use

Locating college and university resources is one of the easiest Internet recruiting methods available. It can be done via the following simple steps:

- Review resources.
- Determine your goals.
- Visit the university site and look around.
- Process your information.

These steps are described separately in the sections that follow.

Step One: Review Resources

The best way to choose college or university sites is to ask, Am I looking local or national? National will obviously give you many more sites to peruse. There are several great directories on the Internet that will guide you to specific collegiate sites. They include:

ScholarStuff at http://www.scholarstuff.com/. There you will find links not only to colleges and universities, but also directories for business, engineering law, and medical schools.

Peterson's at http://www.petersons.com/. One of the best-known resources for colleges, you'll find links to areas of study, financial aid, and more.

Berkeley's Recommended Search Engines and Directories at http://www.lib.berkeley.edu/TeachingLib/Guides/Internet/ToolsTables.html. Each search engine listed will have directions on how to best utilize it.

Halcyon.com at http://www.halcyon.com/investor/alumni.htm. While not comprehensive, the links here will bring you directly to the alumni sites of many universities.

Ask yourself where would make the most sense to explore first. Remember, many universities will have alumni clubs that track where former graduates have gone—you might have a Princeton alumni club in your Chicago backyard (**Princeton Alumni Clubs**, by the way, can be found at http://www.princeton.edu/~alco/regpages.html). Next, consider the types of resources that will be demanded of *you*. Are you only open to conducting interviews on campus? If so, you must factor in the cost of travel, plane tickets, and staff time; if you're only interested in local colleges, of course, that cost would be much less. And what of your own time? Do you have the temperament necessary to conduct effective interviews in person when not at your office? If not, perhaps you should consider just posting your available jobs to one of the many college-specific job banks that are available.

Step Two: Determine Your Goals

Before you even visit university Web sites, first sit down and determine your goals. For whom or what will you be searching? Alumni? Graduating seniors? Opportunities to give career seminars about what one can do with a marketing degree?

Do you want to meet on campus with students? In that case, you should discuss your goals with the career development center, meet with student organizations and offer a free career seminar, and network with the alumni. Do you only want to find résumés? Do you want to establish long-term networking with the college in question? Meeting with the alumni board might be the way to go. It all depends upon what you want to achieve and the amount of time you have to spend.

If you are serious about collegiate recruiting, it might be beneficial to map out a comprehensive recruiting process. Some things to include would be a schedule of universities to visit and a person to organize and conduct the interviews, review the résumés, and make a final determination.

Step Three: Visit the University Site and Look Around

Let's say that you would like to see the career resources at Georgia Institute of Technology. First, we need to determine the location of the Web site. Visit **ScholarStuff** at http://www.scholarstuff.com/ as seen in Figure 11.3 and select Colleges and Universities, then United States, and finally Georgia. You'll find a link to the **Georgia Institute of Technology** at http://www.gatech.edu/. Visit the site; if you're looking only for résumés, see if you can find a way to search the site. In this case we're quite lucky—it's in a very obvious page. On this page, look for `<skill>` resume. For example, to find students with experience in Visual Basic, you'd search for `"visual basic"` resume. Several hundred should be returned.

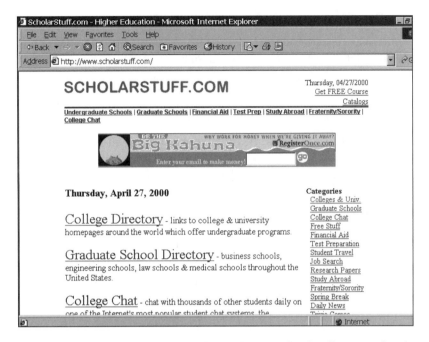

Figure 11.3: ScholarStuff offers direct links to thousands of colleges and universities.

What do you do with these results? Well, what are your goals for contacting students? You might be able to contact seniors and offer an internship, for example.

Next, look for a link on the main page for Career Services. If it's not visible on the main page (which in our example it's not), look for links named Student Services, Student Resources, or the like. Georgia Tech has one named Student Resources—clicking on that will reveal a link for the **Career Services** at http://www.career.gatech.edu/. From here, you can see if résumé books of graduating seniors are available, find out if you can participate in an on-campus interview, and see how else you and the career development center can benefit one another.

Proceed to looking for Alumni links on the main page. Just about every university or college will have their alumni pages most visibly highlighted—Alumni are a very valuable component to universities. In our Georgia Tech example, you'll find the **Alumni** page at http://gtalumni.org/. What can you expect to uncover on alumni pages? Often there will be links to career resources, alumni clubs, jobs for alumni, and more. What about student organizations? Searching through the main Web site reveals that the **Student Organization** section is located at http://cyberbuzz.gatech.edu/. Depending upon the industry in which your business is, you might find student groups that contain superb candidates for your future positions. For example, perhaps your business deals with industrial engineering.

You'll uncover a link to the Georgia chapter of the **Institute of Industrial Engineers** at http://cyberbuzz.gatech.edu/iie/; one of their resources is a **Career Center** at http://cyberbuzz.gatech.edu/iie/résumés/, which offers a free job-posting site as well as a way to request a résumé book.

Step Four: Process Your Information

After you've visited the colleges and universities, process all the information you've uncovered. Have you found résumés of seniors, graduate students, or alumni that look good? Contact them and invite them to visit your site. Remember that quite often, companies will reject college hires because of their lack of experience. Sometimes you can miss extreme gems in this fashion!

Another good use for this information is to build a database of students. Freshmen, sophomores, and juniors will eventually be looking for entry-level positions or summer internships; every year you'll have a new batch of quality students to call and interview. Recruiting can be a long-term project; just because someone isn't a candidate now doesn't mean you should lose out on that person in the future.

Examples

In this chapter, many hidden benefits contained in college and university Web sites were revealed. You can take advantage of free student résumés, student organizations, networking, and more. Let's now apply this to the following real-world searches:

- Find entry-level technical students from Rutgers University.
- Find entry-level engineers near Walnut Creek, California.

These examples will show you how to narrow down your searching based upon job location when recruiting on the Internet.

Find Entry-Level Technical Students from Rutgers University

Anne's company deals mainly with business services—financial, computer, marketing, and the like. Because she lives near Rutgers University in New Jersey, she'd like to see which of their resources can assist her in finding employees and networking.

Whom does Anne need?

Her business is general-purpose, so she is looking for graduating seniors and alumni in the business, computer, and financial academic departments.

What does Anne need to find?

Anne needs to uncover the career development center for Rutgers University, as well as any student organization resources, alumni resources, and the like.

Where does Anne look?

She first visits **ScholarStuff** at http://www.scholarstuff.com/. She chooses Colleges & Universities, then United States, and then New Jersey, and sees that **Rutgers** can be found at http://www.rutgers.edu/. Visiting that site, she notices several things right away. One, there's a lot of information available, but no direct links for career resources! She looks for information targeted towards current students, and finds a direct link to the **Rutgers Career Services** at http://www.rutgers.edu/menus/career.shtml. (Note that the name is Career Services and not Career Development. Different universities will call it different things.) This page has information about the various career options for the different Rutgers colleges and provides detailed information about how to participate in on-campus interviews, job postings, and more.

Anne has found Career Services and learned how it can benefit her.

Next, Anne returns to the main site for Rutgers University and discovers **Rutgers Search** at http://websearch.rutgers.edu/compass/; from there, she can search on specific keywords like business resume. This gives her leads for finding the résumés of students directly and then determining whether it would be beneficial to contact them.

Résumé Searching—*Often you can search for résumés directly on university servers, much like using a typical search engine.*

Anne has located résumés on the university servers.

Anne next turns to uncovering related student organizations. She chooses Student Services from the main page and discovers a link to **Student Organizations** at http://info.rutgers.edu/Services/stud_org/. If she's up for sowing long-term seeds, she can offer to visit organizations like the Computer Science Club and provide a seminar entitled "Careers in the Real World." Exploring further, she comes across a detailed database of **Student Organizations** at http://www.cis.rutgers.edu/StudentOrgs/default.html; this provides her with links to the Undergraduate Student Association for Computer Systems as well as the Women in Computer Science Organization; this last organization presents a list of available job opportunities from several major corporations. Depending upon what she has to offer, Anne can contact the presidents of these student organizations or the faculty advisors and offer to provide free career counseling or a seminar about opportunities in her field.

Anne has now located student organizations of which her future employees might be members.

Anne discovers the Rutgers main page has a direct link to **Alumni Services** at http://info.rutgers.edu/University/alumni/. **Alumni Associations** can be uncovered at http://info.rutgers.edu/University/alumni/assoc/assoc.html, and **Alumni Career Services** are at http://info.rutgers.edu/University/alumni/services/career.html. She sees on that page that every two weeks, alumni networking career meetings are held at the Rutgers Student Center. This might be an excellent opportunity to network with current alumni and sow seeds of interest in that particular community.

Anne has found beneficial alumni resources.

Finally, Anne can try to locate specific academic resources. From the main page of Rutgers University, she chooses **Academic Departments** at http://www.rutgers.edu/Departments/AcademicServers.shtml, and searches for accounting. This leads her to **Accounting** at http://www.rutgers.edu/Accounting/raw/Accounting/. It turns out this site is notable for far more than academic contacts alone; it also includes a plethora of information about the industry as a whole, such as the local accounting organization **New Jersey Society of CPAs** at http://www.njscpa.org/ and the job site **Accountingnet.com** at http://www.accountingnet.com/.

Anne has uncovered more accounting-specific resources from the academic pages.

Find Entry-Level Engineers Near Walnut Creek, California

Let's try another example. John owns an engineering firm in Walnut Creek, California, that provides design specs for electrical appliances. He's willing to bring aboard quality engineering students who have demonstrated a promising potential for the career world.

Whom does John need?

John needs to find engineering students or alumni who would want to work in Walnut Creek, California. He would also be open to uncovering places to post his entry-level jobs.

What does John need to find?

He needs to uncover the career development centers for colleges close to Walnut Creek, as well as any student organization resources, alumni resources, and the like.

Where does John look?

Like Anne, he first visits **ScholarStuff** at http://www.scholarstuff.com/, chooses Colleges & Universities, then United States, and then California, and sees a number of potential universities from which to choose. He decides to start with the **University of California at Berkeley**, and visits their site at http://www.Berkeley.edu/. After selecting the link for **Student Life** at http://www.berkeley.edu/students/, he sees that the **Berkeley Career Center** is located at http://career.berkeley.edu/. There, John uncovers information about the numerous career fairs (some deal with diversity, some deal with biotech, others deal with different academic disciplines) and other ways of increasing his company's visibility. As usual, the link to post jobs is provided via **JobTrak** at http://www.jobtrak.com/. All of these resources provide structured methods for finding and interviewing promising students from the university.

John has found how the Career Center can benefit him.

John's next task is to see if he can find student résumés on the university servers. He returns to the main page and finds a link entitled Search; it brings him to **Searching UC Berkeley** at http://search.berkeley.edu/. First he searches for resume; this leads him to several great results including a résumé **Book Order** from the Electrical Engineering and Computer Science Honor Society at http://www-hkn.eecs.berkeley.edu:80/indrel/indrel-résumébookorder.shtml. This includes the résumés of approximately 100 EECS students who are in the top quarter of their junior class or the top third of their senior class and have demonstrated initiative in their extensive extracurricular activities as well as their academic achievements, as seen in Figure 11.4.

John revises his search to engineering resume and now uncovers résumés that include the word engineering. By meticulously perusing the responses, he

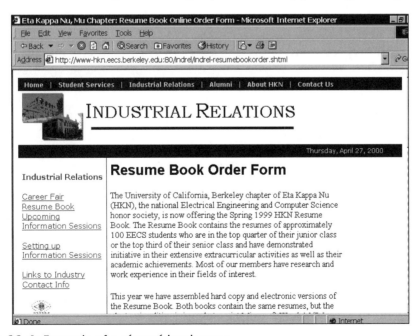

Figure 11.4: Example of a résumé book page.

can determine if some deserve further attention from him and his company; almost all résumés will include the student's home address.

Next, John decides to see the student organizations from which he might benefit. He already knows about the honor society which provided him the résumé books; reviewing those resources certainly would be a good start. He then chooses Student Life from the main page and discovers a link to **Student Activities & Services** at http://www.uga.berkeley.edu/sas/. This will eventually lead him to the actual **Student Organizations** page at http://www.uga.berkeley.edu/sas/student/groupsearch.asp where he can search for engineer. Doing so leads him to several student organizations, job-posting opportunities, and résumé books.

John has located résumés and associations on the university servers.

As John has taken care of finding undergraduate resources, he now turns his attention to alumni and graduate students. The main page of the University of Berkeley has a direct link entitled **Alumni, Parents, & Friends** at http://www.berkeley.edu/alumni/. **Alumni Associations** can be uncovered at http://www.berkeley.edu/alumni/associations/, but unfortunately there's no apparent link for alumni career resources. John revisits the search site for Berkeley and searches on alumni career. Many resources are returned including the **Career Center for Alumni** at http://career.berkeley.edu:80/Alumni/Alumni.stm and the **California Alumni Association** at http://www.alumni.berkeley.edu/. There, he can further his own network.

Making Life Easier

One thing to keep in mind about the previous searches. All required a patient, logical methodology of knowing where either the future employees or resources for employment might be found on the university Web server. Both Anne and John could have instead opted to use some of the college job-posting sites such as:

JobTrak at http://www.jobtrak.com/

CollegeRecruiter at http://www.collegerecruiter.com/

EngCen at http://www.engcen.com/

CollegeGrad at http://www.collegegrad.com/

Golden Parachute at http://www.goldenparachute.com/

While some businesses refuse to consider college grads, others welcome the opportunity to mold new minds. These resources are something you should look into for your own employment needs. When searching through the many resources that colleges and universities offer, be sure to always explore further and see what you uncover.

CHAPTER TWELVE

Forums

Forums are one of the best ways to become known to your targeted future employee audience (in other words, you become the employer of choice). Forums are sections of Web sites that allow visitors to participate in conversations via posting ideas and replies on the Internet. They differ from Internet chat in that they are not real-time; you have to visit a Web site to read the latest posts.

A good analogy for forums are recaps of ongoing, personal discussions. Have you ever been to a business meeting where issues are debated, sometimes for grindingly long periods of time? The most exciting part of such an event is watching two individuals duke it out verbally, each attempting to provide reasons for others to agree their viewpoint is correct. Sometimes other members of the meeting will pipe up with their own comments, other times the dialogues swing off into the wild blue yonder and end up focusing on unrelated topics. Forums are quite similar; the only difference is, instead of verbal communications, people will post or write their ideas, opinions, and questions on a specific page on a Web site, and others will respond in their own turn. They can be an important characteristic of a Web site; often, they will assist in developing a specific, targeted community of enthusiasts in all areas of interest. Consider **OnHealth** at http://www.onhealth.com/; they include a thriving **Discussion** area at http://discussions.onhealth.com/user/onhealth/default.asp. This resource allows anyone to post or answer specific health-related questions.

Networking—*Forums are excellent not only for networking, but also to post jobs, peruse résumés, and broaden the reach of your brand name.*

One neat quality of forums is the exposure they afford you as a professional. One of the best techniques for increasing your visibility among your customers and future employees is to share your information freely at related forums; this will go light-years towards branding your name in the community's mind. I experience this quite often; both my customers and people who have yet to purchase my materials have sent me dozens of e-mails thanking me for participating so fruitfully in forums like the **Recruiters Network** at http://www.egroups.com/group/recruitersnetwork/ and *Inc.* **Magazine Discussions** at http://www.inc.com/discussions/. By willingly answering all questions that come my way, I'm showcasing my skills and value. You can accomplish this, too, for your industry and business. It shouldn't cost you any money; almost always, registration and participation for any forum is free.

Sites often have more than one forum available from which visitors can choose. For example, consider, as seen in Figure 12.1, the **Oracle Forums** at http://www.orafans.com/; one of them is specifically for Oracle jobs, another is just for Oracle résumés, a third is for different aspects of Oracle itself, etc. This demonstrates yet another use of forums; sometimes special niche or career sites use them as mechanisms for employers to post jobs or for candidates to post their résumés. This is an important fact to remember when searching on the Internet for locations to advertise your jobs; you'll see that occasionally employment sections are called Job Forums or Career Forums. In a vital, thriving community, it's a good bet that many individuals will either post their jobs or their résumés online.

The Benefits of Forums

Forums are wonderful because not only do they encourage networking, but they're an excellent vehicle to get your name known in your industry. Once your name is known, people feel they know you, and will be more willing to consider offers from

Figure 12.1: Orafans provides a forum specifically for free Oracle job postings.

your firm. I've had this experience myself! *Inc.* **magazine** has a series of entrepreneurial forums at http://www.inc.com/discussions/. Every morning, I make a point of spending 15 minutes or so, perusing the boards and seeing where I can offer free information.

Imagine my surprise when I recently discovered that one of *Inc.*'s e-mails included a story about me. Can you imagine how many of tens of thousands of people received that e-mail?

Other benefits of forums include:

Targeted visibility. When anyone posts to forums, the messages are available for anyone else to peruse. This will afford you a wonderful opportunity to refresh your business in the minds of the viewers.

Fan club. Post enough, with quality information, and you'll start to develop a following of individuals who eagerly await your latest ideas. The **Entrepreneurial Success Forum** at http://www.ablake.net/forum/ is the home of Tony Blake, a well-known Internet marketing guru—visitors simply wait to see what he posts.

Advertising. Some very popular forums will offer banner advertising. Depending upon the visibility and the targeted audience, this could be an excellent way of getting your company out in front of qualified visitors. Many sites offer advertising benefits on the main forum pages as well as the subpages one level below (that's where people post responses to questions).

Customer Base—*Many businesses and professionals use forums to build a targeted customer and client base. It costs zero to do this.*

Community. Networking is the most effective way to conduct business on the Internet—many sites will include forums to develop a sense of community. **MechanicalEngineer** at http://www.mechanicalengineer.com/ has a forum in which mechanical engineers network and discuss technical issues, **WomenConnect**, a woman's portal, has a series of community boards at http://boards.womenconnect.com/. **Tom Peters**, the world-famous author about change in management, has his own set of forums at http://www.tompeters.com/talk.htm. In all cases, forums exist for the sole purpose of building a loyal following; the more people who participate, the more visitors a site receives, the more publicity for the Web site itself, and the more one can charge for advertising.

You can use forums in the following fashions:

Discussions. By far the most popular use, forums are created to enable Web-based discussions among visitors and professionals alike. **CareerMag** at http://www.careermag.com/ has a message board at http://www.careermag.com/ubb-cgi-bin/Ultimate.cgi where you can read or post about diversity issues, workplace issues, and other career-related topics. **Sun Corporation** has several forums specifically for Java resources at http://forum.java.sun.com/. **Barbara Sher**, the famous career author, has a forum at http://www.barbarasher.com/ubbcgi/Ultimate.cgi.

Job/résumé boards. Forums can be configured as quick fixes to posting jobs or storing résumés. For example, **ComputerTelephony** at http://www.computertelephony.org/ has a **Jobs Wanted** forum at http://www.computertelephony.org/jobs/wanted.html, **ActuarialRecruiters** has a free job board at http://www.actuarialrecruiters.com/jobs/, and the **E-commerce ItToolBox** has a free jobs forum at http://ebiz.ittoolbox.com/jobbank/. Many, many similar sites exist.

Neighborhoods. Neighborhoods are simply discussions that center around a physical community. For example, **NJ.com** has a forums section at http://forums.nj.com/— there, you'll see discussion groups for New Jersey regions, hobbies, and more. And the **DC Registry** at http://dcregistry.com/bbs/welcome.html includes forums specifically for the Washington, DC area, as seen in Figure 12.2, and a free employment board.

Forums can be considered a valuable business tool. The more people who know about your forums (assuming there's quality content), the more people will tell their friends to visit the site and receive the same benefits.

Referrals. This is crucial. Doing your own

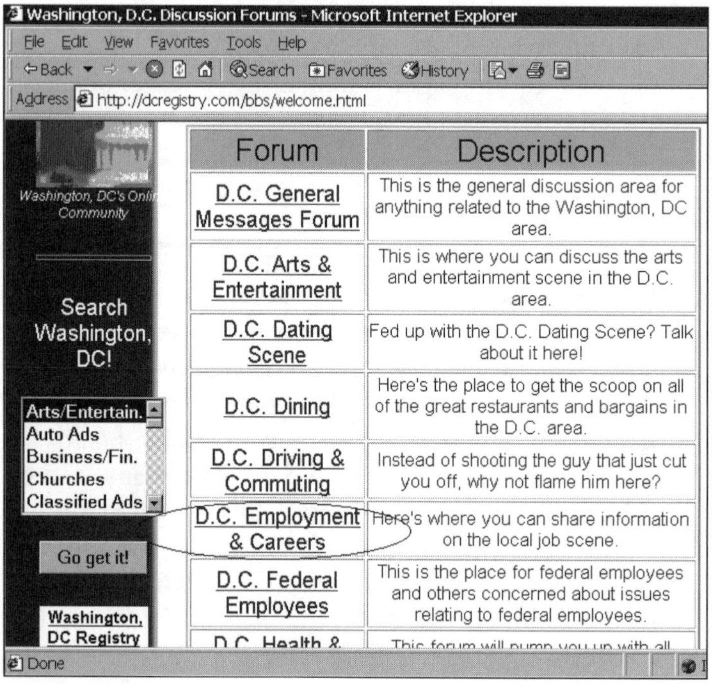

Figure 12.2: Note the employment forum that DC Registry offers specifically for DC residents.

Internet marketing can be time-consuming at best. When customers start telling their colleagues to "check it out," they're effectively doing your marketing for you. This can be applied to not only posting at industry niche forums, but also rolling your own at your company's Web site to allow people to learn about you.

How to Find Your Targeted Forums

Locating targeted forums can be quite simple if you follow these steps:

- Define what kind of forum you want.
- Browse forum directories.
- Utilize search engines.
- Plan your participation.
- Monitor the results.

These steps are described separately in the sections that follow.

Step One: Define What Kind of Forum You Want

First off, ask yourself: What kind of forum would I like to find? Targeted job posting or résumé finding? Local? Regional? National? In what industry?

What are your main goals? Do you want to find someone *right now*, or do you want to build a following? Finding someone right now means you should target your searching to the job/résumé forums—generating a following means you should also consider discussion forums geared towards the industry in question (and not only employment). At these kinds of groups, you simply want to monitor questions and jump in when you can amaze the audience with answers.

Do you want to monitor a local forum to see if individuals post questions about where to find jobs in your area? Perhaps your company deals with financial investment. Are there question/answer sites like those found at **Quicken's Message Boards** at http://www.quicken.com/boards/ where you can answer questions? Not only might you find stellar employees in these locations, but you can also drum up some excellent business for yourself.

Step Two: Browse Forum Directories

If you're looking solely for people to hire right here and now, you want to concentrate upon the job boards that reflect your industry; quite often they'll include targeted forums in which you can participate

Remember our discussion of industry niche sites in Chapter 7 and professional organization sites in Chapter 8? The method of finding job forums is quite similar. Visit those sites you uncovered in Chapters 7 and 8 to see if job boards exist. Remember uncovering the site **ITToolbox** at http://www.ittoolbox.com/? They have several directly related sites where you can post jobs for free.

One popular place to uncover forums is **ForumOne** at http://www.forumone.com/ as seen in Figure 12.3. Visit this site and search for `<industry>` job, `<industry>` career, or `<industry>` employment. For example, if you were looking to hire Oracle professionals, searching on `oracle job` brings you to the site **Orafans** at http://www.orafans.com/, which offers a free résumé/job board. Searching on `management job` returns the **Management Roundtable Networking Forum** at http://www.trainingforum.com/MRT/bbs1.html.

Visit the following sites and perform the same type of search. You'll uncover many forums that will assist you in your Internet recruiting endeavors.

Delphi at http://www.delphi.com/

Egroups at http://www.egroups.com/

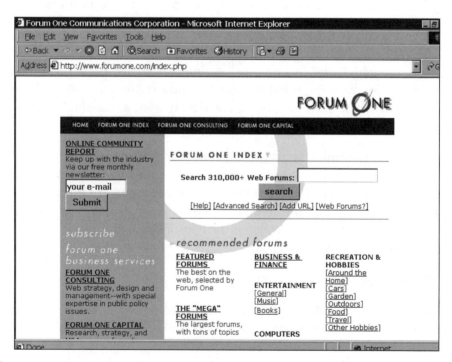

Figure 12.3: ForumOne is a comprehensive directory of Internet forums.

Yahoo! Messages at http://messages.yahoo.com/

The above are excellent ways of uncovering forums that assist you in finding employees. But what if the sites you need haven't yet been listed in these directories? Sometimes, more specific searching will be required; in that case, it's time to revisit your friendly neighborhood search engine. Before we go there, let's review search engine basics and get them straight in your mind:

What am I looking for? Industry-specific forums in which I can network with my peers, post my jobs, or find employees.

What are the keywords that I might use? Industry names and states or cities, such as `accounting`, `computers`, `java`, `unix`, `vision`, `retail sales`, `vermont`, `arizona`, or `silicon valley`, combined with `forum`, `discussion`, `community`.

Step Three: Utilize Search Engines

Quite often, sites will include forums, index the pages via search engines, and neglect to actively list them in the prior forum directories. Luckily, there are many techniques you can utilize that will help you uncover the forums you need.

Job boards (actually, forums in general) are often installed in specific directories, such as `wwwboard`, `bbs`, `ubb`, or `ultimate`, as seen in Figure 12.4. Let's say that you're looking to find accounting individuals. Visit **AltaVista** at http://www.altavista.com/, choose Advanced Search, and use a search string like the following. This kind of searching will work for other industries too; however, you must remember that not every site has been indexed by every search engine. Your mileage might vary.

```
(url:wwwboard or url:bbs or url:ultimate or url:ubb or
url:ultimate) and jobs and accounting
```

The above takes are of the here and now question—you should be able to uncover both free and paid job forums that will assist you in your hiring quests. Let's take this one step further. One of the great benefits of doing business online is to create a following. Followings are beneficial for many reasons—you'll see other individuals doing your marketing for you by referring their friends to your postings, and when you *do* need to find professionals to hire, you'll have much more credibility by being a known and trusted source. Not only can you derive benefits this way, but if your business involves the actual selling of products, you can increase your customer base most dramatically.

Figure 12.4: Notice the keyword wwwboard in the URL of this Las Vegas job board.

How do you actually create a following? Well, one way is to either find or create forums in which your peers, customers, and industry professionals hang out. For example, perhaps you sell home theater equipment. Go to **Google** at http://www.google.com/ and search for "home theater" forum—you might find a link to the **Home Theater Forum** at http://www.hometheaterforum.com/uub/main.html. Visit that site—you'll see how all needs of home theater fanciers are met. A community has been built! Think about it—where would be the best place to find people who would enjoy working with such a product? You got it—that particular, individual forum.

***Special Interest**—Many forums focus on specific, niche interests. If you are hiring in industries that serve this interest, you can often find many people who would be interested in what you have to offer.*

Now, keep in mind that if you don't own the forum in question, you can't simply show up and offer jobs. No no no! Instead, take time to become a valued resource. The Internet is for sharing—the more you offer, the more people will want to hear from you. I've done that myself at several forums where my own customers lurk. My main industry focus is Internet recruiting; I'm also quite skilled in entrepreneurial business. Thus, I can frequently be found at the forum of **RECNET** at http://www.egroups.com/group/recruitersnetwork/, and *Fortune* magazine discussions at http://www.fortune.com/ (see also Figure 12.5). My frequent postings

Figure 12.5: *Fortune* magazine has a career forum.

result not only in increased orders of my book and seminar series, but also in a wide distribution of my brand. In other words, people listen when I post.

How can you implement this yourself? It takes time and patience to develop a following. You need to locate a forum or discussion board where your industry is discussed (not necessarily strictly the jobs aspect). Once you uncover one, join the community and showcase why you're worth paying attention to. You might be surprised by the results.

Step Four: Plan Your Participation

You found the forums in which you would like to participate—now what? Keep in mind your basic goals. If you are looking for the quick fix, the finding of employees fast, you'll want to post your jobs. Remember the basic premise of your job posts—they are advertisements for bettering your candidates' life as well as for how wonderful your company and offered position is! Make it dynamic, exciting, compelling—make it the catalyst for people to learn more about what you have to offer.

If you're in it for the long term, think of what you have to offer. Can you provide industry tips that will showcase your knowledge of what works and doesn't? Can you develop your name in such a way that future employees remember you?

Following are some guidelines to assist you with interacting with specific industry (not solely job-related) forums.

> **Don't blatantly advertise.** Almost all the forums you encounter will have messages in their code of conduct that state no advertisements are allowed. This is because many marketers will visit sites, post ads about their products, and then leave. While this might be considered logical business sense, in reality, it is filled with flaws; the site owner will recognize someone is getting free visibility while he or she is receiving no benefit (such as advertising fees or quality information for the forum). Thus, such messages are generally quickly deleted.

Do provide answers. Instead of advertising, first lurk on the forum and see what kinds of questions are being posted. Can you answer them without making the response seem like an advertisement for your company? Perhaps you are in the exercising industry. Forum participants will probably ask questions about the most effective ways to lose weight after pregnancy, the best kinds of elliptical exercise machines on the market, and maximizing weight lifting routines. By continuously answering these questions, you cause other visitors (which probably will include trainers as well, which would be your future employee market), to heed your name and advice.

Do include your link information. Even though you shouldn't blatantly advertise, you generally *can* include information about yourself in the form of a link back to your site. This gives people who view your writings a chance to click on your link and see what you do have to offer. It's an effective yet unobtrusive way of increasing your own visibility.

Don't flame. For some strange, inexplicable reason, people get the insane desire to start posturing in front of others online, and resort to ugly language, insults, and other components of *flaming* (Internet nasty behavior). This is simply childish at best and dangerous at worst—you never know if the person insulting you is a 13-year-old chemistry student or a 20-something deranged pathological criminal. Should individuals start attempting to embroil you in a useless debate, always take the high road. You'll look better and also generate more respect from the by-standers.

Never Flame—*The anonymity the Internet offers makes it tempting to let go of common courtesy. Never flame in bulletin boards or forums; all you do is look like a fool. Instead, take the high road and continue your networking goals.*

That takes care of how to participate in forums … what if you want to increase your visibility via paid advertising? Consider banners; quite often, forums will have space for individuals to advertise their services. If you don't want to take the time to become a community leader, you can try your hand at advertising your openings and products via banner at appropriate forum sites. Banners generally can appear on the main forum page, on individual answer pages, and on the site in general.

Step Five: Monitor the Results

How can you monitor the results from your forum participation? Simple! Remember, most forums will generally allow you to post a link back to your site once you've participated. When someone clicks on that link and visits your site, that will be recorded in your Web-site log file. Thus, you can keep track of who finds you when you analyze your Web-site logs.

Site hits, however, are not the only benefit you'll receive from forum participation. My personal site, http://www.barbaraling.com/, receives a number of hits from my recruiting mailing list participations, yet surprisingly fewer hits from the Internet marketing forums such as Inc. Discussions or Fast Company (which are places where I post constantly). But that's okay; those two sites are components of the specific magazines, which is where I'd like to get known by the Powers That Be. I'm willing to spend my time offering free information for the chance of getting chosen for an interview or article; to me, that is just as valuable as bringing droves of potential customers directly to my site.

Examples

You learned in this chapter how to uncover forums that will assist you in your Internet recruiting. Let's now apply this to the following real-world searches:

- Locate cosmetics salespeople.
- Locate commercial Realtors.

These examples will show you how to locate needed professionals by taking advantage of forums.

Locate Cosmetics Salespeople

Nora, a manager for a cosmetics store, would like to increase her personal network, both within her industry and in places where her future employees would gather.

Whom does Nora need?

Individuals who are skilled in selling cosmetics, although she'll consider training promising candidates.

What does Nora need to find?

Forums in which she can post jobs and keep abreast of her industry.

Where does Nora look?

First, she tackles her industry as a profession, and visits **Google** at http://www.google.com/ and searches for cosmetic industry. One link that might be returned is the **COSMETIC INDEX Resources on the Web** at http://www.cosmeticindex.com/ci/html/resources.html. Visiting that site reveals a link to the **Perfume 2000** at http://www.perfume2000.com/; this proves to be an industrial site specifically for the perfume industry and includes several forums, one specifically related to jobs and careers. Not only that, but the site also offers free e-mail so that Nora can obtain an e-mail address like nora@perfume2000.net. If she has only an AOL or other ISP address, choosing one that ends in an industry name might be beneficial when communicating with potential employees.

Nora has found an industry niche site that offers forums specific to the cosmetic industry.

Nora then takes a second look at http://www.cosmeticindex.com/ci/html/resources.html; because the words cosmetic and index are included, she decides to investigate the site further. She removes /ci/html/resources.html, the secondary part of the URL, and reloads the main site at http://www.cosmeticindex.com/. There, she'll see links to another job bank, a classifieds section, and even more industry resources.

When examining the main site, Nora uncovered another hidden job bank specifically for her industry.

By poking around these links, she can almost certainly find other industry- and trade-related forums, and get her name known by fellow professionals. This will be beneficial if she ever considers a career change in the future; she'll have a new network in which to ask for suggestions and ideas.

Now Nora knows at least one industry-related site, Perfume 2000. She visits **AltaVista** at http://www.altavista.com/ and looks for other sites that include links to it via the search query `link:www.perfume2000.com -url:www.perfume2000.com`. One site that might be returned is the **American Society of Perfumers** at http://www.perfumers.org/links.html; there she might come across a link to **Cosmetic World** at http://www.cosmeticworld.com/. This site also contains industry-related forums.

Nora has now found organizations for her industry in which she can network with other fellow professionals.

Nora's pretty well set now for her professional industry connections; now she has to consider finding resources for locating employees to work at her store. Ideally she would like someone with previous cosmetic experience. She considers her location, Livingston, NJ, and searches for `nj forum` at Google. She might be returned a link to **NJ.com** at http://www.nj.com/, where she'll uncover many regional forums that include communities as well as businesses. In those forums, she can either answer local community questions or post questions about the best places to advertise local jobs. NJ.com has a great classifieds section, too.

Nora has now found local forums she can use for hiring.

Find Commercial Realtors

Let's try another example. Greg is a manager for a commercial real estate corporation that specializes in the selling of downtown buildings. He'd like to both broaden his network of peers as well as locate places where other commercial realtors might be found.

Whom does Greg need?

Greg needs to hire more realtors within the commercial industry.

What does Greg need to find?

Forums in which his future employees gather, as well as resources where he can market his own services and broaden his network.

Where does Greg look?

Visiting **ForumOne** at http://www.forumone.com/, he searches for `commercial real estate` and comes up with the **CCIM Commercial Real Estate Network Forums** at http://www.ccim.com/. There are several industry-related forums in which he can participate.

Greg has located his first forum where he can post to his targeted audience.

Next, he visits AltaVista to see who else links to this site. The search `link:www.ccim.com -url:www.ccim.com` leads him to the **Real Estate Library's Commercial Links** at http://www.relibrary.com/12c1.htm. This page contains a link to the **Loop Network** at http://www.loopnet.com/; not only is there a direct jobs forum for his industry, but also opportunities to post his banner ad and reach over 75,000 commercial real estate professionals.

By searching for additional resources, Greg has now uncovered more forums and commercial real estate job boards.

How can Greg take best advantage of all the resources that he has uncovered? If he has time to spare, he could start lurking on the various forums and answering questions concerning the managerial aspects of commercial real estate; if not, he can simply post his job advertisements online or create a banner to be displayed during one of the newsletter mailings.

Simplifying Your Hiring

As you can see, forums represent much more than merely places to visit and chat. By using forums and becoming known by your candidate population, your name starts to become known by the very people you want to hire. Not too many employers take advantage of the riches this byproduct of forum participation can bestow upon them; you can get a step ahead of your competitors by actively networking and posting where your candidates will see your contributions. Take advantage of that.

CHAPTER THIRTEEN

Mailing Lists

Mailing lists have been around since the dawn of time. Well, actually, probably a tad later, but the point remains—mailing lists are one of the original ways of communicating on the Internet. Their premise is quite simple; enthusiasts send and receive e-mail to and from one another, but instead of manually sending e-mail to every person on the list (think of the tracking that would require), subscribers to mailing lists instead just send their comments to one main, central location. This location will then blast out the message to everyone on the list.

You can compare this to a memo that gets circulated around your office. Someone comes up with an idea and submits it to the rest of the team for constructive comments and responses. Eventually, the team as a whole hears out everyone else's take on the proposal. Mailing lists provide a similar resource, except the responses are generally in real time and do not require paper to be shuffled from one person to another.

From this description, you might think that these resources have no set guidelines. Nothing could be further from the truth! Mailing lists come in four flavors:

Unmoderated and open—Anyone can join and post anything they'd like.

Unmoderated and closed—People have to be manually added to the list, after the list members approve.

Moderated and open—Anyone can join, but someone acts as a moderator to cut down on the amount of spam.

Moderated and closed—The moderator must give permission for new members to join.

When participating on a mailing list, it is crucial that you follow the guidelines set by the creator. Like with forums, you never want to just jump in and start advertising your services. Instead, as always, become a valued resource first, and the references and quality reputation will follow.

Many professionals find mailing lists an invaluable resource for their business day-to-day operations. Not only does participation help develop a sense of community and networking, it also provides access to good, first-person advice regarding new software to use, sites to visit, and resources to use. The amount of e-mail that might be generated can be staggering; some lists have hundreds of messages that get bounced back and forth every day. One solution that many lists now implement is to allow subscribers to receive daily digests instead.

Nowadays, the trend is moving towards combining mailing lists and forums. Sites like **eGroups** at http://www.egroups.com/ give the option to receive information via your Web browser (that's the forum aspect) or via actual e-mail—see Figure 13.1. Still, there are many mailing lists whose main format is based in e-mail—that is what this chapter will cover.

The Benefits of Mailing Lists

Mailing lists, like forums, assist individuals in creating a sense of community. Their main purpose in life is to allow like-minded individuals a simple way to communicate with one another. They originated long, long ago, back before there was a World Wide Web. I ran several back in the early 90s—the unofficial list for rec.pets.birds, a humor list, and a news update of what was happening during the

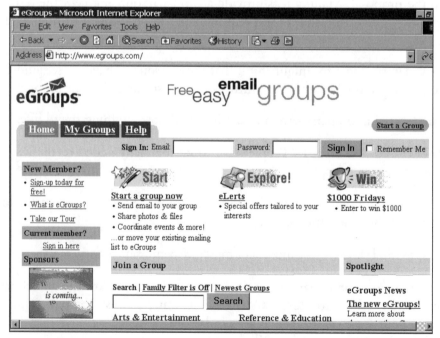

Figure 13.1: eGroups lets you choose from thousands of mailing lists.

student uprising in Tiananmen Square. It was a simple premise—I was a central focus point for disseminating information.

Nowadays, of course, the Internet has taken that concept and run to the ends of the Earth with it. It seems that there are mailing lists for just about any topic you can imagine. Want to find Windows programmers? Thousands upon thousands of mailing lists deal with that topic—questions about programming, systems administration, fine-tuning, hacking, and more. Want to discuss Internet marketing and e-commerce trends instead? You merely have to visit any of the popular mailing list directories to uncover hundreds of choices.

Mailing lists are great business tools—not only do they encourage networking, but like forums, they're an excellent vehicle to publicize your name in your industry. The name of the game here is encouraging individuals to feel comfortable in dealing with you. Perhaps you are in the business of selling homes; you can participate on many of the excellent professional Realtors' lists that are available, such as residential-sales@dealmakers.net. (A whole list exists at **DealMakers** at http://www.property.com/news.html.) Here, you would be networking with your colleagues, sharing information, and, should you need to hire more Realtors, you could ask your peers for advice on the best niche job boards around.

***Jobs by E-mail**—Many enterprising recruiters will create a hot-jobs mailing list in which potential employees can receive weekly notification of all new offers in their field.*

Another popular use of mailing lists is to broadcast hot jobs available at your company. Have you ever visited company Web sites that encourage visitors to sign up for future employment opportunity distribution? This is an example of opt-in marketing and can be invaluable in reaching potential employees.

I've even seen résumé distribution services via mailing lists! Years ago, I was helping a recruiter find NT candidates. Because I was a techie at heart, I was already familiar with some of the guru mailing lists that abound on the Internet, and sent e-mail to Stu Sjouwerman of **Sunbelt Software**, who ran some e-mail lists at http://www.sunbelt-software.com/. When I explained my need to find lead NT systems administrators, he created the specific mailing list **NT System Admin Résumés** at http://lyris.sunbelt-software.com/scripts/lyris.pl. It consists of professionals looking for NT jobs and is running to this day.

Other benefits of mailing lists include:

> **Visibility**—When anyone posts to mailing lists, the message will be broadcast to all members. As with forums, this will afford you a wonderful opportunity to

refresh your business in the minds of the viewers. Visit the **Recruiter's Network Mailing list** at http://www.egroups.com/group/recruitersnetwork/ and search for my posts—you'll see how visible I've become to my potential client and customer base. Figure 13.2 gives a small sample. Additionally, you can append your contact information after every post you make; this ensures that interested parties know how to contact you.

Fan club—Post enough, with quality information, and you'll start to develop a following of individuals who eagerly await your latest ideas. This can be an incredibly valuable resource, especially if you are releasing new products where the community has learned to trust you.

Advertising—Some mailing lists will encourage advertisers to sponsor the list. If you don't have time to participate actively in a mailing list, this might be a great opportunity to gain exposure. Consider **Lockergnome** at http://www.lockergnome.com/—this is a mailing list that reaches more than a hundred thousand fanciers of the Windows operating system. This list is so huge advertisers willingly pay into the thousands for commercial space. The owner, Chris Pirillo, has written a book about running an e-mail list; check out *Poor Richard's E-mail Publishing* at http://www.topfloor.com/pr/email/. It's a comprehensive and excellent reference guide.

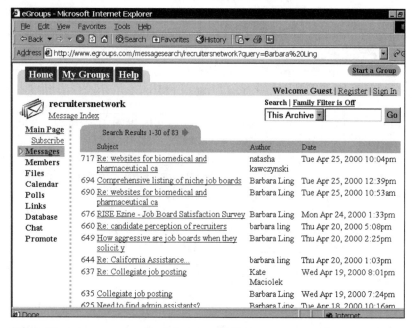

Figure 13.2: The more you post, the more visible your name becomes.

Advertising!—*Many mailing lists will allow advertisers to pay for their offers to be broadcast to the list members. If you have neither time nor inclination to become part of a community, perhaps taking an advertisement out in a targeted mailing list would bring you valuable visibility.*

Community—Networking is the most effective way to conduct business on the Internet—many sites will include mailing lists to foster communications between enthusiasts. A case in point—I'm a member of the **Computer Book Publishers** list at http://www.studiob.com/, where individual contributors are recognized by name and publicly lauded when their newest books are published.

Mailing lists can be used in the following fashions:

Discussions—Want to stay in touch with a hobby group, user group, or professional organization? Lots of lists spring up to meet these needs. You only need to visit **eGroups** at http://www.egroups.com/ and browse Home > Family or Home > Home Business to find useful lists:

home business
http://www.egroups.com/group/-ihomebiz/

Clicker Horses
http://www.egroups.com/group/123horseclick/

Aromatherapy
http://www.egroups.com/group/brandeys/

Let's take this one step further. Can you define any hobbies or interests in your industry niche or employee makeup? If so, you can most likely find mailing lists where friendly bantering will be seen by potential employees.

Job/résumé boards—Mailing lists can be configured in a pinch to serve as a method of broadcasting work opportunities or industry news. Many industry-specific lists will allow such postings given they fall under specific guidelines. For example, **Jobs4Women** at http://www.jobs4women.com/ba/ is a site that allows women professionals in the San Francisco area to receive notification of local jobs (see Figure 13.3) . **RésuméZapper** at http://www.resumezapper.com/ allows individuals like you and me to sign up and receive free résumés via e-mail. And http://www.egroups.com/group/1telecommutejobs/ lets you post your telecommuting jobs for free.

Reading your mailing lists is a great way to start the day. You can build up quite a following by taking the time to participate effectively. Not only that, but you will create many new friends who can help spread your word when you're hiring.

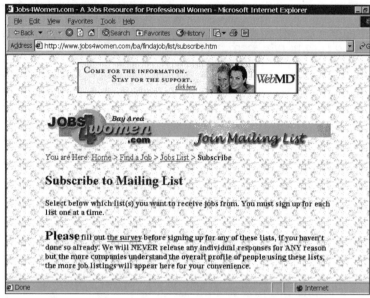

Figure 13.3: Jobs4Women.com has several San Francisco job-related mailing lists.

How to Find Targeted Mailing Lists

Locating mailing lists specifically targeted towards your business is not difficult. It can be done via the following simple steps:

- Define what kind of mailing list you want.
- Utilize search engines.
- Plan your participation.
- Monitor your results.

These steps are described in the sections that follow.

Step One: Define What Kind of Mailing List You Want

Paralleling the technique in Chapter 12, "Forums," ask yourself the following questions: What kind of mailing would you like to find? Job posting or résumé finding? Local? Regional? National? In what industry? With what focus? What are your main goals? Do you want to find someone *right now,* or do you want to build a following? Finding someone right now means you should target your searching to the job/résumé mailing lists—generating a following means you should also consider discussion forums geared towards the industry in question (and not only employment). At these kinds of lists, you simply want to monitor questions and jump in when you can provide your peers with the right answers.

Lots of Possibilities—*You have many ways to use mailing lists. Industry mailing lists are great for networking with your peers; job-related or résumé mailing lists might deliver leads to potential employees to your mailbox on a daily basis.*

Mailing lists are often found in specific directories online. Additionally, they can be found at industry niche and professional organization sites, too. When searching, you want to keep the following goals in mind:

What am I looking for?—Mailing lists.

What are the keywords that I might use?—Topics, careers, or skills such as `Java` or `Marketing` or `Banking` or `Decoration` coupled with the phrase `mailing list`.

Step Two: Utilize Search Engines

If you're looking solely to find people to hire right here and now, you want to concentrate on the mailing lists that reflect your industry. Remember our earlier discussion of finding forums? The method of finding job board mailing lists is similar.

Visit the many mailing list directories that abound on the Internet. The most popular are **Tile.net** at http://www.tile.net/, **Liszt** at http://www.liszt.com/, **Publicly Accessible Mailing Lists** at http://paml.alastra.com/, **Talklist** at http://www.talklist.com/, and **eGroups** at http://www.egroups.com/.

Once there, you should search for your industry followed by the keyword `job`, `career`, `employment`, or `resume`. For example, perhaps you wish to locate jewelry professionals. Searching **eGroups** at http://www.egroups.com/ for `jewelry job` will bring you to the group called **Orchid** at http://www.egroups.com/list/orchid/info.html— further exploration shows this to be a mailing list that is a free service maintained by jewelers for other jewelers. The FAQ Frequently Asked Questions List (commonly called a FAQ) on the Orchid site will bring you to the sponsoring site at http://www.ganoksin.com/, where you'll discover a free classifieds section.

These kinds of searches work for many, many different industries. Need to find free places to post programming jobs? Searching for `programming job` at http://www.egroups.com/ reveals several dozen sites, starting with the **American Association Of Computer Programmers** mailing list at http://www.egroups.com/group/AACP/. Of course, you could be much more specific and search for, perhaps, `unix job`— you'll uncover lists at http://www.egroups.com/messages/a1a-OpSystjobs/, http://www.egroups.com/messages/UNIXJobs/, http://www.egroups.com/list/craigs-list/info.html (that's a list for professionals in San Francisco), and more.

Sites like **Liszt** at http://www.liszt.com/ and **Tile.net** at http://www.tile.net/ have been around the longest, so you might come up with more firmly established lists there. Searching on `job` at http://www.liszt.com/, for example, will return over fifty lists where you can post offerings for free.

The sources discussed so far address the here and now question—you'll find both free and paid job mailing lists that will assist you in your hiring quests.

Consider also the benefits of searching for general, all-purpose industry mailing lists, too. Quite often, professional organizations, associations, and niche sites will include mailing lists and resources for their members' benefit.

It's even easier to locate these kinds of resources. Perhaps you need to hire automotive engineers. Search for `automotive engineer` at Google—you might uncover the **Society for Automotive Engineers** at http://www.sae.org/. Search for `list` or `forum`—you'll uncover a link to their niche forum site at http://forums.sae.org/.

Why search for forums when we're looking for lists? Well, nowadays the line between mailing lists and forums is constantly being blurred—a mailing list can be archived as a Web-based forum, and questions posted to a forum can be received as e-mail. So people have taken to using either word for either style of discussion. Note that the example search for automotive engineers picked up a forum and not a list—we'd have missed it entirely if we'd concentrated on lists.

Our main goal is maximizing the benefits we find. If you're searching for mailing lists and a high-quality forum pops up, don't ignore the lead—it could end up being quite valuable.

Zeroing in on particular skills can also improve your findings. Need to hire technical professionals who eat, live, and breathe Microsoft Windows NT? A search for `nt mailing list` on Google might result in a page like the **Los Angeles NT Users Group** at http://lantug.org/. There, you'll uncover many NT-related mailing lists. This technique holds for the e-mail directories too. Let's say that you need to hire CORBA programmers—visit http://www.liszt.com/ and search for CORBA. You'll find several CORBA-specific mailing lists.

***Seek and Ye Shall Find**—Quite often you'll be able to uncover the mailing lists you need by simply browsing publicly available directories.*

Again, I cannot overemphasize the importance of netiquette when participating in these mailing lists. They are *not*, for the most part, there for you to simply post your jobs! You have to first become an active member of the community, perhaps exchange e-mail with the moderator (if the list in question is moderated), ask for advice about sponsoring messages, and similar actions. It's all about creating a successful following.

Step Three: Plan Your Participation

You found the mailing lists in which you would like to participate—now what? Keep in mind your basic goals. If you are looking for the quick fix, the finding of employees fast, you'll want to advertise your jobs. If the list in question allows for job posting, so much the better—if not, you can simply try to sponsor messages on the mailing list to get your name out.

- If you're in it for the long term, think of what you have to offer. Can you provide industry/business tips that will showcase your knowledge of what works and doesn't? Can you develop your name in such a way that potential employees remember you? In any event, there are specific guidelines you should follow to increase your success with a mailing list. In any event, follow the same guidelines on a mailing list that you would in a forum (see Chapter 12, in the section entitled "Step Four: Plan Your Participation"). There's one additional step for a mailing list:

- Include your signature information. Because you generally participate in mailing lists from your own e-mail application, it's easy to include your signature information in every e-mail message that goes out. Signatures are traditionally four lines long; while nowadays length is unlimited, it's a very good rule of thumb to stay within four lines as often as possible (ultra-long signatures generally appear to be too commercial). Include your name, contact information, Web site address, e-mail address, and perhaps a catchy slogan or two. For example, my signature includes `C Code. C Code Run. Run Code Run ... Please!` Done well, signatures can be visually appealing and tempt a viewer to learn more.

Signatures—*When posting to mailing lists, always be sure to include your signature information; this is an effective way of getting your contact number and site publicized to interested viewers.*

Step Four: Monitor the Results

How can you monitor your results from your mailing list participation? Simple! When individuals start to refer to you by name or post adoring messages about you on the list, you're leagues ahead of your competitors. Here are some posts from lists in which I've participated: "I agree with Barbara's comments. I can't think of anyone who has provided more value to the group in the way of information." This is the kind of response that builds one's reputation. The results I'm experiencing from participating in mailing lists are not unique; every list will have a number of appreciated contributors who give and give and give. You can enjoy the same benefits, too, once you become a member of your chosen communities and provide value to all visitors; word of mouth simply spreads and your reputation grows with it.

Think about how this will benefit your hiring in the future. Let's say that you're a money manager in a business located in Little Rock, Arkansas. If you locate community-related mailing lists and actively participate in them, not only will you have increased your personal network, but you'll also most likely have discovered information about the local Chamber of Commerce and other business-related resources that you'd never have found otherwise. Perhaps your immediate network wouldn't deliver actual employees; however, it's apt to include someone who knows someone who is looking for the opportunities that you offer. Because you've already become a valued member in the network, you should find advertising your positions a lot easier.

Example

In this chapter, you learned how to maximize your benefits from mailing lists. Mailing lists can be used not only to network with potential future employees, but also as an effective vehicle to broaden the scope of your positive reputation. The following example will walk you through a search for technical mailing lists.

Find Technical Mailing Lists

Linda is a recruiter who specializes in matching technical candidates to Fortune 500 companies.

Whom does Linda need?

Linda needs individuals who are well versed in various aspects of technical fields—programmers, developers, systems administrators, and the like.

What does Linda need to find?

She needs to locate mailing lists where her candidates would gather. Additionally, she wants to investigate the possibility of running her own mailing list so interested professionals can sign up to receive weekly hot jobs.

Where does Linda look?

First, Linda visits **eGroups** at http://www.egroups.com/ and searches for technical skills such as `java` and `oracle`. Immediately she learns of dozens of mailing lists that relate to these topics. She doesn't, of course, post her jobs there; she joins several to lurk and see if career questions arise that she can answer. In other words, she starts to become part of that community.

Linda has uncovered several mailing lists.

Next, Linda visits **Google** at http://www.google.com/ and searches for `java mailing list`. She finds a **master list** of them at http://metalab.unc.edu/javafaq/mailinglists.html. These are more resources she can consider to use for her networking.

Linda is pretty well set for now regarding mailing lists.

Remembering the **RISE Internet Recruiting seminar** at http://www.riseway.com/ she took earlier, she considers other aspects of mailing lists. Returning to eGroups at http://www.egroups.com/, Linda searches for `jobs` (as in Figure 13.4). The resulting responses prove to her that many of her colleagues are using mailing lists to keep their candidates abreast of all developments. Linda decides to set one up for herself.

Linda has now incorporated a mailing list into her business.

Next, Linda decides to take advantage of networking with her peers. She returns to **Google** at http://www.google.com/ and searches for `recruiter mailing list`. One site returned discusses **mailing lists** at http://www.riseway.com/mailinglists.html; alas, it's not specific to her industry. However, on that page, she sees a link for Recruiter Goodies, and uncovers the **Recruiters Network** at http://www.egroups.com/group/recruitersnetwork,

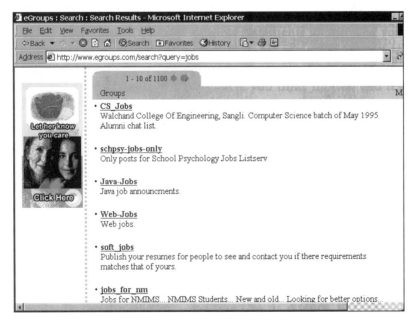

Figure 13.4: Searching for jobs on eGroups returns over a thousand entries.

the **Electronic Recruiting Exchange** at http://www.erexchange.com/, as well as an **HR-related list** at http://www.egroups.com/group/hrnet. A **mailing list/forum** at http://www.recruitersonline.com/ also shows up.

Linda has now found several mailing lists in which she can discuss many different recruiting techniques with her colleagues.

Also Consider ...

Mailing lists offer a great way to communicate with your peers as well as network with your candidate population. As we've seen, rolling your own list can be an effective way of keeping interested professionals up to date with your employment offerings. You can even take that a step further by creating separate mailing lists for different employment needs; if you're in the marketing business, you could create mailing lists for direct marketing tips, techniques for closing sales, learning how to negotiate, and more. The more high-quality information you offer, the more visitors will refer your site to their peers. And that will provide a great boost in your Internet recruiting adventures.

CHAPTER FOURTEEN

Towns, Communities, and Newspapers

Remember those long ago, halcyon days when finding employees was as simple as advertising in your local newspapers? Or when you wanted to know how your local marching band fared in the state regional finals, and all you had to do was pick up the sports section and read all about it?

Many newspapers have now seen the light and started providing active online editions for their print brethren. These Web sites might include daily news, headlines, local neighborhood forums, classifieds, career centers and more. This can be highly beneficial for your recruiting, because quite often the audience includes individuals who would be most willing to consider your employment opportunities. Human beings have a tendency to gather around common interests; in the real world or online the community can prove to be a focal point for many diverse interests, including employment. Think about it; how often have you perused the "help wanted" section of your newspaper or seen thumbtacked notices about community happenings in your local supermarket or library? These resources are becoming more and more popular online as well; often you'll see community business directories listed as a resource, too.

Business Directories—*Often community and town sites will have business directories available online. Depending upon the site, you might discover it's free for you to add your business link.*

The Benefits of Towns, Communities, and Newspapers

First and foremost, the benefit of using town, community, and newspaper Web sites is you'll enjoy a targeted means of finding employees. Think about it. Many of the job boards that are popular on the Internet—Monster.com, Headhunter.net, etc.—are national in scope. Local newspaper, town, and community sites, however, are dedicated to your area.

Sometimes the line between newspaper sites and regional sites can blur. For example, check out **Online NJ.com** at http://www.nj.com/—not only is it chock-full of New Jersey resources—regional forums, classifieds, and the like—it also has news headlines from the *Star Ledger* (a New Jersey newspaper). Thus, when thinking about community sites, always keep in mind community resources like newspapers, too.

Regional sites don't have to be widely publicized to be visible—sometimes all that's required is for the residents of the town to know about them. Consider, for example, the town of **Lynchburg, Virginia**—http://www.lynchburgonline.com/ offers a regional business listings directory (and of course, if your business was in that location, you certainly would want to investigate how to add your link!). **Highland Park, Illinois,** has the same opportunity for local business visibility at http://www.highlandpark.org/bizdirectory.html. And the site for **Madison, Wisconsin,** at http://www.madison.com/, has a direct link to **Classifieds and Employment** at http://classifieds.madison.com/—see Figure 14.1.

Community and newspaper sites offer the following benefits:

Local audience. Most of the visitors to the site or readers of the newspaper are local to the state in question. If you're looking for local employees, you certainly want to take advantage of the classifieds and employment section.

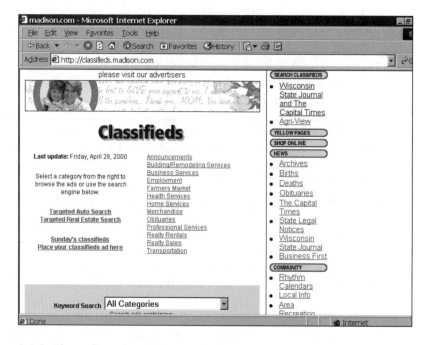

Figure 14.1: The online classifieds section from a city Web site.

Local forums. In an effort to retain viewership, community and newspaper sites will include discussion groups and encourage the visitors to participate. Sometimes individuals will post requests for career assistance in the new town.

Advertising. Many newspaper and community sites will have advertising opportunities. Banners, links, sponsoring sites... if you're looking to hire in the particular area, consider spending your advertising dollars to ensure a targeted audience.

Special sections. Just about every newspaper site (and many community sites, too) will have special sections for their readers on topics such as Business, Technology, Finance, and Real Estate. Along with general advertising, you can often place advertising in specific regional forums that target your hiring area.

Business directory. Because newspaper and community sites are resources, quite often you'll uncover local business directory pages. If your business is regional, certainly submit your link for inclusion—the more visibility the better!

One of the best ways to maximize your benefits from newspaper and community sites is to investigate all the local resources you can uncover. Chambers of Commerce, business networks, the Better Business Bureau, and more usually turn up in even a brief search.

How to Find Your Towns, Communities, and Newspapers

Locating all the community resources you can handle can be quite simple if you follow these steps:

- Define your community.
- Browse city directories.
- Utilize search engines.
- Plan your participation.
- Monitor the results.

These steps are described in the sections that follow.

Step One: Define Your Community

Ask yourself, in what community would you like to search? Most likely, your first thought will be the town in which you need to hire. This certainly can work, but searching on just that location will limit your success. Let's get a tad broader.

Communities are generally located within regions. And regions are almost always located in states. Thus you can search for a community-only site, a regional site, and a state site.

Consider the **Catskill Mountains** area in New York. You can find town links at http://www.catskillguide.com/links.htm, the **Hudson Valley Regional** site at http://www.hvnet.com/, a **Northern New York** site at http://www.roundthebend.com/, and a list of **New York newspaper sites** at http://www.newsdirectory.com/news/press/na/us/ny/. Quite often you'll find similar resources for other areas of the country. Not only can you look for towns, you can broaden your search to include your own region, your own state, even a section of the country itself (like **North West Jobs** at http://www.northwestjobs.com/).

One neat way to uncover regional job sites is to guess at the domain name. For example, consider big cities like **San Francisco** or **Atlanta**, and then visit the sites http://www.sanfrancisco.com/ and http://www.atlanta.com/. In both cases, you'll see resources for visitors and businesses alike. Granted, these sites themselves don't include job resources, but other Web sites with similar names do. **Online NJ.com** at http://www.nj.com/ has many specific local career resources, while **WestOrangeOnline** at http://www.westorange.com/ allows local businesses to add their listings to the business directory. From these resources, it's a simple step to search for pages that include them as links and uncover related sites as well.

Step Two: Browse City Directories

The easiest way to locate newspapers or community sites is to browse related directories on the Internet. For example, a comprehensive collection of newspaper and magazine sites can be found at **NewsDirectory.com** at http://www.newsdirectory.com/ and **MediaFinder** at http://www.mediafinder.com/. From these locations, simply browse or search for the particular state or newspaper in question.

Let's say that you wanted to find newspapers that deal with the region around St. Louis, Missouri. Visit http://www.newsdirectory.com/ (shown in Figure 14.2), select `United States`, then select "`United States`" and then choose `Missouri`. You'll see a link to the *St. Louis Post/Dispatch* at http://www.postnet.com/. Browsing around that site reveals community forums for the Jefferson and Tri-County areas, which include links for local associations, local computer user groups, and of course employment classifieds.

Specific community sites can often be found by browsing **USA CityLink** at http://www.usacitylink.com/. Perhaps you'd like to find community resources for the town of Lakeland in Florida. Choosing `Florida` from the main page, you'll see a

Figure 14.2: NewsDirectory.com has direct links to hundreds of online newspaper sites.

link to **Lakeland** at http://www.lakeland.net/ right on the page. Visit that site—you'll see direct links to **Employment** at http://employment.polk.net/, **Forums** at http://forums.polk.net/, and **Classifieds** at http://classifieds.polk.net/.

Let's take this a step further. Remember how in Chapter 8 we tried finding similar sites by seeing who else listed them as a resource? Communities can often be located online via search engines. Again, let's specify our key goals:

What am I looking for? Communities or newspapers.

What are the keywords that I might use? Community names such as west orange, walnut creek, or monmouth county, coupled with forums, links, or news.

Step Three: Utilize Search Engines

Visit AltaVista at http://www.altavista.com and search for link:www.Lakeland.net -url:www.Lakeland.net. One of the results returned is **Polk-Country** at http://www.polk-county.com/business.shtml; you'll uncover a business directory at http://www.polk-county.com/busdirectory.shtml that will list your link if you put in a request. The more business visibility you can have, the better!

Another great directory to check out is **DigitalCity** at http://www.digitalcity.com/. From here, you can browse different cities and view career-related resources.

Of course, new Web sites are being built every day. Perhaps you'll fail to discover your specific town at USA CityLink. Not to fear—now is the time to invoke the power of search engines. Visit **Google** at http://www.google.com/. Consider finding resources for Springfield, Massachusetts, and search on `springfield ma`. One site that might pop up is **Springfield, MA's Official Site** at http://www.ci.springfield.ma.us/.

Hmmm. The only problem you'll find is there doesn't seem to be any community-encouraging aspects of the site! But since it's an official town site, most likely other Massachusetts Web sites will refer to it.

Jump back to AltaVista and search for `link:www.ci.springfield.ma.us -url:www.ci.springfield.ma.us`. You might come up with a link to **Yahoo's MA listings** at http://asia.yahoo.com/Recreation/Travel/Browse_by_Region/U_S__States/Massachusetts/Complete_Listing/. It's a humongous page—from your browser window, choose Edit|Find and search for `springfield`.

You'll uncover a link to **Virtual-Valley's Springfield** site at http://virtual-valley.com/towns/html/springfield/. Further exploration of this site shows that not only can you add your listing for a small fee, but the main site itself deals with the entire western Massachusetts area. Community links, free classifieds, and more are found here.

CAUTION—*Just because a community site exists doesn't mean it's popular or well known. Anybody can plunk down the $70 or so required to register a domain name for a couple of years, so always first explore a site in its entirety to verify it makes sense to post your jobs there.*

Keep in mind, however, that just because a site is focused upon a particular community, that doesn't mean it's *known* by the community in question! One always has to poke around to see what town and community sites enjoy a high level of focused traffic. If the community site showcases a well-known newspaper, it's a pretty sure bet that it's popular; otherwise, you should take your time and see what traffic-building goodies the site includes.

Step Four: Plan Your Participation

After you've uncovered the specific town/community or newspaper sites on which you'd like to concentrate, now what? Your avenues are wide open! You can try any of the following:

Post employment ads. Many of the community/newspaper sites will offer classifieds at a reasonable rate. Be sure to include your phone number, Web site, and e-mail address if at all possible. Quite often, you'll see your ads appear in the print edition, too.

Advertise. If potential employees are visiting the site frequently, consider advertising via banners or links. Of course, if you're looking for nuclear scientists with experience in management, you might not uncover them in Hacketsville, Texas—you have to have a sense of where your quarry resides.

Add your link. If a business directory exists, you can submit your link for inclusion. Again, the more targeted visibility you can achieve the better. Not only that, but perhaps you can uncover related local businesses with whom to partner and network.

Participate. Participate in the local community forums. Is there a link to the local Chamber of Commerce? Again, that's a great lead! Take advantage of it.

Step Five: Monitor the Results

How can you monitor your results from your town and community participation? Well, you'll know you're receiving excellent results when people send you e-mail and refer to your postings at the local forums or in the online classifieds. Additionally, you can analyze your Web-site logs and see if any visitors originate from the community site in question.

Example

This chapter showed creative ways of uncovering community resources and using them to your advantage for Internet recruiting. Neighborhood job boards, community forums, and local business directories are only three of the great benefits you'll uncover. The following example will show you how to find community sites near Boston, Massachusetts.

Locate Boston Community Resources

Jack is a mortgage professional based in Boston, Massachusetts. He'd like to locate community sites in which he could advertise open job positions, as well as include his business link in appropriate directories.

Whom does Jack need?

Jack needs professionals in the mortgage or financial industry who are local to Boston and have several years of experience.

What does Jack need to find?

Jack needs to locate all the Boston sites he can find, and take advantage of community resources—forums, business directories, classifieds, and the like.

Where does Jack look?

First, Jack realizes that the city of Boston is surely large enough—and sufficiently up to date—to have its own presence on the Web. So he guesses that there ought to be a site at http://www.boston.com/ that would be a logical place in which to start looking. Visiting that site, he sees a link to **Career Classifieds** at http://careers.boston.com/. Right away, he's uncovered a good resource to post his Boston jobs.

Jack has an initial site for Boston interests.

He goes back to the **Boston.com** site, and notices a link for **Chat** at http://talk.boston.com/. True, it's not a forum, but it does provide a real-time method for actively talking with Bostonians, so he makes a note of it. Jack now wants to uncover other Boston sites, and visits **USA CityLink** at http://www.usacitylink.com/ (Figure 14.3). Browsing down to the town level, he uncovers **Visit Boston** at http://www.visit-boston.com/. Alas, that site doesn't seem to have the resources he's looking for, either. Not depressed (not yet, at least), he returns to Google and searches for boston forum. Success! He finds a link to

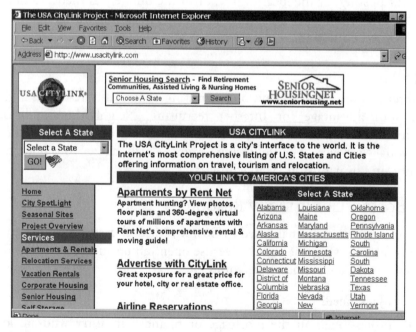

Figure 14.3: USA CityLink is a great resource for finding town and community sites.

About.com's Boston site at http://boston.about.com/; this location includes Boston employment sites, a community site, and more.

Jack has located a definitive resource for Boston. By poking around that site, he'll find many sites that can assist him in his business goals.

Next, Jack wants to find business directories to which he can add his business Web-site link. He visits **AltaVista** at http://www.altavista.com/ and searches for `boston business directory`. Ah, the sites that are returned! They might include **Search Boston** at http://www.searchboston.com/, **East Boston Online's Business Directory** at http://www.eastboston.com/business_dir.htm, and a **Boston Internet Directory** at http://www.webguideboston.com/. All of these sites can be considered for business purposes.

Jack is well on his way to finding business directories in which to list his company.

Finally, Jack decides to see if any more online local newspapers can be discovered. He visits **NewsDirectory.com** at http://www.newsdirectory.com/ and finds his way to the Massachusetts listings. He uncovers many listings, including the *Boston Herald* at http://www.bostonherald.com/; this site includes many resources including **HR Today** for employment at http://www.hr-today.com/ and **Boston-specific forums** at http://www.bostonherald.com/forums.html.

Jack has found the resources he needs to help him recruit locally.

Going Beyond

Towns and communities offer a great way to find forums and local employment opportunities, and also advertising opportunities and networking as well. You can take that one giant step further by monitoring forums to see when visitors post questions about reputable companies to work for. The Internet is meant for sharing information; when you proactively offer to answer employment questions, you stand a good chance of being the first choice in the mind of a potential employee.

Job Fairs and Trade Expos

One of the best-known resources for traditional recruiting is the job fair. Generally extremely well-publicized events, job fairs encourage professionals to seek out new employment, to explore new career possibilities, to boldly go where they feared to tread before. In short, depending upon how well-marketed it is, a fair is a place where you'll find a high concentration of active job seekers all together. This greatly reduces the amount of time you spend recruiting.

But another resource exists that can be just as effective. Trade expos draw professionals from a specific industry—practitioners, vendors, trainers, and more. Virtually all of the visitors can be viewed as passive candidates; people who might be interested in your opportunities if your presentation is intriguing enough. This chapter will explain in detail the benefits of both job fairs and trade expos.

Job Fairs

Traditional job or career fairs are events where the attendees are active job seekers who bring their résumés and interview as many of the exhibiting employers as they can. They exist for many different industries; one popular job fair theme is the high-tech arena—many job fairs are created solely for these professionals. **Network Events** at http://www.network-events.com/ showcases an extremely large number of these events. **Lendman** at http://www.lendman.com/ also provides job fairs for other industries, including sales.

Virtual Real Life—*Job fairs nowadays can take place in both real life and virtual; often Internet sites are dedicated to a physical event. This means you'll receive additional visibility via the sponsor's Web site if you sign up to participate in the fair.*

These places can be wonderful for recruiting! Quite often, the sponsoring Web site will include a virtual job fair page, enabling interested future employees to submit résumés to you online. Consider **BrassRing** at http://www.brassring.com/—originally The Virtual Job Fair, it also includes links to numerous physical career fair locations, as seen in Figure 15.1.

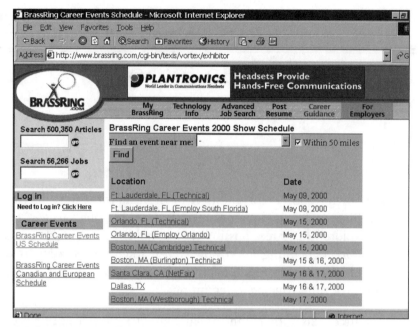

Figure 15.1: BrassRing offers endless opportunities to attend career fairs in person.

The process of attending job fairs for professionals is relatively simple; job seekers hear about the fair in question, brush up their résumés, put on their business suits, and visit the hotel or convention center where it's being held. From there, they will see the hiring companies either at tables or in booths or individual rooms and can then set up interviews on the spot to discuss hiring opportunities. In this fashion, career professionals can easily meet with dozens of companies in one day. You are almost always assured that attendees at these events are people looking to be hired (occasionally you'll see a vendor or two plying their wares). One benefit of these events is that *you* are in control—you have your hiring goals in mind, you know the necessary questions to ask, and you have the luxury of concentrating solely on the candidate without the distractions of your regular job. As mentioned, the Internet can play a large role in this activity. Not only can you uncover local job fairs via online sources, but often the companies sponsoring the job fair will include attending companies' contact information on the fair's Web site as well. Assuming you've chosen your job fair wisely, this will certainly broaden your reach among your targeted candidates.

Job Fairs Consist of ...

Job fairs generally last a day and are usually highly publicized via many different channels; the Internet, newspapers, billboards, and more. By using many of the traditional means of advertising, job fairs can potentially reach a much broader spectrum of individuals—more people might read the newspaper than look at a specific job fair site on the Internet. You can divide job fairs into two major components:

Physical event. The job fair can be viewed as both a hiring vehicle and a networking one as well. Most likely, your colleagues will be present as well, trying to interview the same individuals. You should delegate at least two people from your company if you decide to participate; one to interview and the other to answer questions from interested professionals who are waiting their turn.

Web site of sponsoring company. To increase awareness and visibility of career events, the Web site of the sponsoring company will often list the attending corporations, plus include direct links to their employment opportunities. Additionally, they might register their own events with other job fair directories on the Internet, thus increasing your exposure as well. At times, these sites will be left up after the event has passed.

How to Find Job Fairs

Finding job fairs online can be simplified to browsing job fair directories and utilizing search engines via the following steps:

- Define your industry and region.
- Browse job fair directories.
- Utilize search engines.
- Get the most out of the fairs you attend.

These steps are described in the following sections.

Step One: Define Your Industry and Region

Granted, this is generally a rather simple step. If your business is in the computer industry, you'd probably want a high-tech job fair. If your company instead deals with the retail sales market, finding a sales job fair might yield you more suitable candidates. Of course, you can take this one step further—if you're looking for high-tech sales individuals, attending a tech fair might give you insight into whom to contact (when interviewing technical individuals, ask them if they would recommend their sales colleagues).

Remember, you can define careers by more than simply industry! Is your business minority-owned, or would you like to broaden the diversity in your current workforce? Many diversity organizations will sponsor job fairs that are targeted to their members; participating here would certainly increase your visibility to excellent candidates. For example, the **NAACP Diversity & High Tech Career Fair** site at http://www.naacpjobfair.com/ lists job fairs that target professionals of color; the **Washington State Diversity Network** at http://www.scn.org/civic/diversity/jobfairs.htm lists local diversity job fairs, and **Hispanic job fairs** are found at http://www.saludos.com/.

***Specialties**—Job fairs come in all shapes and sizes, and can target specific regions and industries. Thus, if you're looking to hire sales and marketing professionals, you might find better success at job fairs aimed at the sales industry.*

Additionally, you can take into account your local region, be it city or state. **Carousel Expo** at http://www.carouselexpo.com/, for example, lists fairs specifically in Massachusetts and New Hampshire, as seen in Figure 15.2, while **The Job Fair** at http://www.thejobfair.com/ targets Georgia instead. It merely takes a few moments of digging around in search engines to uncover these resources.

Step Two: Browse Career Fair Directories

You can find several excellent trade show directories on the Internet. They include:

BrassRing
http://www.brassring.com/

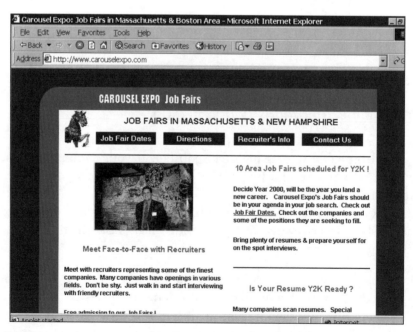

Figure 15.2: Carousel Expo deals solely with job fairs in Massachusetts and New Hampshire.

CareerMosaic Online Fairs
http://www.careermosaic.com/cm/cm35.html

JobDex
http://www.jobdex.com/

JobWeb
http://www.jobweb.org/search/cfairs/ (searchable by many parameters)

Lendman
http://www.lendman.com/

Network Events
http://www.network-events.com/

Professional Exchange
http://www.professional-exchange.com/

Perhaps your business is local to New York City and you'd like to hire programmers for software development. Visit **JobWeb** at http://www.jobweb.org/search/cfairs/, set your State dropdown box to NY, and search. You'll see several career fairs originating from colleges and universities, including a career expo from the New York Institute of Technology.

Programmers, however, deal with the technical industry. You can also visit **Network Events** at http://www.network-events.com/, click on `Career Fairs`, and select `Location` to bring all the New York stuff together; you'll uncover information about the New York High Tech Career Fair as well as the New York DotCom Job Expo.

Sometimes, more specific searching will be required to find the kinds of career fairs that you need; in that case, it's time to revisit your friendly neighborhood search engine. Before we go there, let's review search engine basics and get them straight in your mind:

What am I looking for? Career fairs.

What are the keywords that I might use? Industry names, such as `Sales`, `Health`, `Computer`, or `High Tech`, diversity options such as women or `Latino`, as well as keywords like `job fairs` or `career fairs` or `career expos`.

Step Three: Utilize Search Engines

Finding job fairs via search engines is accomplished by searching for a specific industry, followed by some keywords. This can be done in the following ways:

- Visit **Google** at http://www.google.com/ and search for `<state> job fair` or `<state> career fair`. For example, in our previous example, searching for `New Jersey job fair` might return a link to **NJ Careers** at http://www.njcareers.com/, which has a link to specific career fairs within the state.
- Visit **DMoz** at http://www.dmoz.org/ and search for the same thing—`<state> job fair` or `<state> career fair`. Looking for job fairs that take place in Atlanta? Searching on `Atlanta job fair` might return **The Job Fair** at http://www.thejobfair.com/, a site dedicated to that region.

Usually, it's that simple to locate general all-purpose career fairs that would make sense to attend. Deciding which to attend, however, leads us to the next question—how do you make sure you obtain the most value for your participation?

Step Four: Get the Most Out of the Fairs You Attend

Once you've found the job fairs in which you'd like to participate, the next question is, how do you maximize your returns? It all depends upon your goals. Do you want to gather résumés for future hires? Do you want to hire on the spot? Do you want to uncover leads for future projects?

As mentioned earlier, have at least two people on site for the job fair you choose to use. And don't think that professionals will mysteriously gravitate to your booth whatever you do; you should take the time to create displays that beckon to people to learn more. To maximize your presence at a career fair, include giveaways (freebies get people to stop), set out a fishbowl for attendees to submit their business cards for a raffle (you can include that information in your database when you return), and make sure your signs present compelling copy that spells out in simple, bold letters why your preferred professionals should consider you.

***Raffles**—You can run a raffle at your booth. Collect business cards from professionals who visit, give a prize to one winner, and take all the cards back to your office and transfer the information into your future contacts database.*

How will you interview the participants? Remember, you'll be on a schedule, and will want to ensure the process flows as smoothly as possible. What kinds of questions will you ask? What are the key skills and qualities you would like to determine from interviewing during a job fair? When you plan out all these variables in advance, you'll maximize the benefits you obtain.

Also remember to make sure your company name and Web site URL is listed on the job fair Internet site as well. You want to receive the most exposure for the money you spend.

Example

We've seen in this section how one can take advantage of job fairs and get the most out of participating in them. The next example demonstrates how one can uncover career fairs near New Jersey.

Find New Jersey Career Fairs

Judi, a corporate recruiter for a large telecommunications firm based in New Jersey, decides to participate in local job fairs to gather résumés from high-quality professionals and network with other businesses as well.

Whom does Judi need?

Judi requires both local technical professionals and introductions to other business owners.

What does Judi need to find?

She needs to uncover technical job fairs close by her corporation. Job fairs too far away would require relocation expenses, thus she wants to save money by staying within a reasonable commute.

Where does Judi look?

She visits **Professional Exchange** at http://www.professional-exchange.com/ and searches for her location, finding several events that will take place in the coming months. She notices that participating companies have their business Web site addresses included in the "participating companies" page, and makes a mental note to ensure her company is added as well.

Judi has located a career fair near her.

Next, Judi visits **Google** at http://www.google.com/ and searches for NJ career fairs; she's returned a link to the **Workforce New Jersey Public Information Network** at http://www.wnjpin.state.nj.us/ as depicted in Figure 15.3, as well as to **NJ Careers** at http://www.njcareers.com/. These sites contain additional links to other career fairs that are going on throughout the state of New Jersey.

She has found numerous career fairs to consider for her company.

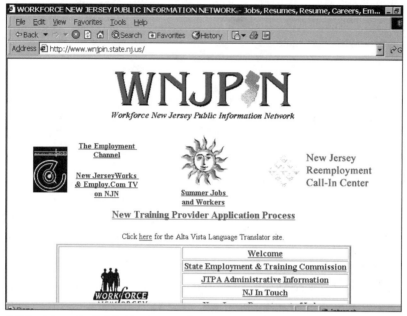

Figure 15.3: Many individual states will have specific career fair information.

Developing a Database

Career fairs can be considered as yet another avenue to find and hire employees. You can use the Internet to locate specific fairs that will meet your industry and regional needs; it only requires logical searching to uncover them. Remember to take advantage of all the résumés that flow in; when you return back to the office, assign someone the task of entering them into your employment database. Even if they're not suitable for your current positions at this time, they might provide an excellent resource in the future when new hiring needs emerge.

Trade Expos

Trade expos can be valuable for your recruiting efforts. The key, of course, is how effectively you use them. In general, trade shows consist of vendors, exhibitors, classes, seminars, and keynote speeches targeted to the industry in question; often, it's a full-day event in which a great amount of networking can be accomplished. Think of the most popular shows like Comdex or MacWorld; hundreds of thousands of individuals attend these events. You simply cannot find a more targeted audience than at a trade show in your own industry.

Let's compare trade expos and job fairs. All the attendees of job and career fairs are actively looking for new positions (this is good!). Visitors to trade expos, on the other hand, are more focused on the technology or industry presented. Careers are generally in the back of their minds; they are instead concerned with the advances on display. In the world of recruiting, these people are perfect passive candidates; professionals who are most likely quite happy where they currently work but who might be open to learning about new opportunities.

Let's think about this for a moment. Both your peers and the people you would like to hire often show up at these kinds of events. If your business has invested in a vendor booth, you could divert a portion of the space from your products and services to showcase the great opportunities the people who work for you enjoy. Your future employees are right there in front of your eyes!

Front and Center—*When you exhibit at a trade show, you are smack dab in the middle of a huge group of potential employees. Certainly you should market your products and services; consider adding exciting information about how terrific it is to work for you. It's an added bonus to working a trade show.*

The hidden secret about this phenomenon is that many companies that exhibit *focus only on selling their wares;* they ignore the possibilities of hiring future workers for their own business growth. Since your best possible candidates are right there in front of you as an exhibitor, you should certainly take advantage of this and present your company's employment opportunities in their best light.

Trade Shows Consist of ...

Trade shows are events that last from a day to several. Anywhere from hundreds to thousands to hundreds of thousands of people can pass the entrance gates, depending upon the industry and popularity of the show.

Trade shows generally consist of:

Keynote. Quite often a well-known speaker delivers the keynote address to the attendees. Steve Jobs, for example, has given keynote speeches for MacWorld and Bill Gates has given keynote speeches at Windows-related events. The president of the National Association of Realtors often provides the main keynote speech for their annual event. Keynotes are popular in general and often draw standing-room-only crowds.

Breakout meetings and seminars. Most likely, you encounter many roundtables, seminars, and breakout meetings in which different industry topics are discussed or taught. Quite often, different tracks are created, enabling attendees to enjoy a well-rounded group of meetings. The goal here is to take away new ideas and skills to apply in future business dealings. Teaching one of these seminars is a dynamite way to get known to potential employees; if you present at one of these conferences, you have the entire room's focus directed at you and your company. Generally, it's easier to become a seminar leader than a keynote speaker.

Vendors. Vendors will exhibit at trade shows. Each will purchase booth space, and spend time and money on displaying their company and their wares to their best possible advantage. Here is a great opportunity to showcase your career opportunities.

Social events. Trade shows will have social networking. Breakfasts, dinners, shows, and the like can be part of trade shows. Additionally, sometimes you can create mini-seminars in your booth and invite participants to listen to your offerings.

Discounts. Vendors at trade shows will often offer a show discount. This is great for you both as a businessperson and as a way to locate complementary businesses with whom to network.

Often, professional industries will host trade shows (or call them conventions). This by itself offers a whole new range of networking opportunities.

How to Find Trade Shows

Finding trade shows is as easy as zipping over to a typical trade show directory or search engine on the Internet. Offline, scanning trade magazines and spotting billboards on the highway are other traditional means. Here are the steps to follow:

- Define your industry.
- Browse trade show directories.
- Utilize search engines.
- Get the most out of the expos you attend

These steps are described in the following sections.

Step One: Define Your Industry

Granted, this is generally a rather simple step. If you're in the plumbing business, you most likely would look for plumbing trade shows. If your business focuses instead upon printing and publishing, you would most likely search for printing/publishing trade shows.

Of course, you can take that a step further! Do you print or publish for a specific industry, such as advanced certification/degree testing? If so, you might want to consider the scholastic industry. Look around your current workforce, client base, and product or service offerings; to what industries would they appeal? Sometimes one product or service can cut across many different business fields; these could all be avenues to explore.

Step Two: Browse Trade Show Directories

You can find several excellent trade show directories on the Internet:

Trade Show News Network at http://www.tsnn.com/

ExpoWeb at http://www.expoweb.com/

Exhibitions World at http://www.exhibitions-world.com/

Perhaps your business deals with producing software for the gaming industry. Visit the **Trade Show News Network** at http://www.tsnn.com/, as seen in Figure 15.4, and select Computers—All from the dropdown menu. You'll see a tremendous list, including Comdex, NetWorld, Outsourcing Ebusiness, and many more.

Figure 15.4: The Trade Show News Network is a directory of hundreds of trade shows.

Choose the `Gifts Games Hobbies and Toys` dropdown. You'll find links to casino gaming trade shows, which, if that's the kind of gaming your business promotes, would be a wonderful expo to attend.

Let Your Fingers Do the Walking—*Many directories on the Internet list a broad range of industry trade show categories. These directories often include links to individual trade shows, where you can learn who is expected to attend, what it costs to exhibit, what types of speakers will be present for roundtables, and more.*

But what if your gaming deals with the teenage and younger set and focuses on video games? It's time to use search engines! Let's review our goals:

What am I looking for? Industry trade shows.

What are the keywords that I might use? Industries such as `sales` or `high tech` or `engineering` or skills such as `Unix` or `NT` or `Oracle` and the keywords `trade shows` or `trade expos`.

Step Three: Utilize Search Engines

Finding trade shows via search engines requires that you home in on either the skill set required or the region desired, or both.

This can be done in any of the following ways:

- Visit **Google** at http://www.google.com/ and search for `<niche>` expo or `<niche>` convention. For example, in our previous example, we could search on `video game` expo and find an article entitled **Classic Video Game & Computer Expo Draws Big Names** at http://www8.techmall.com/techdocs/TS980731-1.html—this site provides a phone number for the expo. You could call and find out where the next one will be held and possibly learn of other trade shows in that industry.
- Visit **DMoz** at http://www.dmoz.org/ and search for the same thing— `<niche>` expo or `<niche>` convention. Looking for expos that deal with the marine industry? Searching on `marine` expo might return the category **Maritime Expos** at http://dmoz.org/Business/Industries/Transportation/Ships_and_Shipping/Maritime_Expo_and_Events/, and lead you to **Ship Technology Exhibitions** at http://www.ship-technology.com/exhibitions/ and **Sea Japan** at http://www1.kcom.ne.jp/seajapan/english/, among others.

It's generally that easy to find expositions, conferences, conventions, trade shows, and the like on the Internet. Another characteristic to consider is regional— sometimes states or towns or cities will have region-oriented trade shows. Other times, large convention planners simply move a popular show from one state to another, depending upon the interest. The Web site of a professional organization regional chapter will often highlight the show when it comes to town.

What about the national trade associations and professional organizations themselves? Almost always, you'll see yearly meetings (and great big blowouts they can certainly be!) in far-away locales; for example, the National Association of Home Builders has its **Remodelers Show** at http://www.RemodelersShow.com/ that meets in Detroit, and the annual **Society for Human Resources Management** at http://www.shrm.org/conferences/annual/ meets in Las Vegas. If you are looking to hire professionals in these industries, trade show expos are simply the best places to find them. And it's not difficult at all to uncover this information; simply refer to Chapter 8, "Professional Organizations." This time, however, instead of searching for places on sites to post jobs, you would look for current information about their conferences or industry expos.

Trade Associations—*Trade associations quite often sponsor industry expos. If you are looking for professionals with specific business skills, visit the trade association in question and see when its yearly conference takes place. Quite often, you'll be able to exhibit and include employment information as well.*

The preceding discussion provides some easy ways to locate expos that suit your business recruiting needs. The next question, of course, is what do you with them once you find them?

Step Four: Get the Most Out of the Expos You Attend

Once you've found the trade expos that look promising, the next question is, how do you maximize your returns? First you have to centralize your goals. What would you like to achieve? Do you want to promote your business only, or take advantage of the recruiting aspect by including information about what it's like to work at your company? Will you have a way to take down interested professionals' names and incorporate them into your database when you return? How much will you want to spend? Registering for the expo as an exhibitor will cost a certain amount of money—bringing in material to jazz up your booth can become a completely different set of expenditures!

Of course, it doesn't have to be horribly costly. Whenever I exhibit at a conference, I bring my Expo-in-a-suitcase—40 or so covers of my book, which I then arrange into a collage, party favor stars to brighten up the back wall of the exhibit, tape, and some paper clips. You can usually count on getting a table that can hold your promo material or business samples or a laptop—all you have to do now is intrigue individuals to stop by and see what you have to offer.

Expo-in-a-Suitcase—*You don't have to spend a gazillion dollars to create a world-class exhibition display. Take advantage of your current brochures and press releases, visit a party shop for backdrop material, and presto, you have an exhibit that will draw visitors admirably well.*

Because you want to take advantage of the recruiting opportunities, be sure to have a large sign that presents compelling, punchy copy such as "Unlimited Career Potential" or "Unlimited Career Benefits." Like everyone else involved in the recruiting industry, you want to excite your participants and make them want to learn more.

Example

In this chapter, you've learned how to gain superb benefits from job fairs and trade expos. As well as interviewing potential future employees, you can create your own database of passive candidates from all the résumés you receive. The next example will detail a search for New York area trade expos.

Find New York Area Trade Expos

Tom, a project manager for a consumer software vendor, has been given the go-ahead to hire two new developers.

Whom does Tom need?

Professionals in the computer industry who have had years of experience developing software under a stringent deadline.

What does Tom need to find?

Because Tom is anxious to achieve a sterling year-end review, he decides to bundle finding new employees with marketing his company's products in one grand adventure. He needs to find trade expos that deal with the software industry in general.

Where does Tom look?

First, he visits the **Trade Show News Network** at http://www.tsnn.com/. He selects `Computers—All` from the menu and sees literally hundreds of possibilities. Because he wants to show his management that he is cost-conscious as well, he redefines his query and restricts it to a city within driving distance, `New York City`. A number of shows are returned, including **eShow** at http://www.eshowny.com/.

A consumer Internet event, it's a fair bet to draw a good number of both attendees and exhibitors who will be interested in his company's products and knowledgeable about the Internet as well. After finding out how much it would cost to exhibit, Tom meets with his marketing manager to plan a dual trade show visit; she'll work the product line, while he'll create the handouts about employment opportunities.

Tom has located one trade show in which he can find employees as well as sell his company's products.

Next, Tom visits **Google** at http://www.google.com/ and searches for PC expo. One of the first links returned is **PC Expo in NY** at http://www.pcexpo.com/, which just happens to be close by his office. Because his company's software is developed on a Windows-based platform, and because lots of programmers attend computer expos, he realizes that exhibiting here as well will get his company's opportunities out in front of his target audience.

He has now uncovered a niche expo that would increase his company's visibility to his audience.

Shopping at Expos

Industry expos can provide you with a wonderful opportunity to showcase your opportunities in one location to as big a targeted audience as possible. Try to get extra mileage out of the expense by including product or service sales in addition; this will help you increase your company's profits while finding new employees to hire. In addition, consider giving away something emblazoned with your company's advertising—T-shirts, magnets, or pens, for example. I've seen companies create clever T-shirts that the attendees wear after the expo quite often; this results in quite a lot of free advertising. Should you go this route, be sure to include your company's URL in the design as well.

CHAPTER SIXTEEN

User Groups

By now, you've become aware of the many resources that can assist you in locating employees on the Internet; they run the gamut from professional organizations to trade associations to newsgroups to niche Web sites and more. But back before these Web sites became popular—even back before there was a World Wide Web—there was another resource you could tap, that of skill-based user groups. User groups can be among your best resources for finding employees, or they can be the kiss of death. There's quite often very little in between.

The Dawn of Time—*Well, actually not, but user groups were around long before AOL or MSN or the World Wide Web came into existence. The Usenet is one of the original organizations that allowed professionals to communicate with each other about specific, technical topics.*

User groups have been around since the dawn of the Internet (and probably eons prior). At their heart, they are collections of professionals who share a common passion, almost always technical in nature. Want to learn how to make a Unix system wail? Join the **Systems Administrator's Guild** (otherwise known as SAGE) at http://www.usenix.org/sage/. Microsoft Windows professionals might be members of their local NT user group, Oracle professionals might be members of their local Oracle Tools user group, and Java enthusiasts might check out the local meetings of their nearby Java user group—and they're easy to find, as the Yahoo! search illustrated in Figure 16.1 shows. You'll notice that these examples all center around technology; user groups almost always form within a technical environment. If you are looking to hire non-techies, don't waste your time with user groups; instead turn your attention to professional organizations or trade associations.

Before the arrival of Web sites, user groups mainly kept in touch via mailing lists and group meetings. Their main purpose was to share information among the members and provide needed resources. Because user groups are so technical, the majority of members hate (I mean *hate*) unsolicited e-mail. Thus you have to be extra-careful in your approach to them.

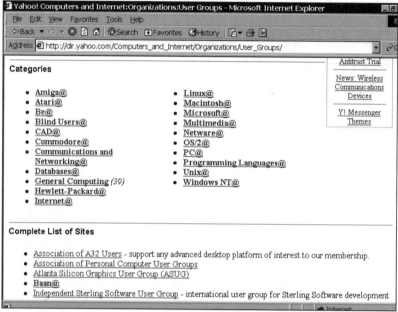

Figure 16.1: Yahoo! offers a tremendous list of user groups.

User groups haven't changed much over the years, although their Web sites now might offer a local means to post jobs. Like any other organization presidents, the folks who run user groups want to provide benefits for their members. Sometimes they will let enterprising companies sponsor a meeting in return for the chance to broadcast employment opportunities to the membership. Other times, they'll invite different scientists or well-known professionals in the field to offer seminars on technical topics.

User Groups Consist of …

Like professional organizations, user groups can offer a number of resources:

Meetings. User groups often have monthly meetings to discuss various and sundry technical topics. If you're hiring, you might want to consider sponsoring a user group meeting; you can offer to pay for refreshments, provide discounts for your services, and the like.

Sponsors. Some user groups actively encourage corporate sponsorship—you pay them money, they promote your site and resources. Additionally, they might highlight your job opportunities above those of other companies on their Web site.

Other user groups. Find one user group site, chances are it will contain references to similar or related user groups. This is a great way to hop from one site to another. Consider a New Jersey Linux user group Web site; you'll probably uncover links to the New York Linux user group and several others.

Job openings. More and more user groups are seeing the value in allowing job postings, either free or paid, either on their site or distributed via a discussion group or a mailing list. The **Twin Cities Linux Users Group** at http://www.mn-linux.org/, for example, has a jobs mailing list at tclug-jobs-subscribe@mn-linux.org; the **San Francisco Java Users Group** at http://www.cityjava.org/ has a jobs page located right at its site.

Forums. Sometimes user group Web sites will have forums for their professionals to discuss related technical issues. The **Professional AutoCAD Users Group of Denver** at http://www.paug.org/ has several forums including AutoCAD questions, résumés, and job opportunities.

Benefits. Some user groups will offer benefits that members couldn't achieve on their own. Software discounts, access to a member directory, and more fall under this category.

Local Jobs—*User group Web sites will often provide a section for local jobs to be advertised. Sometimes this service is available for free.*

The first thing to take into account when considering contacting user groups is to answer that age-old question, "What's in it for me?" If you can persuade the president or board of a user group that your participation will benefit their members, you'll be that much closer to being able to put your company front and center where your future employees might be.

How to Find User Groups

It's quite simple, as is almost all Internet searching, to locate professional organization sites. It can be done via the following easy steps:

- Define your user group.
- Browse user group directories.
- Utilize search engines.
- Get the most out of the user groups you choose.
- Post your jobs and monitor the results.

These steps are described separately in the sections that follow.

Step One: Define Your User Group

What skill does the person you need to hire have to have? This is one way you can define a user group to target. Perhaps you need a Visual Basic developer. Certainly, you will want to find Visual Basic user groups, but can that category be enlarged?

Visit **WhatIs** at http://www.whatis.com/—that's a glossary of hundreds of computer terms. Selecting Visual Basic will show it can be applied in all aspects of the computer industry—databases, active server pages, and more. Thus looking for active server page user groups might also give you an indirect resource to uncovering professionals skilled in Visual Basic.

Next, determine if you are hiring locally or nationally. If your positions span the nation or you're willing to pay to relocate a new employee, you can consider contacting user groups all across the country. If you want to concentrate upon one location, your choices are that much more limited.

Another way to define your user group is to ask your current employees what groups they've chosen to join. As a matter of fact, if you're serious about creating win-win relationships with user groups, being sponsored by a group member might make your life much easier. Yes, this might seem like overkill; still, if this is uncharted territory for you, the more guidance you can uncover the better.

Step Two: Browse User Group Directories

You can find several all-purpose user group directories on the Internet. Alas, however, quite often they are not as comprehensive as the professional organizations databases. Be that as it may, you might cut your searching time down by scanning some of the available online directories. They include:

Ash Nallawalla's Master List of Computer User Groups on the Web
http://easyrsvp.com/ugotw/

Association of Personal Computer User Groups
http://www.apcug.org/

Yahoo! listings
http://dir.yahoo.com/Computers_and_Internet/Organizations/User_Groups/

Perhaps you need to hire NT and Windows professionals. Visiting Ash Nallawalla's site and browsing NT reveals a few NT user groups, including the **Los Angeles NT User group** at http://lantug.org/. But think for a second. NT is a huge arena—certainly there must be more than four user groups! Go to Yahoo's site and you'll uncover a subcategory for NT user groups that includes a dozen or so regional groups. Yes, that certainly is more information, but it's not comprehensive. How can you pinpoint even more user groups? It's time to turn to search engines. Let's specify our key goals:

What am I looking for? User groups.

What are the keywords that I might use? Skills or regions such as `oracle`, `nt`, `delphi`, `middletown`, or `gilford`, coupled with the phrase `user group`.

Step Three: Utilize Search Engines

Finding user groups via search engines requires that you home in on the skill set required, the region desired, or both.

This can be done in any of the following ways.

- Visit **Google** at http://www.google.com/ and search for `<skill> user group` or `<location> <skill> user group`. For example, if you were looking to uncover Unix user groups in California, you'd search on `California unix user group`. Sites that pop up might include the **UNIX Users Association of Southern California** at http://www.uuasc.org/, and a whole bunch of **Linux groups** at http://www.linuxstart.com/support/usergroups/unitedstates/california.html. (Linux is closely related to Unix, and the site owners tend to use the same keywords.)

- Visit **DMoz** at http://www.dmoz.org/ and search for `<skill> user group` or `<location> <skill> user group`. Need to find Oracle user groups? Searching for `oracle user group` will bring you to the specific category at http://dmoz.org/Computers/Software/Databases/Oracle/User_Groups/, where you'll uncover listings for **Houston Oracle Users Group** at http://www.houg.org/, the **Oracle Users Group directory** at http://www.vb-bookmark.com/OracleUserGroupUS.html, and the **Connecticut Oracle Users Group** at http://www.coug.org/.

That was pretty simple. And, as with all our other searches on the Internet, you can do much more. Whenever you find a site worth pursuing, it's a pretty good shot that it will include links to other, related sites that will benefit your searches. Visit **AltaVista** at http://www.altavista.com/ now. Let's assume that you've come across the **San Francisco Perl Mongers** at http://sf.pm.org/. Search now for `link:sf.pm.org -url:sf.pm.org`, which will point to other sites that list this particular user group—see Figure 16.2. One of them is a category from Yahoo! for **Perl User Groups** at http://asia.yahoo.com/Computers_and_Internet/Programming_ Languages/Perl/User_ Groups—there, you'll uncover a link to the

Figure 16.2: Sample results from searching for sites that include links to the SF Perl Mongers.

main **Perl Monger** site at http://www.pm.org/. Not only are **established groups** listed at http://www.pm.org/groups.shtml, but a **Perl jobs mailing list** can be found at http://www.pm.org/mailing_lists.shtml.

Remember, sometimes user groups will allow you to post jobs or scan members' résumés. This is an excellent way to uncover more resources to assist you in finding employees.

Step Four: Get the Most Out of the User Groups You Choose

Once you have a number of user group sites, what do you *do* with them? If a career section already exists, you simply determine whether it makes sense to post your jobs or look through résumés there. If a career section doesn't exist, you can contact the group's board (generally such information will be available on the site) and ask if one can be created. It doesn't have to be anything elaborate—it can even be a mailing list for professionals who would be interested. Are there any local user group meetings? If so, offer to sponsor a pizza party or other refreshments, or ask the moderator if someone could announce your job opening at a meeting.

In either case, you can also look for forums where you can participate and become a valued member of the community. This is a great way to increase your visibility to the people you want to reach. Do you or any of your employees know much about a particular technical skill that's in high demand? If so, answering questions in the local discussion groups is a great way to increase your visibility.

Vendors.... What about vendors? Some professional organizations include detailed lists of vendors who have paid to be included. Vendors quite often have contacts within the industry in question—perhaps you can establish business relationships with local vendors and see how you can benefit one another. *Never* spam the membership directory lists! It just will not endear you to the community. Again, politeness and netiquette count more than anything when recruiting on the Internet. Always respect whatever communications you receive from user groups. Sometimes they will politely ask you to refrain from contacting them, other times they will ignore you, and often they'll engage you in professional business negotiations.

Network—*One of the best benefits you can derive from working with user groups is the quality of network you will develop, especially if you showcase how your company benefits the members in general.*

Step Five: Post Your Jobs and Monitor the Results

Ideally, by implementing the first four steps, you'll have uncovered user group Web sites in which you can post your available positions for free. Remember the audience for this kind of information; they are generally extremely well versed technically. Don't try to hide little white lies in your job advertisements; all you'll succeed in accomplishing is looking like a fool. Be open, honest, straightforward, and as specific as possible in your descriptions. This will greatly help to increase your success.

Example

Charles has the need for some high-quality systems administrators, professionals who have actually had real-world experience that goes beyond simply maintaining machines at colleges or universities

Whom does Charles need?

Professionals with technical skills who can oversee computer systems and keep them running smoothly. Some of the operating systems involved would be Unix, Linux, and NT. Quite often, job seekers who know how to turn on a computer will call themselves experienced systems administrators; these are not the technical employees Charles wants.

What does Charles need to find?

He needs to find user groups in which he can post local jobs, as well as offer to provide a seminar about maintaining security in a computer environment made up of heterogeneous platforms. By doing this, he effectively shows his audience that he has an in-depth understanding of their field.

Where does Charles look?

First, he visits **Google** at http://www.google.com/ and searches for `unix user group`; he comes upon the **Harrisburg Unix Users Group** at http://www.huug.org/. The first thing he notices is a direct link to **SAGE System Administrators Guild** at http://www.usenix.org/sage/—this is one of the original Unix groups on the Internet. On that page, he'll see a jobs site at http://www.usenix.org/sage/jobs/sage-jobs.html where he can post his position for free. Additionally, a list of **local SAGE groups** can be found at http://www.usenix.org/sage/locals/localgroups.html.

Charles has found a number of excellent user groups.

Now that he knows one jobs list appears at http://www.usenix.org/sage/jobs/, he can visit **AltaVista** at http://www.altavista.com/ and search for similar links. Querying on `link:www.usenix.org/sage/jobs/ -url:www.usenix.org/sage/jobs/` might result in the **SunSITE Croatia—Systems Administrator's Corner** page at http://hlapic.srce.hr/tutorial/computing.html. Exploring that page leads to the discovery of the **Unix Gurus' Universe** at http://www.ugu.com/. An extremely comprehensive site, it allows employers and recruiters to post Unix positions for free.

Charles has now found a free niche site to post his jobs.

Next, Charles wants to uncover professionals who belong to NT user groups. He follows the same method as before, and searches for `NT user group` on **Google**. Dozens of user group sites are returned; some of them provide the ability to post NT-related jobs for free.

Charles now has more user groups than he knows what to do with.

Netiquette Rules

User groups can be yet another resource to assist you in locating the technical professionals you want to find. But remember, always be sure to follow netiquette when contacting user group members. The majority of technical professionals dislike unsolicited e-mail in the extreme—you never want to be perceived as a company not worthy to work for. Paying attention to Internet good manners and netiquette in general will go a long way in ensuring you come out ahead in the long run.

CHAPTER SEVENTEEN

Classifieds and Web Rings

Internet-based classifieds and Web rings are two rather powerful resources you can use as another tool in your quest to find and hire the right professionals. Remember the classifieds in the Sunday newspapers? Quite often, you'll see them on the newspaper's Web site, too. And Web rings are collections of sites, all relating to a certain theme and hooked together by a sequence of links. You generally use rings to look for resources that will give you *leads* for the job sites themselves, rather than as places to post your actual jobs. This chapter will showcase how to benefit the most from these potential gems.

Classifieds

Internet classifieds, at their most general, offer the same sort of deal as newspaper classifieds—people post items for sale, job openings, services, products, and the like online. If you're at all leery of the computer yet want to benefit from Internet recruiting, using classifieds is one of the easiest ways to explore the new opportunities.

Classifieds are popular for a number of reasons. Because they're an old-style method of advertising (you only have to go to your local library and peruse newspapers from hundreds of years ago to see their early form), they provide a comfortable format for both newcomers and experienced Internet surfers. The premise is generally the same; for a low price or free, one can submit advertisements of a specific length that are then published on various sites. For example, horse enthusiasts can peruse free classified ads at **DreamHorse** at http://www.dreamhorse.com/, individuals looking to sell computer components can advertise for free at **CompuMarket** at http://www.compumarket.net/, and **comic book classifieds** show up at http://www.comicdepot.com/class/. This phenomenon is finding its way into the jobs and careers markets too; the **Seattle Java Users Group** offers free Java-jobs classifieds at http://doubleologic.com/seajug/seajug.html, **WasteWater International** offers free classifieds for that industry at http://www.wwinternational.com/pages/classifieds.htm, and the **Civil Engineer Online** site includes niche job advertisements at http://www.cenews.com/Classifieds.html.

Classifieds pages are also some of the easiest Web pages to incorporate into a site. Thus, as you saw in the preceding examples, many special-interest or industry niche sites will include a classifieds section, as will most online newspapers and magazines.

Classifieds Everywhere—*Internet classifieds are one of the most common Internet applications you'll see. Easy to set up, they allow for sites to advertise help wanted notices as well as items for sale.*

One of the most popular general classifieds sites is **Yahoo!** at http://classifieds.yahoo.com/, as seen in Figure 17.1. Visit that site now—you'll see ads for homes, roommates, business opportunities, and even job offerings. And because Yahoo! is such a high-traffic site, there's a good possibility your ads will be seen by at least some of your target audience.

One thing to remember, however, is just because a classifieds section exists on a Web site, that doesn't mean that it's either popular or well known among your quarry. Classifieds are very easy to set up on Web sites; their popularity is generally determined by how strategically the section is placed in the site in question. For example, if an industry niche site has a thriving traffic that consists of potential employees *and* highlights on every page that the classifieds section is *the* place to go to find help wanted ads, you'll have a much better chance of finding the professionals you need than if the site's classifieds section was positioned as an

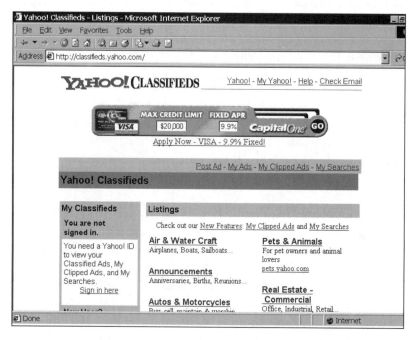

Figure 17.1: Yahoo! Classifieds provides free job posting advertisements.

afterthought with a tiny link at the bottom of the home page. You need to take time to poke around and see who is advertising. Are the majority of ads "make money fast" or "incredible work-from-home" offers? Sites filled with these types of ads are sites you want to avoid.

Classifieds Consist of …

Classifieds generally consist of your advertisement, including a Web site and e-mail address as a contact. As mentioned, they can appear in just about any type of Web site. Visit **Google** at http://www.google.com/ and search for medical job classified—you might be returned **MediMatch's Classifieds** at http://www.medimatch.com/Web/mcpro/mcpro_index.htm. Searching for sales classified might bring you to the **Palm Beach Classifieds** at http://www.the.palmbeachclassifieds.com/—you'll uncover an employment classifieds section there that includes sales positions.

Classifieds on the Internet differ from their printed brethren in that the ads can often run much longer for no additional charge. The criteria might allow ads to stay for one day, one week, one month—you might be able to include hundreds of words. Classifieds are popular with the Internet marketing crowd; several software packages, including **PowerSubmitter** (at http://www.becanada.com/), will help you post to a number of classifieds sites at one time.

Your focus on classifieds should, of course, be directed to employment. Just about every online newspaper will have an employment classifieds section—quite often, however, industry niche sites, professional organizations, and others will also include this type of resource. Be sure to keep in mind the goal of a classified ad—you don't try to close the sale within one, you try to evoke a concrete call to action such as visiting your Web site to learn more about your opportunities. Once someone gets to the site, you can finish the pitch and persuade them to submit a résumé. One of the traps many classifieds users fall prey to is trying to get the sale in the limited number of words available, instead of leading the viewer to visit the advertiser's Web site—which then inspires further action, such as submitting a résumé. You'll receive a much higher rate of response if you concentrate upon piquing people's curiosity to learn more about your employment opportunities.

How to Find Classifieds

You can uncover Internet classifieds by searching via the following easy steps:
- Define your needs.
- Visit the general classifieds sites.
- Utilize search engines.

- Get the most bang for your classified buck.

These steps are described in the sections that follow.

Step One: Define Your Needs

What are your specific needs for classifieds? Often, you'll want to approach classifieds as yet another free or inexpensive way of getting your employment message out. Rarely do you want to rely upon classifieds alone; they are simply another tool to help you gain visibility for your employment opportunities. Consider your target groups of professionals as well; if they're not in the technical industry, you might have a better chance of finding the people you want by placing your ads in the online section of your newspaper classifieds (which will automatically put them in the print version as well). Perhaps you need to find administrative assistants for your furniture store; these professionals will often scan the newspapers to see what's available, sometimes even before looking online.

You can focus your classifieds as industry niche ads (for example, advertising your petroleum manager position at a petroleum-specific site) and as a local resource (placing your Madison, Wisconsin, ad in the Madison newspaper). When debating what site to use, ask yourself, would the people I'm looking for be likely to see the advertisement? Would it be in the Help Wanted section? Is there a more structured format such as Employment Opportunities? Are the classifieds linked to the main page, or do you need to dig around to uncover them?

The Newspaper Connection—*Many of the Web sites for local newspapers have a comprehensive classifieds section available. This is a great way to find non-exempt employees as well as professionals in fields where the Internet doesn't yet have much impact on the job market.*

When searching for classifieds sites, keep your eyes peeled for the whole range—all-purpose sites such as Yahoo!, industry niche sites, the local sites. Again, classifieds are merely another tool to assist you in increasing your visibility to your targeted candidates.

Step Two: Visit the General Classifieds Sites

Before searching for industry niche sites, visit the following general classifieds sites. These sites have a huge amount of traffic, which increases the probability that your ads will be seen by the right audience.

Yahoo! Classifieds at http://classifieds.yahoo.com/

Recycler.com at http://www.recycler.com/

Epage at http://www.ep.com/

CityNews at http://www.citynews.com/

Generally, you will want to place classifieds in the Employment section of a general site. If you'd like to zoom directly to newspaper classifieds, just visit **NewsDirectory** at http://www.newsdirectory.com/ and browse to your state. You'll uncover direct links to many of the popular newspaper sites online. These sites in turn often have links to their Classifieds in a very prominent place on their main page.

Remember some guidelines. For sites that allow a large number of words, be certain to include keywords that relate to your position, contact information, and some of the perks included (think back to Chapter 5, "Sing a Song of Job Posts"—especially the section entitled "How to Make a Blah Job Post Rock"). And along with the large directories, you should consider finding niche classifieds that would benefit your visibility. Let's review search engine basics and get your goals laid out:

What am I looking for? Classifieds sections on Web sites such as newspapers, industry niche sites, and career resources.

What are the keywords that I might use? States, cities, or industries such as `California`, `Texas`, `New York`, `Seattle`, `Triangle Park`, `computer`, `Oracle`, `Sales`, combined with the keywords `classified` or `classifieds` or `post`.

Step Three: Utilize Search Engines

Perhaps you would like to locate skill-specific classifieds hosted on industry niche sites. You could visit **AltaVista** at http://www.altavista.com/ and search for `post oracle classified`. You might come up with site **Orafans** at http://www.orafans.com/—oracle-specific classifieds are available there. Because classifieds hardly ever stand on their own, however (usually they are merely part of a larger site), you'll generally have much better success if you first search for the industry niche sites and then look for classified opportunities on them. Another way to search for classifieds is to target your town. For example, visiting **Google** at http://www.google.com/ and searching for `Kansas classifieds` might lead you to several of the popular newspaper sites that contain help wanted ads. Again, though, you could have simply visited NewsDirectory and browsed to the newspapers in question. When searching for classifieds, it's generally much easier to search for their parents (industry niche sites, newspaper sites, professional organization sites, etc.) instead. This is one example where search engines can be less effective than other Internet search tools. Please refer to Chapter 7, "Industry Niche Sites," for more information.

Step Four: Get the Most Bang for Your Classified Buck

Once you've uncovered the classifieds sites you'd like to use, how do you maximize the return on your investment? Certainly you should post your jobs (and make sure to include all those superb aspects that make your job stand out—perks, career growth, location, benefits, anything that would tempt the viewer to visit your site and learn more). Because most classifieds are free, you generally don't have to agonize over money spent. Ask yourself:

- How popular is the site? Have I heard about it in advertising? Is there a well-defined career section? If so, is it targeted to my industry?
- Are there opportunities for me to gain more visibility for my jobs, such as preferred viewing (jobs in bold, perhaps)?
- Can I have a banner about my company installed on a logical page?
- Are there links to any community forums where I can monitor the activity or post contributions? Often, classifieds sites will partner with other places to provide community resources.

The more yes answers the better, but only the first set is essential. There's no point in listing on a dead site, or a site that doesn't interest your target audience. Many businesses and recruiters who use classifieds only see the obvious benefits of posting one's job to a broad audience. However, if you take the time to comb through relevant sites, you might come across ways of increasing your visibility at no extra cost.

Example

Eric needs to hire busboys and waitresses for his restaurant in Salisbury, Maryland. Because these are low-paid jobs that won't come with relocation benefits, he realizes he'll get the best response by posting in the local newspapers or community sites.

Whom does Eric need?

Local hourly workers; experience, while nice, isn't mandatory.

What does Eric need to find?

He needs to uncover logical places on the Internet such as general all-purpose classifieds sites for his town, as well as the classifieds sections that spring from newspaper sites.

Where does Eric look?

First, Eric visits **Yahoo! Classifieds** at http://classifieds.yahoo.com/. There, he takes advantage of the free job advertising that is offered. Because he can specify the town and state, he's assured that individuals looking for positions in his area will have a good chance of coming across his opportunities. Next, he visits **USA CityLink** at http://www.usacitylink.com/, browses to Maryland, and sees there's a specific site listed for **Salisbury, MD**—it's http://www.salisburymd.com/. Unfortunately, he discovers no classifieds at that site. However, the site does give information about another local paper, the *Salisbury News & Advertiser.* He visits Google and searches for Salisbury News and Advertiser and is returned the headquarters of the paper at http://www.newszap.com/sna/. Because this is a weekly for the community, it certainly would make sense to advertise his classifieds there.

Yahoo!—*Yahoo! Classifieds is one of the most popular classifieds directories on the Internet. Currently job posting is free there, and other sites often rebroadcast Yahoo! jobs, doubling and redoubling your reach without costing you a penny.*

Eric has found a local newspaper in which he can advertise.

Eric then visits **NewsDirectory** at http://www.newsdirectory.com/ and browses to the Maryland newspaper page. There, he uncovers a link to the *Daily Times* at http://www.shore-source.com/times/, which is a newspaper published in that region. Alas, there aren't any classifieds there either—but that's okay; not every community has a specific classifieds or newspaper site dedicated to it. Eric returns to the **NewsDirectory** page and sees several other sites that do include jobs classifieds, such as the *Baltimore Sun* at http://www.sunspot.net/ and the *Star Democrat* at http://www.stardem.com/; that site leads him to directly to **Chesapeake Classifieds** at http://www.chesapeakeclassified.com/. All of these sites can be useful for his job posting.

Eric's quest has been successful.

Remember, your success with Internet recruiting largely depends on how Internet-savvy your target audience is. Some professionals still haven't made the transition to online job-hunting; in this case, using classifieds that will also show up in a print edition will get your ad out in front of the people who are interested.

Web Rings

Web rings are collections of sites relating to a certain theme and hooked together in a numerical format. The theory is that visitors could start at one site on the ring, and then visit the next, and the next, and eventually end up where they began. Web rings provide a simple way of targeting specific interests on the Internet, and first popped up in 1995. Originated by Sage Weil, the first Web ring was **ESLoop**, centered on English Language teaching and learning at http://www.tesol.net/esloop/esloop.html. Nowadays, over eighty thousand Web rings, spanning virtually all areas of interest, are operating on the Internet.

When it comes to Internet recruiting, Web rings are somewhat different from the other resources mentioned in this book. Unless the Web ring in question is specifically focused on employment or an industry niche, you generally *don't* search for rings expecting to locate places to post your jobs; instead, you look for resources that will give you *leads* for the job sites themselves. Thus, if you were looking to hire game developers, you would search for game development Web rings and then branch out to locate those sites that contain game development employment resources. Perhaps you'd like to learn more about truck drivers and similar workers; a **teamster Web ring** can be found at http://www.Teamster.net/ring/.

Local Networking—*Web rings are useful for finding personal and noncommercial sites of interest in all aspects of hobbies and industries. By following the links of a Web ring, you can uncover other sites with which you can exchange links, thus increasing your own visibility to a targeted audience.*

You can even create your own Web ring. It costs nothing and can be a very useful business tool. If you're part of a local business community, you could begin a community Web ring and network; if your site is focused on a particular industry, you might be able to start a Web ring for your clients.

Web Rings Consist of ...

Web rings consist of one or more related sites that are linked together to provide easy navigation for visitors. For the most part, these sites are independent of each other; they focus on the common theme yet are maintained by individual enthusiasts. Each site can be as simple as one page or as comprehensive as an industry niche location. Remember the nature of the Internet—to share resources and information. Web rings allow fellow devotees to unofficially band together and make it easy for visitors and site owners to find one another. And the range of topics is staggering; be it hobbies, industries, professions, games, health, religion, or what have you, there will a Web ring dedicated to it.

Some Web rings are designed to help organizations stay linked with one another. For example, the **Beta Sigma Phi Web ring** at http://www.geocities.com/Wellesley/5982/webring.html is geared specifically towards keeping the sorority sisters in touch. Businesspeople in Denver have their **Denver Area Businesses and Organizations Web ring** located at http://www.1cosmos.com/webring/denver.htm. Other Web rings target hobbies and sports, such as **All Star Sports** at http://members.aol.com/HeckJH/Webring.html (over 200 sites are included), and **Vintage Barbies** at http://members.aol.com/VintajBebe/barbie/ring.html. Still others focus on jobs, such as the **Ring of Employment** at http://www.ardennais.com/webring/. Of course, as we've seen so far, such a broad focus (the whole world of employment) might be too general for targeted searching, but it's nice to know the resource exists.

How to Find Web Rings

You can locate Web rings on the Internet by searching via the following easy steps.

- Define your needs.
- Visit WebRing.
- Utilize search engines.
- Make Web rings spin for you.

These steps are described in the sections that follow.

Step One: Define Your Needs

What are your specific needs for Web rings? Will you have the time necessary to travel through each site in the ring and search for publicity opportunities, or can you delegate that to someone else?

You can decide either to use a Web ring, create your own, or become part of one that already exists. If you are looking to hire someone soon, you probably would want local business or industry niche Web rings. Don't approach Web rings expecting to find people to hire right away; Web rings are generally much more effective for overall Internet publicity. Still, you might be able to uncover leads for other job-related sites by this means.

Step Two: Visit WebRing

Before searching for Web rings, visit the **WebRing site** at http://www.webring.org/ (shown in Figure 17.2). This is considered to be one of the most comprehensive Web ring directories on the Internet. Like Yahoo!, it's a browsable site and allows you to drill down to locate Web rings of interest. For example, you can choose `Directory` and then `Business and Economy`; Web rings of all sorts of business interests will be revealed. Alternatively, you can search for specific needs; searching on `game developers` will return **Designated Ring of Game Developers (Programmers)** at http://www.cyberramp.net/~bigba/drgd.htm. Can you post jobs here? Of course not, but by traveling through the Web ring, you can probably locate resources where job-hunting game developers would gather.

If WebRing.org doesn't meet your needs, you should consider finding niche Web rings that would benefit your visibility. Let's review search engine basics and get your goals laid out:

What am I looking for? Web rings that will provide leads for employment resources

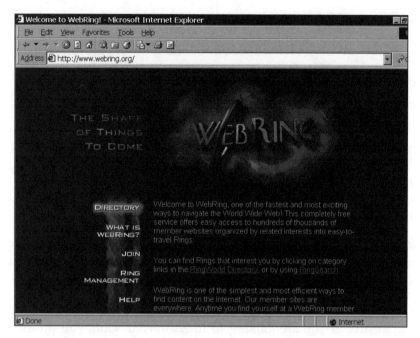

Figure 17.2: WebRing.org is one of the most popular Web ring directories on the Internet.

What are the keywords that I might use? States, cities, or industries such as `California`, `Texas`, `New York`, `Seattle`, `Triangle Park`, `computer`, `Oracle`, `Sales`, combined with the keywords `web ring`.

Step Three: Utilize Search Engines

Perhaps you would like to locate Web rings for women. You could visit **Google** at http://www.google.com/ and search for `women web ring`. You might come up with site **Phenomenal Women** at http://www.phenomenalwomen.com/; the group has a Web ring at http://www.phenomenalwomen.com/webrings/. The same type of searching holds for industry sites as well; a casual search for `sales web ring` results in the **Sales Force Automation Web ring** at http://www.resource-grp.com/sfa_web_ring.htm.

Step Four: Make Web Rings Spin for You

Once you've uncovered the Web rings you'd like to explore, how do you maximize the return on your investment? The best way is to exchange links with the sites you come across. Certainly, you can also search for locations to post your jobs, but one of the strengths of Web rings is the way they increase traffic passing through them. If you can exchange links with these sites, you'll have effectively increased your own exposure on the Internet.

Why should someone want to list your site? You have to answer that age-old question: "What's in it for me?" when approaching them. For example, perhaps your company deals with multilevel marketing for products such as Amway or NuSkin. Does your personal Web site contain lots of beneficial resources for potential customers? If so, you can contact sites from MLM Web rings, invite them to peruse your resources, and then respectfully inquire if they would be willing to add your link. This is called *Internet publicity*. I've included some excellent ideas and examples for you at **Poor Richard's Internet Recruiting resource site** at http://www.topfloor.com/.

Example

Sue needs to locate network marketers who want to work out of their homes yet enjoy meeting customers face to face. Because this industry is rife with dream-seekers, she wants to ensure her employees understand the commitment required and set forth realistic goals.

Whom does Sue need?

Anyone who is people-oriented, can travel locally for customer meetings, and can set up and organize a following (commonly known as a down-line).

What does Sue need to find?

She needs to uncover places where home-based industries are discussed. Ideally, the sites should have forums or mailing lists so she can educate her customers about the realities of network marketing.

Where does Sue look?

First, Sue visits WebRing at http://www.webring.org/. She searches for `network marketing` and comes up with several rings dedicated to Internet marketing (network marketing can be done on the Internet, after all). Some of the rings returned include direct MLM resources she can explore. Others, however, are make-money-fast portals; that isn't what she's after. She revises her search to `marketing` and comes up with the **Internet Marketing Web Ring** at http://www.rwm.net/imring/; this Web ring includes links to many of the entrepreneurial boards that abound on the Internet.

Sue has found places to advertise and also to discuss business dealings.

Web rings can be used for direct Internet recruiting, but you can best benefit from them by finding similar sites and exchanging business links.

Taking It a Step Further

Web rings and classifieds sites should be viewed as additional tools in your Internet recruiting arsenal. If the Internet classified section you choose to advertise in is tied to a printed newspaper, you might have additional benefits from your ad appearing both online and in print. This can greatly increase your visibility on the Internet.

Let's take it one step further. If you include great career or industry resources on your own Web site, you can designate that section to be part of many different Web rings. This will serve to drive the kind of traffic you need to your site—and not just from the rings; comprehensive resources generally encourage visitors to tell their friends to check out your site as well.

CHAPTER EIGHTEEN

Your Own Web Site

Ah, your Web site. Your business Web site. The place where customers can find all those fantastic products and services you offer.... Tell me, have you taken advantage of that traffic and included links describing how wonderful it is to work for you?

Think about it. You or your company own the site in question—*someone* must have the authority to enhance it. If you are hiring and don't showcase how great it is to work at your company, you're missing out on a major opportunity to uncover potential employees.

Your Business Goals

What are the business goals of your Web site? If you say your goal is to sell products or services, you could be correct. If you say instead that it's to get your name known by your customers by providing community-building tools or resources, you might be right as well. You can sum up both of these statements by realizing your business Web site's main purpose in life is to *ultimately enhance your business revenue and profits*, either directly or indirectly. And allowing people the opportunity to explore careers with you of their own volition will save you time, money, and resources.

There are countless books that go into what makes an excellent Web site. For our purposes here, however, I would like to concentrate on the employment aspects. Added to an already outstanding business Web site, they will complement your services and products admirably. Let's take a look at a typical business Web site; you'll see links for the products or services available, information about the company, perhaps free resources or discussion boards to encourage community building, an order form, and the like. Ideally, you'll want to encourage visitors who either share your passion or are interested in what you have to offer to come, explore, and keep coming back, again and again.

Depending upon what you offer, you might find either aficionados or individuals considering employment perusing your site. By including a highly visible link entitled Careers, Employment, or Work at <Company Name>, you can tempt interested visitors to explore why they should consider working for you.

***Ready-Made Audience**—Ideally, people visiting your Web site are already interested in what you have to offer. Such professionals can make excellent employees; by showcasing the benefits you offer in a prominent area, you can increase your Internet recruiting success without extra effort.*

Your Employment Section

Employment sections on business Web sites can range from the mundane (click here to send us your résumé) to the comprehensive, well-thought-out package that sells itself. And the great news is that the high end doesn't have to require an incredible amount of effort, either.

Your employment section should include these features:

Our Benefits. What are the great benefits people acquire when working for you? Look beyond money, perks, or stock—benefits could also include the opportunity to work in a dynamic, cutting-edge atmosphere, monthly group lunches, community involvement, mentoring younger people who have an interest in the industry, being on the forefront of innovation, and the like.

Our People. Include brief descriptions—perhaps with photos of people already on the job. Giving an insider's view can help familiarize and humanize the environment individuals are considering. If you use photos, pick your subjects so as to reflect the whole range of people you're looking for; applicants are much likelier to step forward if they see that people like themselves have already been successful.

Our Company. Why is it so wonderful to work for you? This goes beyond the benefits question—here, you extol the history, goals, and accomplishments of your company.

Available Positions. If you have more than one position open, you might want to consider including a way for candidates to pick and choose from the jobs available. I'll go more into this later in this chapter, in the section entitled "Adding Your Jobs to Your Site."

Submit Your Résumé. Granted, this might sound like common sense, but you'd be surprised how many companies fail to include some crucial guidelines. Make sure you cover these points:

- How should the résumé be submitted? Do you prefer only text, or would you like Microsoft Word attachments? If the latter, how will you verify on your end that the attachment is virus-free?

- To whom should the résumé be submitted? Are different individuals responsible for different skill sets?

- Do you want only the résumé, or would you like additional information such as the person's goals, strengths, dreams, and the like? If so, adding a small questionnaire in the résumé instructions will help clarify the process.

Contact Information. Make life easy for your visitors. Always ensure contact information such as the phone number, name of person receiving the résumé, fax number, and e-mail address is readily visible.

As you can see, the information required on an employment site is not laborious to gather. A fair amount can be gleaned by just talking with your HR department and current employees.

One final, extremely important requirement of your company's employment section is to make it visible *on the main page*—preferably high enough to show up without scrolling. I've heard stories from Human Resource departments about how Marketing controls the site, and well, gee, the main thrust *has* to be on selling, and after all, people really *can* take their time to poke around, and.... Forget it. Marketing certainly is important—hiring future superstars is equally so. For today's supersonic product development, you want to take advantage of every single strength you possess. And a dynamite employment section on your site will power up your chances of finding the right person dramatically. If, by chance, another department does have control over your business Web site, try to obtain its manager's buy-in by demonstrating how that department will benefit from an employment section. For example, marketing directors would now have an effective vehicle for advertising their own positions. In other words, don't fight about it; merely answer the "What's in it for me?" question posed by the department that controls the site.

Win-Win Politics—*If your company Web site is owned by a department that is extremely territorial about what gets put up, offer to showcase that department's open positions in a prominent area in exchange for including a career section. Always try to present new ideas that answer the other person's What's In It For Me question.*

Let's take a look at some well-designed corporate employment sites. Visit **Marriott Hotels** at http://www.marriott.com/; you'll see a link to the company's **career center** at http://www.careers.marriott.com/ near the bottom of the page. Clicking that link will get you to the page shown in Figure 18.1.

Figure 18.1: Marriott's Career Center is warmly inviting to potential employees.

The Career Center copy reads:

INFINITE POSSIBILITIES. ONE COMPANY

> *You've done some searching. Congratulations! You've found a place where boundaries have no meaning. Where your future, your choices, and your potential are wider than you can imagine—and where the landscape of opportunity continues on and on. Welcome to Marriott International, Inc.*
>
> *At Marriott, you'll be part of a remarkable team, enjoying the support, the training and the career development programs of a company that knows how important it is to make everyone feel comfortable (really comfortable). You'll excel with the corporation whose presence is international ... that is growing at unprecedented levels ... that was listed by Fortune magazine as one of "The 100 Best Companies To Work For in America" ... and ranked by Business Week as of the "Top Ten Companies For Work and Family."*
>
> *Learn more about our exciting growth ... our many business units and departments— Our Many Businesses, our functional areas—Your Field, view our current opportunities—Vast Opportunities, our college recruiting—The College Thing, and make sure to visit our company culture and benefits—The Extras. For more information on hourly opportunities, call our easy 24-hour, 7-day-a-week toll free number: 1-888-4MARRIOTT.*

This is absolutely superb. It focuses on the viewer—"at Marriott, you'll be part of a remarkable team." Well, who doesn't want a wonderful team atmosphere? "You'll excel with the corporation"—again, it speaks to the viewer, making them eager to "make sure to visit our company culture and benefits...."

Notice how the site doesn't say, "We're a great big ol' hotel and we're hiring." No indeed! It includes excitement. Ideas. Possibilities. Direct links to all the goodies a visitor would want to see. Immediate, visual contact information. In short, it's a fantastic tool to help draw an active job seeker to submit a résumé.

Let's check out another example. **Kulicke & Soffa Industries, Inc.** at http://www.kns.com/ is a firm that focuses on back-end semiconductor assembly. When you click on the site's Employment link, you'll see a section entitled "Why Work at K&S?"— complete with an array of interesting reasons (the employees, the benefits, the area features, and the like). Information about corporate values is also included, covering topics that are important to potential employees. A direct link to current employment opportunities is also available.

Why Work Here?—*By including a link entitled Why Work Here you are creating a natural path for interested visitors. Everyone would like to know why a particular company is great to work for.*

Nowadays, it's simply not enough to plaster employment opportunities on your site and expect to net the best. You need to talk to the candidate's heart and showcase how, by working in *your* company, *they'll* reap desired benefits.

This technique can work in all areas of business. Consider a summer camp like **Wingate*Kirkland** at http://www.campwk.com/. Its main page has the headline "Become a WK Staff Member" that leads you to http://www.campwk.com/newstaff/. Here you'll see "Why Work at WK?" complete with bullet points that interest potential staff members ("We have sunny, warm days, comfortable nights and no bugs. Why be stuck in the woods of Maine?"), former counselor essays (testimonials), salary information, and more.

Think about this for a moment. The site is for camping! Yet the owners of the business made the most logical decision to include additional information about how great it is to work there. The site includes an online application, so when positions do open up, camp personnel have only to respond to résumés they've already collected. Very effective, indeed—big companies, small companies, any companies—all you have to do is write *from the heart* about why individuals should consider employment at your business.

Or consider **Storr Office Furniture** at http://www.storr.com/. Its employment page describes a "Fun Committee"—a group whose sole purpose is to arrange activities for Storr employees. Everyone deals with work-related committees during the day—a Fun Committee certainly would tickle anyone's fancy.

Keep in mind the goals of such Web site content. Companies are looking to invoke that call to action so crucial in today's job market—submitting the résumé. Elaborating on *all* the great reasons why someone should consider the company's employment opportunities is merely good business sense.

Within Walking Distance!—*Because your employees will probably spend at least a third of the day at your office, including information about great dining and cultural attractions within walking distance will be perceived as yet another perk of working in your company.*

Your Industry Resource Site

Your industry resource site is a gold mine for your business. Imagine it—targeted visitors flock to your site. They refer your site to their colleagues (who quite often are in the same field). Your reputation starts to spread like wildfire. People return again and again. Isn't that a outcome worthy of your goals? Your industry resource site will help you achieve this admirably.

What's an Industry Resource Site?

Simply put, an industry resource site is merely a collection of industry-related information that will appeal to your targeted audience—customers, clients, vendors, and future employees. Here are some useful things to include:

Headlines. Dynamic, changing, targeted content can influence visitors to return often. Perhaps you're looking to hire individuals in the cable industry. If you include headlines about said industry, you're making it easy for your visitors to see information in which they are interested. **Moreover** at http://www.moreover.com/ allows you to pick up headlines linking to almost any line of business you can imagine, and all for free.

Industry sites. Do you know of any trade or industry-related organizations, or perhaps niche sites? Perhaps links to industry expos? Listing them on your site gives your visitors more opportunities to become knowledgeable about the industry in question.

Industry stock prices. With the explosion of interest in the stock market, including the stock prices of, say, the five major players in your industry would be a thought-provoking addition. **Quote.com** at http://www.quote.com/ is one site that provides such information.

Relevant information. Can you provide guidelines that will educate your visitors about your product or service? Perhaps you are a manager for a travel agency— can you provide information about how to maximize travel benefits? How to prepare children for long trips? Current exciting destinations that would intrigue your visitors?

As you can see, creating an industry resource site on your Web site is not that difficult at all. And it will provide you with one killer benefit nothing else can: a noncommercial reason for the entire world to link to you.

Why Have an Industry Resource Site?

The hallmark of the Internet is resource sharing; many more individuals will be willing to exchange links with you if your links point to resources they can actually use than if you're just selling widgets and trying to recruit widget-makers.

Free Publicity—*When you have a comprehensive industry resource center on your site, you'll be offering a great reason for noncommercial entities to link up. This greatly broadens your visibility to your target population.*

Let's apply this to finding future employees online. Perhaps your business is in the sports industry. If you can create and market a sports-resource center, you now have a higher probability that sports-minded people will discover your site (due to its being listed as a resource on other Web pages). If you are looking to hire salespeople for your sports stores or planners for your sports marketing, you'll now have a more highly targeted stream of people enthused about your industry visiting your site! Ensuring your careers link is visible on your resource site now gives these people a direct stepping-stone if they are in the market for a new position.

Consider another example. Perhaps you manage a jewelry store. Quite often, individuals come into your store looking to buy engagement rings. On your Web site, it certainly would be swimming to include a link to the **Diamond Engagement Ring Frequently Asked Questions** list at http://www.wam.umd.edu/~sek/wedding/mlynek.html (like the link that **Holmdel Diamond Exchange** has at http://www.lingstar.com/jewelry/bridal.html). Are you instead looking to hire technical consultants? Incorporating information such as computer-based testing, user groups, local weather, and the like will certainly relate to your potential employees; consider **Devon Consulting's Resource Center** at http://www.devonconsulting.com/consult/ (see Figure 18.2) There, you'll see that many of the resources it presents focus on satisfying the needs of Devon's staff.

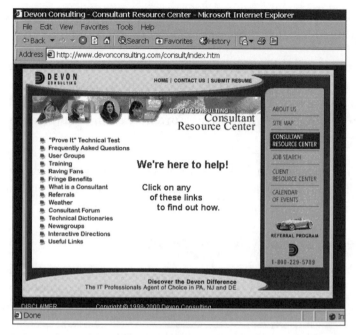

Figure 18.2: Devon Consulting has an excellent example of an industry resource center focused on current and future employees.

When you include information like this, *you're educating your visitors*. This is something that will stand out in their minds. And if said visitors ever decide to look for a career in your industry, chances are that your site is one they will remember to visit again.

How to Create an Industry Resource Site

Creating your industry resource site does not have to be a major undertaking. Indeed, it can be as simple as a few pertinent links—or as comprehensive as links to hundreds of sites. The first thing you have to ask yourself is, what would empower my visitors to make a more informed decision? Perhaps your ideal recruiting goal is to locate aspiring office managers for your toy store distribution center. What would spark interest? What would make an impression?

Well, one thing might be links to the history of toys, such as Discovery Channel's **How Our Favorite Playthings Came to Be** at http://www.discovery.com/stories/history/toys/toys.html or the **History of Toys** at http://www.historychannel.com/exhibits/toys/. Such links give an engaging, interesting, and personal look at the industry. Another idea would be to include links to child safety for toys, such as the **Consumer Product Safety Commission** at http://www.cpsc.gov/kids/kidsafety/. What about actual industry-related stories? You can uncover links to news stories about Mattel, Toys "R" Us, and leisure activities in general at **Moreover** at http://www.moreover.com/.

Does this directly compel your visitors to apply for your jobs? Of course not. But if your industry resource center includes a way for them to add their e-mail address to your free e-zine (more about that shortly), or a link that ties in directly to your career opportunities, you can stay in touch with potential employees who would have escaped you before. Your purpose here is twofold—you want to obtain a way to contact visitors in the future in a netiquette-friendly fashion, and you want to put your career opportunities in the forefront without jarring distraction. People interested in your industry will most likely add their e-mail addresses to keep up with industry news.

What would interest *your* future employees? A great way to figure this out is to poll your current workforce. Send out e-mail or a memo that states you'll be enhancing the company's Web site and you want to highlight how wonderful your business is and also include key information to entrance visitors. What would interest them? Offer a free dinner for the individuals who come up with the most creative, useful ideas—*turn it into a team-building exercise.*

Tap Current Employees—*One of the best ways to create your industry resource center is to ask your current employees what kinds of information they find relevant and interesting.*

Once you have the topics you'd like to include in your industry resource center, finding resources for them is easy. Simply visit **Google** at http://www.google.com/ or **Yahoo!** at http://www.yahoo.com/ and search for your quarry.

Consider Denise, the manager of a big city financial institution. Among the individuals she needs to hire are stockbrokers, financial planners, and office assistants. What might interest these types of people? One thing, certainly, would be how to max out their salary and earning potential. She can visit Google and search for Become a financial planner—she might be returned links to the **Certified Financial Planner Board of Standards** at http://www.cfp-board.org/, the **Motley Fool** at http://www.fool.com/, and others.

Because Denise's business deals with securities, a link to the **National Association of Securities Dealers** might be a valuable resource. Searching for national association of securities dealers should return a link to the group's home page at http://www.nasd.com/. This is easily incorporated into her industry resource center.

What about office assistants? Because her business is not geared towards office assistants (it's financial, after all), she might want to add sites that appeal to administrative workers to her career section of her Web site. What would interest office assistants? What about career growth? **CareersPrep** at http://www.careersprep.com/html/ofcadmin.htm describes many different types of office positions.

The financial institution manager's site is a perfect example of how you can tie aspects of your industry resource center to your employment pages. Remember, nothing is cast in stone about your Web site—you can always try different things as they suggest themselves.

Let's consider another situation. George needs to hire software professionals. Because his industry is dynamic, growing, and quite competitive, he needs to ensure his industry resource center has links that speak directly to the candidates' needs. One thing that certainly assists the kinds of professionals George requires is certification, so it's a good idea for him to visit **Google** at http://www.google.com/ and search for computer certification. There, he'll uncover **About.com's Certification Center** at http://certification.about.com/ or **NetCerts** at http://www.netcerts.com/. These sites provide resources for technical professionals to increase their marketability by studying for and passing relevant exams.

Free Positives—*When you include information that benefits your visitors without obliging them to give you a résumé, you make a positive impression. Links to resources that help visitors increase their earning potential, for example, can make a visitor want to learn more about your current offerings.*

As well as finding potential employees and persuading them to fill his job openings, George faces the ever-growing problem of current employees' being seduced away by the lure of pre-IPO stock dreams. We covered this back in Chapter 2, "Know Your Goals," but let's now approach it from a different angle—that of actively discouraging the dreamers. Because George has to stay abreast of all new business innovations, he's quite aware of **Garage.com**—one of the most popular sites about start-ups on the Internet today. Visiting that site and clicking on **Newsroom** at http://www.garage.com/newsroom.shtml, he encounters **Stories From Hell** at http://www.garage.com/hellStories.shtml—this page contains some enlightening tales of the downside of IPOness—as shown in Figure 18.3.

People who work in George's industry often make rather handsome salaries but work ridiculous hours; their hobbies can include video games, *Star Trek,* and other nerdly pursuits. George can include links for financial planning, sound investing, money management, time management, cutting stress levels, winning popular video games, creative fiction, and the like.

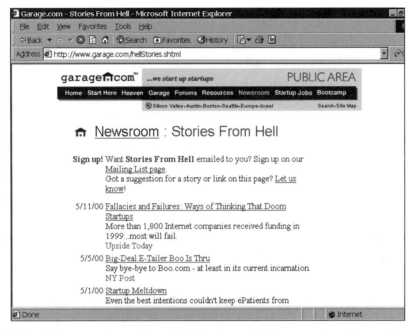

Figure 18.3: Garage.com provides "Stories From Hell"—a section that makes great reading for those seduced by dreams of Easy Street.

Do you see this idea coming together? Your business site should certainly glorify your business—your products and services. At the same time, adding an industry resource site gives an added texture and flavor that makes visitors want to urge their friends to visit it.

Your Opt-in E-zine

Imagine the following. You provide a method for visitors to tell you their e-mail addresses. This gives you an in-house database of individuals interested in what you have to offer. So you offer it in a weekly e-zine. Every week, your name is in front of these viewer's eyes. Every week, these individuals are reminded of you and your wonderful service and products. And every week, you can include key information about your business, including available employment opportunities. Sounds great? It certainly is!

Permission Marketing—*An opt-in e-zine or newsletter allows you to contact potential employees again and again, thus branding your name in their minds. This helps ensure that when they are in the market for a new position, they'll first think of you.*

What's an Opt-in E-zine?

An opt-in e-zine, or e-mail publishing list, or electronic newsletter is simply a means for you to send out weekly information to people who want to see it. Granted, that's a generalization; you can include just about anything of note to your visitors in your opt-in e-zine. I run one for recruiters and HR personnel—the RISE Entrepreneurial Twist e-zine—and every week I send out a couple of hundred words on various recruiting and employment topics. One week I might comment on effective uses of user groups, another week I might discuss what compels candidates to change jobs, still another week I might reveal search engine secrets that allow recruiters to zoom to hidden résumés on the Internet. That's the *informational* content.

The benefit for me is I *also* make sure to include a "message from our sponsor" (myself) that details where my next seminar will be. I might also mention a sale on my other products with a direct link back to my site. In short, I'm including information that immediately benefits *me and my business*.

Let's apply this to you. What can you or your employees write about, week after week? You can comment on industry trends. If you're in a local, town-oriented business, you can comment on last week's news and how it affected your neighboring businesses. You can even include an opt-in e-zine about current positions in your various locations as well!

Realtors have this down to a fine art. **Judy McCutchin's Dallas Homes site** at http://www.dallashomes.com/ has both a real-estate opt-in newsletter and a cute informational site about her dog at http://dom01.dallashomes.com/cstories.nsf. What a great way to get her customers to remember her! Additionally, she offers school reports, town information, and more.

Think about this from your own business perspective. You know the kinds of people you need to employ—you ideally have a handle on what interests them. Take advantage of that, put together a couple of paragraphs every week, and you'll have a powerful marketing tool. It's a tool that will enable you to remind your present and future customers and employees about what you have to offer—and make them glad to hear about it.

Why Have an Opt-in E-zine?

You want to have an opt-in e-zine simply because you want to contact your potential customer base in as effective a method as possible. When you run your own e-zine, you're putting a name and a virtual face to your actions. Your customers will start to feel like they know you. And if they're in the same industry as you are, they'll be quite receptive should they hear of job opportunities that are originating from your business.

Because the e-zine is sent to individuals who actively sign up for it, you have in essence received permission to contact them again via this mechanism. And when you do, including information about your own products, sales, and employment opportunities is an effective way to subtly get your own commercial message across. I've found this quite useful when marketing my own products; every week, scores of people sign up to receive the **RISE Entrepreneurial Twist e-zine** at http://www.riseway.com/. This means that every week I have more and more potential clients who hear about my name in a favorable light.

How to Create Your Opt-in E-zine

It doesn't take that much effort to create one, either. There are two main components to creating your opt-in e-zine—providing a way to accept and store e-mail addresses, and then creating the content to send out. Many services today on the Internet allow you to run your own e-zine, including

Messagebot at http://www.messagebot.com/

eGroups at http://www.egroups.com/

Lyris at http://www.lyris.com/

And that certainly isn't a comprehensive list. I urge you to check out the book *Poor Richard's E-Mail Publishing* by Chris Pirillo, who runs one of the largest e-zines in the world—**Lockergnome** at http://www.lockergnome.com/. Additionally, to learn more about e-zines, visit the following resource sites:

EzineSeek at http://www.ezineseek.com/

ZineZone at http://www.zinezone.com/

Once you have one or more e-zines going, you can incorporate them in your business site as components of your resource center. That way, future visitors will always be able to see the benefits and free information you offer. You can uncover more resources and information at **Poor Richard's Internet Recruiting resource site** at http://www.topfloor.com/.

Adding Your Jobs to Your Site

There are two ways to include jobs on your company Web site. Host them yourself or include a direct link to an employment site that does it for you. Both possibilities are described in the sections that follow.

Do It Yourself

Hosting your jobs yourself doesn't have to be difficult, but it will require the creation of additional job pages. You can use a simple text editor to create a jobs page and copy and paste your job announcements to it.

Additionally, you can create individual pages for each job you offer. Any Webmaster can easily put together a template for you to enter your jobs and incorporate them into your Web site. Consider a **sample client Web site** like http://www.virtual-coach.com/clients/ejp/jobs/. All the jobs posted were created by entering data into a template—the resulting HTML code not only formatted it professionally but also created a page the owner could index in the major search engines.

This is a major benefit for your Internet visibility within search engines. The neat thing about job postings that are directly on your site is that they contain many keywords relating to the careers you offer, as depicted in Figure 18.4. If you choose to submit them to search engines, you might increase the probability that your site will pop up in the top ten for queries like San Francisco Unix job or New Jersey engineering recruiter or jewelry sales job or the like. Never underestimate the types of queries people will enter in search engines; often professionals will search on Connecticut computer job or similar types of constructs.

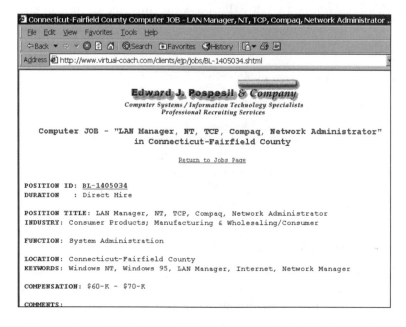

Figure 18.4: Note how this job post Web page is packed with keywords to enhance search engine visibility.

Use a Service

Another resource to consider is a career service that provides you with a direct link to all your jobs. Many services offer a "post once/populate a zillion times" option—i.e., post your job one time and it will be broadcast out to hundreds of career-oriented sites—which can be a real advantage.

One easy service is **Jobvertise** at http://www.jobvertise.com/. There, you can post your jobs for free (effectively hosting them off of Jobvertise) and include direct links to them without having to format them yourself. Additionally, you can use many of the paid boards that exist and hook your job offerings directly to that site. For example, consider **XiTech Staffing** at http://www.xitechstaffing.com/; its job link goes directly to its Smart Office at Recruiters Online. And **Rapid Design Service** at http://www.rapid.com/ points visitors to its jobs at Monster.com. The benefit to this is you don't have to worry about formatting your own job output; it's done for you by the services that you choose. If you don't want to spend the time or effort of hosting jobs directly on your site, it's a great time saver.

After the Résumé Is Submitted ...

After a visitor gives you a résumé, you have to *do* something with it. The question is, what? Many résumé databases on the market will let you store incoming résumés:

Gopher at http://www.resume-software.com/

Personic at http://www.personic.com/

PCRecruiter at http://www.pcrecruiter.com/

Pursuant at http://www.more-o.com/

RecruitMAX at http://www.recruitmax.com/

ResPro at http://www.chaparralsystems.com/

Résumé Inspector at http://www.nerdssoftware.com/

Simpatix HireTrack at http://www.simpatix.com/

Winsearch at http://www.winsearch.com/

The best way to determine which package is right for you and your business is to poll other employers, managers, or HR professionals and see what best matches your own situation. You can find these individuals at the **HRNET mailing list** at http://www.egroups.com/group/hrnet/. Questions for you to answer include

- How many résumés will you want to store?
- Will you need to export the data to other applications?
- If customization is required, who will do it?
- What kind of learning curve can you handle?

After you've derived the answers to these questions, you're in a much better state to choose the right software package—one that will grow as your company does at a budget you can afford.

Tell a Friend

Your Web site is far more than just a place to advertise your products and services. Take advantage of your visitors' potential interest in learning more about your career opportunities and offer them compelling, dynamic copy that encourages them to send in their résumés. It can help cut your recruiting costs dramatically.

But don't stop there! You can embed in your site a link that encourages visitors to tell their friends about the resources you offer (often called a "Tell-a-friend" or "Refer-a-site" script). This enables professionals to easily notify their peers about your resources in a netiquette-friendly way. One place to find this script is at **BigNoseBird** at http://www.bignosebird.com/carchive/birdcast.shtml; adding it to your own Web site will provide additional marketing value at no cost or effort to you.

CHAPTER NINETEEN

Certification and Telling the Truth

Certification and training are becoming increasingly important in today's economy. They're a measure of learning and an incentive for management to pay more salary to those individuals who pass critical tests and earn the certification. You only have to casually peruse today's industry news to realize how quickly certification and training are evolving and changing—especially in the technology arenas. With such a frantic pace as the norm, employers need some way of establishing that their employees are up to date on the latest and greatest of industry happenings.

Benchmarks for the Best—*Certification is an excellent way to assist you in determining if potential employees have the skills you require. Virtually all industries have either certifications or continuing education classes.*

Alas, one negative side effect to this fact of life is the way more and more professionals are stretching the truth of their credentials. It's easy to claim mastery of different skill sets, especially if the interviewers are not educated in the subject matter themselves. This chapter will go a long way in demystifying what certification is all about, the benefits your people will derive from it, and how to lessen your chances of being burned by out-and-out liars.

What Is Certification?

A certification is earned by professionals' passing exams in a given industry. The tests are often quite difficult and comprehensive, requiring hours of detailed study and real-life experience to pass.

A certification can provide an added criterion when hiring employees. If you are actively seeking computer administrators, developers or programmers, financial advisers, Realtors... indeed, just about any professional, you can research what certifications are available in the industry that would help you in assessing candidates for your positions. Keep in mind, of course, that you also need to research what is required to pass exams. What checks are in place to ensure the person taking the exam is actually the person in question? How is the testing delivered? What percentage of the industry takes the exam?

Individuals can become certified through many vehicles. In the computer industry, schools for certification exist in various and sundry hardware and software platforms. Vocational schools also might have programs that lead towards specific certification within different industries. Businesses like **GoCertify** at http://www.gocertify.com/ (see Figure 19.1), which have sprung up all over the Internet, include links to certification resources, CD-ROMs to assist individuals in passing exams, and magazines and other resources dedicated to certification.

As an employer, you might find certification makes your hiring decisions easier. After all, passing the certification exams generally requires quite a lot of dedication and work, which are certainly desirable employee qualities. The certification tests themselves are generally created by the software vendor or professional association in question, and often include problem-solving skills as well as rote memorization. For example, according to **Microsoft's testing criteria** (presented at http://www.microsoft.com/trainingandservices/), their exams call upon test takers to *apply* their knowledge to a situation, analyze technical solutions, solve problems, and derive decisions that work. Because no two real-world problems are exactly the same, understanding how to deduce the correct solution based upon several variables

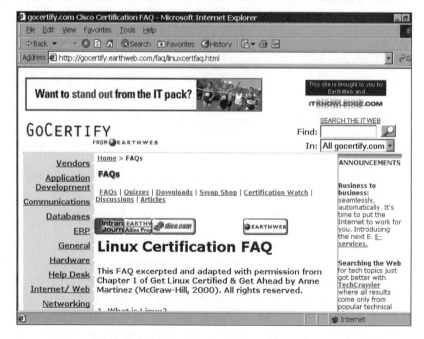

Figure 19.1: GoCertify.com has many resources for different technical certifications.

is a far more exacting skill than parroting technical information. Consider some of the skills that one must master to pass the "Updating Support Skills from Microsoft Windows NT 4.0 to Microsoft Windows 2000" exam:

- Install Windows 2000 and describe tools used for unattended installations.
- Install, configure, and troubleshoot the DNS Server Service.
- Explain the relationship between Active Directory structure and network organization.
- Install and configure Active Directory in a network.
- Populate Active Directory and manage Active Directory objects.
- Upgrade a Windows NT 4.0 network to Windows 2000.
- Install and configure RIS.
- Deploy RIS images to workstations.
- Manage desktop environments by using Group Policy.
- Manage software by using Group Policy.
- Install and configure Terminal Services.
- Configure and support Routing and Remote Access in Windows 2000.
- Configure smart cards, security policy, Internet Protocol Security, and the Encrypting File System.
- Support DHCP and WINS in Windows 2000.
- Manage file resources in Windows 2000.
- Create and manage dynamic volumes.
- Implement disaster-protection and disaster-recovery techniques in Windows 2000.

Unless you are technically adept, you probably don't understand the majority of these requirements. However, if you need to hire someone to upgrade your network to the latest and greatest, knowing that your prospective employee has mastered these requirements should provide some reassurance.

Master of All—*Many certification exams require the test taker to master a number of critical applications and skill sets involved in the technology in question. These comprehensive exams are often a challenge to pass.*

Anytime a new skill appears, a new technology comes along that improves the way business works, or your industry undergoes a paradigm shift, resources spring up that enable individuals to prove their expertise by becoming certified in the new material. Years ago, the World Wide Web didn't even exist; now, one can become a Certified Internet Webmaster courtesy of **ProSoft Training** at http://www.prosofttraining.com/.

The skills required include electronic commerce fundamentals, law and the Internet, security, and much more, and the exams have been endorsed by the International Webmasters Association, the Association of Internet Professionals, and the Internet Certification Institute International. Were you aware that your Webmasters should be proficient in these matters?

Benefits of Certification

An important benefit of certification for you as an employer is the way it enhances your company's *knowledge base;* that is, the sum total of career-related skills that employees bring to the job. The theory is that certified professionals have an in-depth understanding of the requirements needed to succeed in a particular field. The premise makes sense; to become certified, professionals must answer a multitude of rote questions and also solve real-world problems without any reference material at hand. Knowing how to logically deduce answers in a given scenario gives any professional an edge.

When you hire certified professionals, you also benefit by being able to reassure your customers about the quality of your employees. If you're in a support industry, for example, or some other field that puts you in contact with customers on a daily basis, revealing your people's credentials might be the deciding factor in persuading someone to go with your company.

Certification training can be a valuable perk for your employees—psychologically and financially. Taking exams costs money, as does investing in the exam materials and course books. Luckily, you now have many options to decrease the cost dramatically, including the following:

> **Web-based training classes**. Web-based training classes present the material your employees need to know in a fashion that doesn't require travel or hotel expenses. Because it's delivered over the Internet, students can go through the exercises at their own pace and level. Some technical Web-based training sites include **TeachMeIT** at http://www.teachmeit.com/ and **O'Reilly** at http://training.oreilly.com/; nontechnical certifications available via the Web include the **American Society for Quality's Certified Reliability Engineer** certification at http://www.asq.org/, the Personal Watercraft Safety Test at http://www.pwcsafety.com/test.htm, and a variety of disciplines at http://www.test24hour.com/.

> **CD-ROM training classes**. Some training materials have been distilled to CD-ROM versions, where students use their computers to work through the exercises. CD-ROM training specialists for the Information Technology industries include **Transcender** at http://www.transcender.com/, as seen in Figure 19.2, and a whole slew of them at Yahoo!.

Figure 19.2: Transcender is one vendor that provides study materials to help you pass certification exams.

Onsite or offsite training. Many corporations will offer classes for certification purposes. You can locate them at Yahoo! and other directories.

As noted earlier, almost every industry has its own certifications available. You should always be able to uncover what the current hot skills in your industry are and what certifications show comprehensive understanding of them.

How to Find Certification Resources

You can find certification resources on the Internet by searching for the most commonly used words via the following easy steps:

- Define your industry niche.
- Browse certification directories.
- Utilize search engines.

These steps are described separately in the sections that follow.

Step One: Define Your Industry Niche

You may often need to hire certified professionals outside your own core industry. For example, perhaps your business centers around the national hauling of freight. If you've been given the task of finding someone to coordinate and oversee daily computer operations, of course you will want to interview technical computer professionals instead of truck drivers. Keep in mind that any given business can span many different industries; you'll always need to concentrate upon the most important skills your interviewees should possess.

If your target turns out to be unfamiliar, don't initially worry about details; set your search criteria to pick up as broad a category as possible and *then* narrow them down. For example, perhaps word has come down from above that you need to hire engineers to design new products for your company. That's all the boss tells you. Of course, you should request specifics; but in the meantime, you already know the basic industry is *engineering* and one required skill is *design*. Put those two words together and you get "design engineering." This leads you to three precise questions:

- How do engineers design?
- What tools do they use?
- What certifications are available?

Finding the answers to these questions can be relatively simple. You can visit **Google** at http://www.google.com/ and search for `design engineer resource` or even `engineering certification`. You might then find out that design engineers often use the Pro/E software package on the job, which indicates that proficiency with that software might be a useful quality to look for in potential employees. Remember, the more thorough you are in spelling out crucial career-related skills, the higher the probability that you'll interview the right group of professionals.

Step Two: Browse Certification Sites

Once you have your industry and skills defined, you can browse or visit several of the certification and training sites that abound on the Internet.

Technical

About.com's Certification site at http://certification.about.com/. Perhaps you want to hire a Microsoft Certified Systems Engineer for your new software position. Visiting this site reveals several links to the requirements such as **Microsoft's information page** at http://www.microsoft.com/mcp/certstep/mcse.htm, **free cram sessions** at http://cramsession.brainbuzz.com/cramsession/microsoft/, and other resources.

GoCertify at http://www.gocertify.com/. Someday, you might need to hire network developers. Included on this site is a link for Communications; here you'll uncover information about the Certified Network Telephony Engineer (CNTE) certification, the (Computer Telephony) Solution Developer certification, and others.

BrainBuzz at http://www.brainbuzz.com/. A comprehensive site with free study guides for Linux, Novell, Microsoft certification, and more, BrainBuzz also presents IT news headlines, forums, columnists, and more.

Nontechnical

Yahoo! at http://www.yahoo.com/. Yahoo! is a great directory for general information. For example, perhaps you are interested in locating certifications in the purchasing industry. Searching for `purchasing certification` reveals that the **National Association of Purchasing Management** at http://www.napm.org/ offers the Certified Purchasing Manager (C.P.M.) and the Accredited Purchasing Practitioner (A.P.P.) certifications.

Hoovers at http://www.hoovers.com/. An extremely comprehensive business resource site, Hoovers has an industry directory you can browse for organizations that deal with whatever industry you need to research. As noted earlier, quite often professional associations will offer certifications for many of their careers; navigating to `insurance` leads to a link for the **Society of Actuaries** at http://www.soa.org/, where you can uncover thorough exam information.

Free!—*Many sites on the Internet provide free training and tests to assist professionals in passing particular certification exams. Consider CertReview at http://www.certreview.com/—open to Microsoft certified professionals, it provides communities, test assistance, and more.*

As you can see, the process for actually locating niche sites is rather simple. Remember our earlier discussion about search engines; it's easy to become overwhelmed by information overload. Take it methodically and carefully; don't get flustered by all the possibilities that abound.

What if you can't find the necessary certifications in the directories I've mentioned so far? It's now time to turn to search engines. Let's review the basics of what you'll be searching for:

What am I looking for? Certifications for specific skills.

What are the keywords that I might use? Industries or skills such as `IT`, `Oracle`, `banking`, `sales`, plus the general keyword `certification`.

These steps are described in the sections that follow.

Step Three: Utilize Search Engines

Let's say that you need to hire employees for your bank and want to find out what, if any, certification requirements exist. Searching on **Google** (http://www.google.com) for `banker certification` might return the page **AIB Southern New England Chapter: Diplomas and Certificates** at http://www.sneaib.org/diploma.htm This page refers to The American Institute of Banking, a service of the American Bankers Association. You can then return to Google and search for `American Bankers Association Certification`; you might find the official site for the **American Bankers Association** at http://www.aba.com/, and then uncover links for **training and certification** at http://www.aba.com/aba/ProductsandServices/ps98_training_aib.asp. This site describes certifications in Bank Operations, Commercial Lending, Consumer Credit, General Banking, and Mortgage Lending, as well as Customer Service Skills, Securities Services Skills, and Supervisory Skills. Thus you can incorporate questions about these certifications in your employee interviews.

You can use this technique when searching for other industry certification as well. Are you looking to hire sales professionals? As well as focusing on the amount of revenue generated during a candidate's last position, you can also ask about their views on their industry's certifications. Searching for `sales certification` at Google might return a page from the **National Association of Sales Professionals** at http://www.nasp.com/certifcont.html, which details how to become a certified professional salesperson or CPSP. Keep in mind the ongoing debate in some industries about the value of certification; some professionals insist it's a waste of time that could be used for actual business transactions.

Another way to locate potential certifications within your industry is to visit **Yahoo!** at http://www.yahoo.com/ and search for `<industry> certification`. For example, searching for `manufacturing engineering certification` might lead you to the **Society of Manufacturing Engineers** at http://www.sme.org/, where you'll find several descriptions of available certifications.

The next thing you'll have to accomplish is to determine if the certifications available are truly a requirement for your career opportunities. Ask yourself

- How important are certifications compared to real-life experience?
- Will my customers expect my employees to be certified?
- Can I send a potential employee for certification training?

This last step is rather important. Offering certification training as a perk will certainly be perceived as a benefit. But you do want to ensure that employees don't try to obtain positions with you simply to become certified for free and then gallivant off to a different employer; you want to realize a hefty return on your expenditures. As a recruiter trainer, I've heard horror stories from employers who are used by professionals simply for the free training they provide. Guard against this by spelling out the requirements for receiving certification education.

How to Quiz Your Future Employees About Their Skills

One of the challenges when hiring is ensuring that potential employees are actually proficient in the specific skills claimed on their résumés. Alas, lying on one's résumé is more and more commonplace; people see the stratospheric salaries some top-notch computer professionals and contractors command and decide they want to get into the action. Because that particular industry reinvents itself constantly, they might not want to take the time required to learn the necessary skills prior to being hired.

It's your responsibility as an employer to determine that your employees are knowledgeable in the skills you require. There are several ways to accomplish this:

- Web-based testing
- Face-to-face quizzes
- Former employer comments
- Background checks

These are described in the following sections.

Web-Based Testing

Many Web-based testing sites are available on the Internet. These locations quiz individuals on specific skills and industries, and then report their scores to the test taker as illustrated in Figure 19.3. Here are some of the most useful sites:

Brainbench at http://www.brainbench.com/

IT Crunch at http://www.itcrunch.com/

proveit.com at http://www.proveit.com/

ShowMe Tests at http://www.showmetests.com/

When individuals take Web-based tests, they are actively demonstrating they have a firm technical understanding of the skills required. Unfortunately, however, passing a test—especially a Web-based test—doesn't automatically imply that a candidate is *the* person you should hire. The candidate may well have memorized (or looked up) the required facts, and may know enough to deal with hypothetical problems but not enough to cope with the ones that arise on the job. Real-world experience can be just as important as factual knowledge.

Face-to-Face Quizzes

If you currently have an employee you trust who has knowledge in the skills required for a new position, you can always ask that person to quiz a candidate. I remember when I was responsible for quizzing systems administrators; I would encounter individuals who thought that knowing how to turn on a computer without causing dire bodily harm to themselves qualified them as competent in systems administration. Sometimes it takes a knowledgeable person in the industry in question to verify another's claims.

What if you don't have such a person on hand? You can network with your peers and ask if they know of anyone, or, failing that, visit your local bookstore and pick up a book on the subject. Granted, this may not be too helpful if your quiz deals with advanced career-specific information, but can be useful for weeding out those individuals who have filled their résumés with keywords they can barely define, let alone apply on the job.

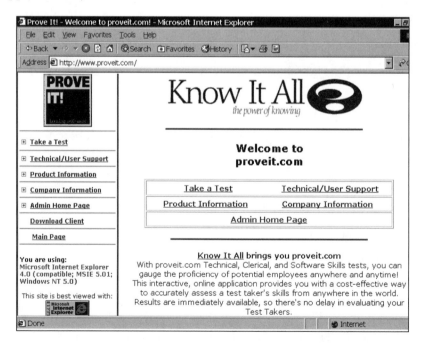

Figure 19.3: You'll find a variety of Web-based testing at proveit.com.

Former Employer Comments

Former employers can be useful in assessing an applicant. If someone claims to have built an e-commerce system from scratch that brought in over twenty million dollars of profit during the past year, it should be a relatively simple process to verify that with the former employer. As with anything that deals with personal relationships, however, always be aware that emotions can color a person's evaluation. If the person you are considering hiring left on bad terms with the previous management, you might receive a biased report on their skills that contains significant errors.

Tap Current Employees—*If you have professionals working for you who are knowledgeable about the required skills, you can ask them to quiz interviewees and evaluate their knowledge.*

Because today's job climate encourages job hopping, potential employees might have a number of former employers you can contact for skills evaluations. In any event, you should always take the time to verify that people you consider hiring actually can deliver on the promises they make. It will cost your company quite a lot of money should you hire someone you need to fire due to poor performance after three months.

Background Checks

Sometimes it's beneficial to run a background check before you bring someone into your workplace. Many resources and companies on the Internet will assist you in performing this action and uncovering public information. Here are two samples:

HireCheck at http://www.hirecheck.com/

Knowx at http://www.knowx.com/

It's *Your* Hiring Decision

Certification exams, verbal quizzes, former employer contacts, and background checks can assist you in fine-tuning your hiring process. No matter what information you need to uncover, the Internet will almost always be a valuable supplement for your traditional recruiting resources.

Don't let certification become the be-all and end-all in your hiring decisions, however. Certification is simply one additional tool you can use to determine if you should hire a prospective employee; other qualities such as real-world experience can be just as important. Hiring the right person is a critical step for your business; always take into account crucial variables such as proven ability to solve problems and avoid trouble spots as well.

CHAPTER TWENTY

Mastering Paid Job Boards

If you've read this book from the beginning, it's now rather apparent: Given the time and the energy, one doesn't have to spend thousands of dollars to find high-quality candidates on the Internet; countless locations let you both advertise your open positions and review targeted résumés in your industry either for free or for a low monthly fee. You'll receive the best responses if you network with others in your industry and take the time to ensure the career aspect of your Web site attracts the best candidates possible.

But perhaps you *are* willing to pay to cut to the chase and use the brand-name job and career boards. Perhaps you don't have the time to locate industry niche sites; maybe you don't have any other resources that you can delegate to search out free professional organization job boards; or it might be your management has it in their heads that One Must Use What Everyone Knows. If this is the case for you, this chapter will show you the benefits and drawbacks to the various large careers sites and explain how to choose one that best meets your needs.

Benefits of Paid Job Boards

First and foremost the benefit of paid job boards is popularity and immediate availability of candidates. Many of the large paid job boards can afford to charge big bucks for access because they have tremendous traffic, brand-name recognition, and public relations advertising. In other words, hundreds of thousands of professionals are already aware of their existence and choose to investigate their offerings. As we've already seen, access to a number of the large boards is absolutely free for candidates; after all, their résumés are some of the products being sold. Thus, it costs job-seekers nothing to submit résumés to these boards and benefit from their career resources.

Another benefit of a paid job board is that it satisfies the preconceived expectations of many management professionals; sometimes it's human nature to go with the best-known services. This way, when writing up their own end-of-year performance review, managers can state with confidence that they attempted to increase their number of hires by using the most popular job boards known on the face of this planet. Companies such as **Monster.com** at http://www.monster.com/ (as seen in Figure 20.1), along with Hotjobs, DICE, and other big-name boards have spent millions of dollars getting their name out in front of humanity via many different routes. By branding their names indelibly into people's minds, they have quite successfully upped the odds that when managers think of hiring new employees, they'll turn to those boards first.

Immediate Availability—*Large paid job boards are chock-full of candidates that are immediately available, instead of professionals who might or might not actively consider a new job opportunity.*

Other benefits of a paid job board include:

Possibly unique candidates. Nowadays, the trend is towards résumés of professionals that don't appear anyplace else on the Internet. Privacy is a valued commodity.

Job agents. Job seekers can specify their requirements and receive job descriptions that match them via e-mail. Not only is this convenient, it also contributes to keeping the name of the job site in the professional's mind.

Figure 20.1: Monster.com offers one of the most popular job boards on the Internet because of its high visibility.

Automatic résumé matching. Some of the large paid sites set up specific criteria and then e-mail you incoming résumés that match them.

Communities. Setting up *communities* (a buzzword in Internet recruiting) basically means carving out a section on a Web site dedicated to a specific industry such as sales, or Java, or engineering. Within this area you can generally find resources targeted to that particular industry—and people chatting away about them and building relationships with each other. Again, it's a great way of encouraging visitors to return.

Local career information. Many of the paid job banks provide the means to target specific regions of the country. This is accomplished by specifying a state or city via a drop-down menu like Monster's **Jobsearch** at http://jobsearch.monster.com/, creating metro sections as **DICE** does at http://www.dice.com/jobsearch/metro/, or setting up individual servers like **Computerjob's Atlanta** site at http://www.atlanta.computerjobs.com/.

***Regional Resources**—Many big-name job boards provide regional career sites so you can target only those professionals who are local to you.*

Career advice. The large, expensive job boards know how important traffic is for their bottom line. Thus they often go all out in providing crucial career resources such as job advice, résumé information, dressing for success, and the like. Information like this is easy to prepare yet valuable for site visitors. You might find it gathered under the name "Career Center" or "Career Resources."

Career links. Smart big boards know they can't be everything to everyone, so they include career resource links on their site. For example, perhaps a big board doesn't want to develop a résumé-writing workshop of its own. In that case, it might choose to either barter or provide advertising space for professionals résumé writers to handle that aspect of the business. The inclusion of career links offers more of a "one-stop shopping" motivation for candidates to utilize the service, thus providing more potential employees from which companies can choose.

Life links. When considering a new career, professionals have far more to worry about than merely finding a new job; they might have to deal with relocation, increased job stress, being part of a both-parents-work household, and other related career issues. Thus, you might find links for these topics on the large job boards as well.

Although directed primarily to job seekers, these features offer benefits to employers as well. When job seekers browse around a comprehensive site to see what else is available for free, they often decide that this is the place to post a résumé. This tendency builds the site's collection of immediately available candidates, especially in the nontechnical industries, where job seekers are relatively unfamiliar with the Internet and are apt to have heard about the big job boards but not about other resources. They go to Monster.com or one of the other big boards, discover what looks like a whole world of helpful features, and never look anywhere else—which means that if you want candidates of this type, you'll find them here in larger numbers than anywhere else.

Paid Job Boards Consist of...

The only broad difference between paid job boards and free job boards is publicity. For every **Monster.com** (http://www.monster.com/), you'll be able to find a **Flipdog** (http://www.flipdog.com/) reaching for your business. (Flipdog is the up-and-coming job board that intends to provide just what Monster.com does for a much lesser cost.)

This is not to say one should not use Monster.com, not by a long shot. Recently I conducted a poll about Internet recruiting job boards and Monster.com was rated quite highly by a number of the participants. I prefer to liken job board choices to traveling via coach or first class; both will get you to the same location; one will cost considerably more money, but will also at times be the most direct, fastest route.

As we've seen, paid job banks can offer much more than merely job posting and viewing résumé. Serious players in the industry are focusing on the recruiting process as a whole and positioning themselves as a way to streamline the entire process. Remember, finding and hiring new candidates doesn't simply finish when you find a potential employee—you need to interview, evaluate, and convince that person to take the job. Thus you might find the following components of the large paid job sites useful as well:

> **Certification training and exams.** One of the easiest ways to evaluate employees is to see how well they fare in passing certification and training exams. Several large job boards are taking advantage of this and partnering with test-administration companies; consider **DICE** at http://www.dice.com/, which offers MeasureUp, an online testing and certification product, or **CareerPath** at http://www.careerpath.com/, which has partnered with **Brainbuzz** at http://www.brainbuzz.com/ for the same type of services.

> **Psych tests.** Career evaluations to see what kinds of jobs would suit your personality are becoming more prevalent on the Internet. Some job boards such as **Headhunter.net** at http://www.headhunter.net/ have partnered with organizations that offer such evaluations at a discount.

Freelancing. Not everyone wants to find a new career via the old-fashioned recruiting process. Some individuals enjoy being in the driver's seat and offer their skills for auction. **Monster's Talent Bank** at http://talent.monster.com/ is one place where these freelancers can be found.

Company research. Smart job boards know that providing as much information as possible will help impress job candidates, so they include comprehensive information about the companies that advertise on the site. Examples include **JobCircle** at http://www.jobcircle.com/ and **FoodIndustryJobs** at http://www.foodindustryjobs.com/.

These are only some of the additional benefits you might see at the paid job boards; you should always be on the lookout for what else might be available. Remember, too, that many paid job boards will offer package deals such as cheaper rates in return for an extended period of subscription service. This brings us to the next important topic—how to evaluate a paid job board.

How to Evaluate a Paid Job Board

With all the choices available, how can you ensure you make the right decision concerning what paid job board to use? As with any service you buy, you should ask a number of questions prior to sending any payment:

What are your services? Paid job boards generally have at least two services available; posting your jobs and viewing professional résumés. These two services should have comprehensive features—you should be able to post your position once and see it appear in numerous places; to search for résumés according to location, date of posting, skills, and more; and to set up job or résumé agents so you are automatically notified when a potential match occurs. Sometimes you'll find that job posting and résumé viewing are two separate services and have individual costs.

Cost of Services—*Sometimes posting jobs and viewing professional résumés are two distinct products on a job board. Make sure you understand exactly what services are included in any job board offering.*

How new are your résumés? Unless you are a recruiter searching for those wildly desirable hidden, passive candidates, you need a résumé database that is chock-full of people actively looking *now* for a new career. So ask, How many new résumés come in each day? Can you search via date to ensure you see résumés no more than a day old?

How targeted are your résumés? This is an important question. What delivers results beyond measure to a computer-oriented business might bring close to zero results for a construction firm. If a sales rep extols the 3,000,637 résumés in the board's database, don't be swayed solely by that fact! Sheer numbers are useless; you're after quality and professionals you can actually hire. You can extend this question to inquire about how many local professionals use the service as well.

Where do you get your résumés? As you have seen throughout this book (especially in Chapter 7, "Industry Niche Sites," and Chapter 8, "Professional Organizations"), you can find free résumés all over the place. You want to ensure you are getting what you are paying for—high-quality résumés of individuals who really are looking for employment right now. It would be easy enough to create a script that sucks up résumés all over the Internet, put them in a database, and then charge to access them. Job boards can also get résumés by hiring telemarketers to call up individuals and ask for their information, then add the crop to the résumé database. Unfortunately, neither the script nor the telemarketer will bring in the best résumés—those from people who just made a personal decision to actively look for another job.

How will I receive information about new résumés? Many job boards offer a service in which you can specify the criteria for particular candidates and then receive e-mail whenever a résumé matches your request. This saves you the time of actually logging on and performing searches.

Do you offer any free trials? It's at this moment, when you're actively discussing buying a membership to a particular job bank, that you might hear the site doesn't offer free trials. Every job board should offer at least some sort of free trial or, failing that, a money-back guarantee. It shows confidence in the service.

What packages do you offer? As I was writing this chapter, some boards required that you sign up for three months at the minimum; others offered a year at a discounted price. Be sure to list all of the components of the packages—job posting, résumé viewing, and whatever else—are included. For example, some job boards might charge per user, meaning that if two of your managers use the board to find future employees, you'll pay more money than if just one does.

Who are your competitors and why should I choose you? Every job board salesperson should be able to discourse learnedly about the marketspace and point to the company's benefits with ease.

How do candidates know about you? It doesn't matter what benefits a job board offers if your targeted candidates don't know the board exists. Examine the site in question. Do resources beckon candidates to return and refer their friends? Ask what kinds of targeted advertising gets the word out about the job board to your future employees. Ads in trade magazines, on television or the radio, via Web site banners, and the like are all good responses; referrals are also an effective marketing tool. **Hotjobs** at http://www.hotjobs.com/ (as depicted in Figure 20.2) not only invests in these marketing methods, it also creates a humongous banner that is dragged behind airplanes at the Jersey shore. The only word on that sky banner is *Hotjobs.com*. Now *that's* effective advertising.

Another way to evaluate job boards is to contact the people who are posting their jobs and ask how useful the board has been to them. Often you'll find very helpful comments. Be certain to choose businesses that are in your own industry, though—access to the best computer programmers in the world won't help you if what you need is a pastry chef.

When you discuss job boards with their sales staff, you might hear of different usage rules from one board to another. For example, one company said I should buy a single job post that would give me an 8.5-by-11-inch piece of paper on which to

Figure 20.2: Hotjobs takes advantage of many marketing avenues to build its brand name recognition.

write my ad. That simply meant I'd have the space to write quite a lot of information. I was also told that, as in a newspaper, once an ad was posted it couldn't be changed unless I bought the bigger package.

You Are the Customer—*When investing in a paid job board service, remember that you are the customer. You have the right to buy only what you need and to understand exactly how a paid job board service benefits you. Never spend a dime until you are confident the service in question meets your needs.*

Be wary of salespeople who try to sell you more than you need. For example, some job boards split their sites into numerous boards that handle different industries such as technical, sales, and health; they might try to sell you a discount if you invest in two instead of one. The problem is that, prior to using a new job board, you simply don't know if you'll receive the benefits you deserve. That said, paid job boards might deliver results if you simply don't have the time to search for the hidden resources yourself. Just be careful and prudent when spending your money.

List of Large Job Boards

In alphabetical order, here are some of the big job boards that are currently available. Some of them are general, others are industry focused.

Career Builder at http://www.careerbuilder.com/. This general site has partnered with many newspapers and powers a number of regional job boards.

Career Mosaic at http://www.careermosaic.com/. One of the longest-lived all-purpose job boards on the Internet.

CareerPath at http://www.careerpath.com/. Another general site that powers a number of newspaper and regional job boards.

ComputerJobs at http://www.computerjobs.com/. A very popular technical job site.

ComputerWork at http://www.computerwork.com/. Another very popular technical job site.

DICE at http://www.dice.com/. Ditto. You'll find similar (and sometimes the same) people at this board and the two preceding it.

Flipdog at http://www.flipdog.com/. Uses sophisticated technology to gather job posts from all sorts of fields all around the world, as well as provide excellent employer tools.

Guru at http://www.guru.com/. A popular talent-for-hire site—especially good for freelancers and other contractors.

Headhunter.net at http://www.headhunter.net/. One of the earliest and most user-friendly job boards, with a nice line in managerial candidates.

Hotjobs at http://www.hotjobs.com/. Very popular all-purpose job board.

Job Options at http://www.joboptions.com/. Formerly eSpan, a comprehensive board that tries to have somebody for everyone.

Medzilla at http://www.medzilla.com/. Popular biotechnology, pharmaceuticals, science, medicine, and health care job site.

Monster at http://www.monster.com/. One of the best-known (and therefore best-supplied) all-purpose job boards on the Internet.

NationJob at http://www.nationjob.com/. Another popular all-purpose job board.

SixFigureJobs at http://www.sixfigurejobs.com/. Job board targeted towards executive positions.

Passport Access at http://www.passportaccess.com/. One of the earliest job boards, still a lively source of résumés in nontechnical fields.

Techies at http://www.techies.com/. As its name indicates, this one is aimed at the real tech-heads; it's gaining in popularity among its target audience.

Managing Your Investment

Choosing to use a job board is an investment of your time and money not to be taken lightly. Always try to pre-qualify job boards as much as possible before spending your hard-earned money; nothing is more frustrating than paying for a service that fails to deliver what you need.

If at all possible, take note of responses you receive from job boards. By tracking the job boards where applicants find your job postings, you can determine which resource provides the most benefits for your particular needs. **Flipdog** at http://www.flipdog.com/ and **eQuest** at http://www.equest.com/, for example, will provide you with these types of statistics.

Chapter Twenty-One

The Benefits of Recruiters

Throughout this book, we've seen that the Internet brims with free and low-cost resources for your hiring needs. No matter what kinds of employees you want to find, you'll almost always be able to uncover leads, targeted job banks, industry niche sites, and the like to assist you in pursuing your goals. It's all a matter of time management and creativity; done diligently, Internet recruiting reveals hidden resources at every turn. The only drawback, of course, is the amount of time you might need to spend.

Alas, not everyone has the luxury (or the self-discipline) to carve out time from a busy schedule for Internet recruiting, even if that time is only 15 minutes a day. These things happen; after all, you are getting paid to do your own job and not to spend a lot of time recruiting on the Internet. So what do you do if you realize you lack either the time or the inclination to take advantage of all the resources offered by Internet recruiting? You turn to recruiters to save the day.

Choosing the right one for you can be an adventure; how can you ensure you end up with a recruiter who delivers what you need? This chapter will outline several key points to assist you in your choice, describing the skills great recruiters possess, the way recruiters locate qualified candidates, the questions to ask potential recruiters to determine their skills, and more.

What's a Recruiter?

Recruiters are generally skilled professionals who are paid by companies to locate potential employees they can interview. Once an interview takes place and a candidate is hired, the recruiter receives a nice fee. Sounds simple, eh? Just find candidates, send 'em out to interviews, and then sit back and collect the money. The reality is far different. Competent recruiters are worth their weight in gold; they offer a whole bag of tricks and job skills:

Candidate database. Recruiters often have a database of past, current, and future candidates. This database will include the professionals' résumés, contact information, work status, specific skills, and the like. Recruiters who have been around for years might have information on thousands of people; this can make finding candidates to interview (note, I didn't say "hire") as easy as browsing through the available records.

Candidate network. Recruiters are known by word of mouth via candidate networks. When a recruiter successfully places someone, delivering exceptional service in the process, the happy new employee generally tells friends and colleagues about the stellar treatment. Likewise, if a recruiter treats candidates poorly, that will be broadcast as well—as you'll see in the various contractor message boards such as **RealRates** at http://www.realrates.com/ or **CEDaily** at http://www.cedaily.com/.

Knowledge of the industry. Many industries are undergoing dynamic changes. Specialized recruiters can talk to candidates in their own language, point to current hot skills that would increase a candidate's marketability, know what sites to visit to stay abreast of industry trends, and the like. Never underestimate how important it is to "talk the talk" when interviewing a potential employee; it will greatly assist you in determining the skill level of the candidate and communicating on the same level.

Get the Clearest View—*Recruiters often have an unbiased view of the industry in which you are recruiting, as they are actively involved with its employment aspects on a daily basis. Thus they are often the first to hear of cutting-edge trends and desirable skills.*

Pre-qualifiers. Competent recruiters know how to pre-qualify candidates so you don't get stuck interviewing shoe sales specialists for the position of software marketing lead. As we saw earlier, many candidates will simply lie on their résumé (forgive me, I meant "fudge the truth a weeeee bit") in hopes of landing a better job. I've quizzed a lot of professionals in the technical IT fields, and it never ceases to amaze me how people who can barely spell "UNIX" will declare themselves competent at systems administration.

Inside corporate knowledge. Every organization has its own environment and customs that make a big difference to the people who work there. Additionally, within large corporations there can be different cultures and mores; some departments are more political than others, other departments are calmer, etc. If you are in charge of hiring someone within your corporation but don't know the specifics of the supervisor's group, choosing a recruiter who is on the preferred vendors list and has years of experience with your company might deliver excellent though intangible benefits.

As you can see, recruiters can save you time and effort by presenting only those top-notch candidates whom you would like to hire. The cost initially can seem quite high; depending upon the type of recruiter, it can range anywhere from 10 percent of the compensation package to 35 percent and higher. Thus if you plan on hiring an employee for a yearly salary of $40,000, you might end up owing the recruiter anywhere from $4,000 to $14,000. But put this cost in your own context; if you find yourself lacking time to recruit, qualify, and hire others yourself, recruiters can save you time (you'll know the only people you'll be interviewing are qualified candidates) and money (the longer you are without the candidates you need, the more money your company loses)—your company may well spend more if you do the recruiting than if you engage a specialist to do it for you.

There are three broad types of recruiters—contingency, retained, and corporate:

Contingency. Contingency recruiters are by far the most common. These recruiters will take on a job order for no cost; you only pay if you accept and hire the candidate they propose. The fee is agreed to up front and is paid upon hiring. As professionals, contingency recruiters generally draw a base salary from the agency they work for plus commissions for any of their candidates who are hired.

Retained. Retained recruiters are paid no matter what. Often used by corporations, one-third of their fee is paid upon agreeing to take on a search, one-third is paid halfway through the search, and the last third is paid when the search is complete.

Corporate. Corporate recruiters generally have jobs in a company's Human Resources department, and are charged with finding employees to hire. Because they are employed by the corporation, they are generally paid as salaried employees.

What type of recruiter you use depends upon your business needs. A good way to pick a high-quality recruiter is to poll your peers and colleagues and see who they use.

Benefits of Good Recruiters

Recruiters offer many more benefits than merely finding potential employees for your business. For example, perhaps you are in the telecommunications industry and would like to hire individuals who have extensive work experience with MCI or Sprint. Or possibly you're getting ready to pump up your new dot-com and want to find seasoned executives to oversee the financial aspects of the business. Recruiters can help you achieve all this and more:

- Cost savings
- Competitive intelligence
- Sales closing
- Outplacement

These four points will be described in the following sections.

Cost Savings

If you choose not to become skilled in Internet recruiting, using a high-quality professional recruiter can save you money in the long run. When thinking about costs, companies generally think only of the recruiter's fee. (Eeeek! It's several thousand dollars! I can buy a membership in Monster.com for that!) Compare that to these possible savings:

Your time. The amount of time you spend recruiting on the Internet is time you could use for your actual job.

Your money. If you hire the wrong person, i.e., someone you soon have to fire, all the money you spent finding that person is lost. (If a candidate from a recruiter doesn't work out, you may get a free replacement.)

Remember, one of your main goals when recruiting on the Internet is to find your future employees fast and at low cost. If you lack the time to bring yourself up to speed on Internet recruiting, it will be faster to choose a good recruiter to locate candidates for you—and if you're really under the gun, chances are that you'll even save money compared to an ineffective effort of your own.

Competitive Intelligence

The best kinds of candidates for recruiters are those known as "*hidden*" or "*passive*" candidates; i.e., professionals who aren't actively seeking a new job. Recruiters find these individuals from many of the time-honored recruiting methods—cold calling, referrals, and networking through candidate databases. Thus if the people you need to hire all seem to be working happily for your competitors, a recruiting agency may well be able to showcase your opportunities in ways that you couldn't manage and to attract attention among those who are not currently looking for new jobs.

The employment market is tight, especially in the IT industry. One only needs to peruse the technical niche sites such as **ZDNet** at http://www.zdnet.com/ or **ComputerWorld** at http://www.computerworld.com/ and read some of the many articles that bemoan how difficult it is to lure new employees. Remember the section entitled "Know Your Goals" in Chapter 2, which walked through the process of defining why candidates should choose you? The tighter the labor market, the more difficult it becomes to find employees. Recruiters are well trained at targeting corporations or industries and finding candidates who wouldn't have noticed your opening but are now eager to learn all that you offer.

Passive Candidates—*Experienced recruiters are often highly skilled at uncovering passive candidates—those professionals who are not actively looking for a new position, yet are open to learning about career opportunities.*

Sales Closing

As you've seen throughout this book, a good portion of successful recruiting depends on "closing the sale"; in other words, on showcasing all the benefits you offer to persuade candidates to consider choosing you for their next career assignment. Successful recruiters are superb salespeople at heart; they know how to present the job opportunity in its best light. They also are well equipped to deal with individuals who want to bargain or play games; sometimes people who act like potential employees were never serious to begin with (they only want an offer so they can return to their current employer and negotiate a raise). Would you recognize when this is happening, or feel comfortable in actively debating it? It's part of a recruiter's daily job.

Not everyone excels at sales (I can't sell my way out of a wet paper bag); if this is not an activity you enjoy, definitely consider recruiters.

Closing the Deal—*Often you will require excellent sales and negotiation skills to hire professionals. If you take to sales like elephants take to mice, recruiters will definitely be a benefit for your company.*

Outplacement

If you've received word from Up Above that cuts must be made in your employee numbers, you might want to contact a recruiter and ask them to prepare a career seminar on other opportunities in the industry. This will provide two benefits; you cushion the "alas, we have to let you go" message with a "but here are some career resources and seminars that I've found to help you find a new position," and you also get to see from a third-party perspective just how good a particular recruiter is. After a career seminar, you can ask your current employees to evaluate the recruiter's understanding of the industry, knowledge of available job opportunities, and general effectiveness.

Outplacement can also be used when you need to fire individuals for other reasons besides management decrees. Sometimes the person you hire to fill a position simply doesn't work out; the skill set turns out to be a mismatch, the employee's personality doesn't fit with the job (think of a hermit trying to sell computers door to door), or similar things. True, the end result is this person will be fired. However, you will look much better and it will also benefit this employee's career if you can provide an introduction to a reputable recruiter to assist in finding a new position.

Disadvantages of Sub-Par Recruiters

It's sad to say, but a few poor recruiters can affect the whole industry like poison ivy affects your prized rose garden. Certainly, there are still desirable flowers to be discovered within, but hardly anyone will want to risk the painful irritation of exploring it further.

Because recruiters are ultimately paid by their clients, it's tempting at times for them to forgo the matching process and simply try to make placements in order to receive a fee. Recruiters who are driven by money and nothing else are the recruiters to avoid at all costs. How can you determine if a potential recruiter is going to do the job for you? This is covered in detail later in this chapter, in the section entitled "How to Choose a Recruiter." In the meantime, asking Human Resources professionals who deal with recruiters on a daily basis can provide you with some excellent recommendations; these people participate at mailing lists available at **The Electronic Recruiting Exchange** at http://www.erexchange.com/ and **HRNET** at http://www.onelist.com/group/hrnet/.

How Recruiters Operate

Ever wonder how recruiters actually do their job? It's not that every single time they receive a job request, they automatically have a candidate at their fingertips to fulfill it! Many steps might have to be taken before they ferret out the right candidates to present for interviews; searches can be as simple as skimming through the company database or as complex as spending weeks scouring their personal network and the Internet.

Remember, you've seen how one can find more than résumés on the Internet. *Resources* for résumés such as niche job boards, user groups, and professional organizations can be uncovered with great frequency! If one avenue turns out to be a dead end when searching for competent candidates, a skilled recruiter can turn on a dime and utilize another source instead.

The actual process can be outlined as follows: The recruiter who receives your job requisition first checks the agency's database to see if anyone on file looks right for the opening. If the database doesn't turn up enough suitable candidates, the recruiter will check with his or her personal recruiting network, use the type of Internet recruiting resources described in this book, and make some "cold calls" to people who look suitable but aren't currently looking for jobs. The recruiter will initiate contact with candidates to determine their interest, pre-qualify them to see if it seems likely they can deal with the job in question, and get references. After checking the references, the recruiter will have face-to-face meetings with the candidates who have survived the pre-qualification and reference checking process and then set up interviews for you to meet them.

A recruiter should go through all of these steps on every search for candidates for your job opportunities. As you can see, it's quite time-exhaustive and can require a great focus on details and follow-up. The benefit you derive is you only interview people who are a good match for your position, thus freeing you from the hours that would be wasted interviewing impossible candidates.

How to Choose a Recruiter

If you decide you'd like to use a recruiter to assist you in locating people to hire, you want to choose a reputable professional who knows both the recruiting industry and your own business. Anyone can put up a Web site and claim to be a recruiter; you want to be sure the person you partner with is one who will deliver the results you deserve. But if this is a new venture for you, how can you tell if you're making the right decision?

Questions to Ask Yourself

When you choose to use a recruiter, you are committing yourself to a business partnership (albeit one that is structured client–customer). Certainly you can try hard-line negotiations down to the last penny, but remember—good recruiters normally have more work than they can handle. Treat them as you would like to be treated by another company who views you as a supplier.

Before determining which recruiter to use, first you must answer some key questions about yourself:

- What is your industry?
- What are your goals and expectations?
- How much time can you spend?
- What is your definition of success?

These four questions are explored in the following sections.

What Is Your Industry?

Some industries—such as the information technology sector—have an overabundance of recruiters. This can be beneficial, as it offers you a great deal of choice, and confusing as well, because you'll have so many firms from which to choose. Other industries, such as the food technologies or steam professionals, have only a few specialized recruiters. No matter what industry your business is in, however, you should still be able to network with your peers either personally or via industry niche sites and see which recruiters stand out. The customers of excellent recruiters generally will be quite happy to extol their virtues, as would any other satisfied clients in an industry.

What Are Your Goals and Expectations?

Sometimes people expect miracles from their Internet recruiting and their recruiters. Often, however, they'll hamper their own success by some of the following methods:

Underpayment. Imagine this situation. You have an insane desire to create the world's Next Big Thing—a portable e-commerce network. Doing so requires the skills of a top-notch Web developer, database administrator, and a few other in-demand professionals. So you offer $40,000/year for these positions, figuring the glory would be enough. I have news for you; it just doesn't happen that way! Certainly, there are professionals who will hedge their bets and be willing to work at a severely undervalued salary, but you *must* give something else in compensation. I cannot count the number of times I've spoken with managers who want the world (and several galaxies, too) but are only willing to pay a flea-market price. Never think that skilled professionals don't know what they are worth—there are many discussion groups and sites on the Internet that freely showcase rates, salaries, and wages. For a few samples, check out **WageWeb** at http://www.wageweb.com/, **JobStar** at http://jobstar.org/tools/salary/sal-prof.htm (as shown in Figure 21.1), **Available Jobs Salary Survey Links** at http://www.availablejobs.com/_pges/preferred_salary_survey.htm, and **RealRates** at http://www.realrates.com/.

Unrealistic Expectations. I polled several recruiters from the **Recruiters Network** at http://www.recruitersnetwork.com/ about hidden ways of shooting oneself in the foot when working with recruiters. The responses from these professionals, all of whom have been in the business for many years, were numerous and quite eye-opening! Consider the following from Porter McManus, a recruiting director from Kelly Law Registry, who discusses the importance of timely responses and internal communications:

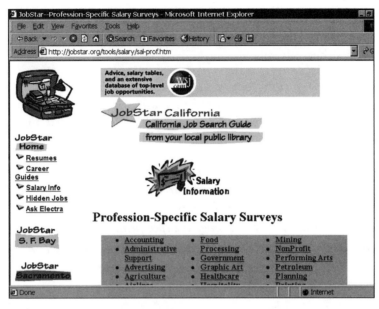

Figure 21.1: JobStar provides direct links to industry-specific salary surveys.

By far the most recurrent problem I have run into is lack of timely response from the client. The lag causes the entire process to lose its momentum. As a result, recruiters in the office lose enthusiasm to recruit for the client and candidates lose faith in the strength of their recruiter's relationship with the client. It's the old "hurry up and wait".... That aside, with certain clients I also see evidence of a lack of internal communication between the Hiring Coordinator and the department and/or individual person requesting the hire.... In instances where my contact is limited to the Hiring Coordinator, my information is then confined to a one-paragraph (or often one-line) summary of the requisition. When I take a look at the requisition and then run through the obvious fill-in-the-blanks questions, the Hiring Coordinator is either at a loss or is afraid and/or unwilling to either go back to the GC [General Counsel] or put me in touch ... directly, and basically says, "Just fill it, okay?"

It's like someone ordering a pizza from me without specifying whether they want pepperoni or mushrooms or onions or extra cheese, and then expecting it to be just what they had wanted when it arrives at their door. As a result, our recruiters' searches are not as clearly defined as they should be, and candidate submissions may be off the mark. This strains both client and candidate relationships.

Porter McManus
Recruiting Director, Kelly Law Registry
http://www.kellylawregistry.com/
Boston, Massachusetts

Sherri Dresser, a recruiter who runs Dresser Search and Consulting, points out the importance of effective communications between the hiring employers and the recruiters themselves:

As an independent recruiter, my message to clients is "Help me to help you." Clients sometimes do things that can cause the recruiting process to slow to a crawl and become ineffective, costing both the client and the recruiter lost time, money, and good candidates, including:

- *Lack of providing accurate and detailed information and/or a solid job description for each position causes a recruiter time and frustration in trying to gather the details to determine where and who to search for, and usually results in having to change the specifications mid-stream.*
- *Changing the specifications drastically in the middle of a search costs money and time for the recruiter, who must then shift gears and start the networking and search process all over.*
- *Slow response time by the client to qualified candidate résumés or when trying to set up phone screens/interviews often results in losing the candidate to the competition due to the current hot job market.*
- *Clients who expect ridiculous guarantees for replacement of candidates or unrealistic refunds of fees or low fee percentages only ensure that recruiters will work much harder and more quickly to fill other clients' searches who have more reasonable terms and higher fee percentages.*

Treating recruiters with disrespect and trying to circumvent their efforts in the process will only cause the recruiter to lose interest in the search, eroding the recruiter/client relationship, and making the search ineffective, more time consuming, and costly.

Clients should be more than willing to help recruiters in the process of getting good candidates to the table and getting them hired. After all, the client is hiring the recruiter to get the job done well and quickly. They should realize that we are working for THEM!

Sheri Dresser, PHR
Dresser Search and Consulting
Marietta, Georgia

Always remember that recruiters are in a service industry. You're not after *only* the cheapest possible fee settlement; you're after the chance to hire the professionals you need as soon as is humanly possible. Make sure your recruiter wins by taking you on as a client, and you'll receive the best service available.

How Much Time Can You Spend?

Another key point that will assist you when using a recruiter is having the time to discuss your needs in detail as well as schedule interviews with potential employees. Sometimes managers forget the time-sensitive nature of in-demand candidates and try to set up interviews two or three weeks down the pike. By then, it's almost guaranteed that candidate will have been submitted for another position. Remember, gone are the days when companies could pick and choose whom to hire and when to deign to interview; if you're slow on the scheduling, the candidate might slip through your fingers. And if that person would have matched the position you had open, that would truly be a shame.

It Takes Time to Save Time—*Always spend as much time as necessary to answer your recruiter's questions concerning your open job positions. The more information recruiters have at their fingertips, the easier it is for them to start lining up the right candidates for you to interview.*

Never think you can initially simply call up recruiters, dump a job description in their laps, and expect to hire the next day. Done well, recruiting is a fine art that involves a comprehensive understanding of the client's needs and expectations as well as of the candidates' goals. You *must* expend the time necessary to answer all questions the recruiter might have, provide names of business competitors from whom they can source, and be available when needed. Doing this will increase your opportunities for success.

What Is Your Definition of Success?

Defining "success" isn't as obvious as you might think. Your definition of it might hinge on any of the following:

Time. The faster a future employee is found and hired, the better.

Quality. You're willing to wait and pass by several plausible candidates in order to find the best one you can afford.

Savings. The bottom line at the end of the year is the most important result from your hiring endeavors.

Additionally, however, another factor might come into play—that of your own boss, who might have decreed that you are the contact specified for a particular recruiter. What are your boss's expectations? Always be certain you're both operating from the same page; failing to achieve your supervisor's ideals of success might be detrimental to your own career goals as well.

The questions discussed in this subsection and the preceding subsections are all useful in helping you as an employer or hiring manager shape your own expectations and needs for a recruiter. But when you choose to actively search for one, you might become overwhelmed with all of the possibilities available! How can you determine which company and which recruiter will be the best match for you?

Questions to Ask a Recruiter

As with any other supplier or vendor, you should research and evaluate recruiters before you make a decision. It's a good idea to have a face-to-face meeting if at all possible and see how the two of you will work together. In any case you need to get answers to the following basic questions:

- How do you find candidates?
- Why do candidates choose to work with you?
- What references can you offer?
- How long have you been in the business?
- What do you know of my industry?
- What are your guarantees?
- What are your fees?

How Do You Find Candidates?

As you've seen from Chapters 8 through 19, you have dozens of ways to find future employees on the Internet. But recruiting doesn't have do depend upon that at all, not by a long shot.

Keep in mind that traditional recruiting was done via the telephone and networking long before the Internet came into existence. High-quality recruiters can use the Internet as yet another tool for uncovering candidates, but will also rely on their company database, their ability to source into competitive companies, and their networks within the industry. Referrals are another powerful source of candidates for these recruiters; it's human nature to want to share good resources with one's peers, and a professional who is treated well by a recruiter will quite often refer the recruiter to a whole circle of friends. Some recruiters will also encourage referrals by offering a finder's fee to candidates who suggest their colleagues.

What if a recruiter simply doesn't have a potential candidate for you? Recruiters will often band together and share what they call *splits;* this occurs when one recruiter has a position that another recruiter can fill. Several networks exist for recruiters to participate in splits, including **Recruiters Online Network** at http://www.recruitersonline.com/ (as seen in Figure 21.2), **Top Echelon** at http://www.topechelon.com/, and others. Clients aren't part of these arrangements; you'll simply receive candidates to interview.

How else can recruiters find candidates for you? As with direct sales, simply picking up the phone and calling potential candidates, time after time, can yield results. Recruiters can also network with their peers via some of the many industry niche sites such as the **Recruiters Network** at http://www.recruitersnetwork.com/, the **Electronic Recruiters Exchange** at http://www.erexchange.com/, or the **Sourcer's Apprentice** at http://netrecruiter.net/sa/. Competent recruiters will always have several resources available to which they can turn when trying to fill a job order.

Why Do Candidates Choose to Work With You?

Because recruiting is nowadays more than ever a service industry, any recruiter you evaluate should be able to present several reasons why candidates choose to work with them. After all, candidates are entrusting their careers to these people; they

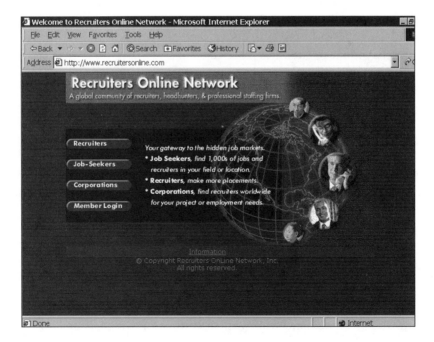

Figure 21.2: Recruiters Online is one of several excellent recruiters' networks available on the Internet.

almost always have reasons why they want to work with specific firms. The list of reasons might include the following:

Trust. Recruiters who have demonstrated they are worthy of a candidate's trust quite often will have that candidate for life. If they actively disclose the truth about job opportunities, don't fudge the facts about the skills required or compensation offered, and otherwise work in good faith, they will spark loyalty in those candidates who use their services.

Candidates Network, Too—*Candidates often share with one another the names of recruiters who treat them well and deliver on services promised. Recruiters should always be able to point to happy candidate testimonials and to provide references as well.*

Honesty. There are times when recruiters simply don't have positions available for candidates. The wise ones will disclose that immediately, and offer to send those candidates to another resource. Because this has the short-term effect of removing a commission, it makes quite an impression on the candidate. Often, that candidate will check back again to see if the situation has changed.

Industry knowledge. Candidates enjoy knowing the recruiter they deal with understands their industry and can converse knowledgeably about the types of positions open. People who have worked in a field often have their fingers on the pulse of the industry and understand the specific needs you might have (having experienced them themselves).

Career counseling. Smart recruiters, when discussing a candidate's career goals, will try to find out exactly why a candidate is searching for a new position. What need isn't being met in their current job? Career counseling and guidance targeted to the candidate's best interests provides a compelling reason for professionals to choose a particular recruiter.

If you hear any of these reasons and can verify them, you're one step closer to finding a recruiter who will solve your staffing needs.

Why Do Clients Choose to Work With You?

Competent recruiters understand and can discuss the reasons why clients choose them to find candidates. It's much the same as with candidates; clients work with recruiters who don't overpromise, who explain in detail how the recruiting process works and what to expect, and who work with them as much as possible to turn up candidates who offer a real match to the available opportunities, providing both the technical skills and the interpersonal assets needed to do well on the job with minimal orientation time.

Keep in mind, of course, that the answer to this question is rather subjective. After all, a recruiter could simply fudge the truth and talk like the Yoda of the industry. You need to follow up with reference checking, as described in the next subsection.

What References Can You Offer?

Truthful references are important; competent recruiters have lots of happy customers, which usually means lots of happy candidate testimonials to share. Often, you should be able to receive a list of current clients who will vouch for a recruiter's skill in finding the best possible match for certain job opportunities. Granted, sometimes recruiters do operate under nondisclosure agreements, meaning they cannot reveal the names of current clients or candidates. In this case, consider all the other methods for qualifying your recruiter.

Generally, however, you'll find many clients who are willing to share their experiences. Frequenting some of the recruiter or HR mailing lists that have already been mentioned is a good way to get referrals as well. Additionally, the recruiter's Web site might also have customer testimonials in a prominent location.

How Long Have You Been in the Business?

There are no regulations, so anyone can put up a Web site and claim to be a recruiter. Some people do take exams and become certified as recruiters, but such tests are purely voluntary. It's just like contracting; anyone can pick up a hammer and claim to be a building contractor. I experienced that rip-off firsthand (the building contractor in question turned out to be an insurance salesman); you always want to check into a company's background.

On the other hand, just because someone just started out shouldn't immediately disqualify them; they might have been corporate or agency recruiters in the past and are starting their own business now. Thus you should verify the recruiter's personal experience in all aspects of the industry and recruiting if at all possible. And it's not always true that the longer a company has been in business, the better it has to be; the recruiting industry is changing so much that overall success is more important than longevity. I've seen recruiting businesses come and go, only to reappear with a different name... you want to focus upon the quality within when making your determination.

What Do You Know of My Industry?

Many recruiters, alas, are not as skilled in their industry as they should be. For example, I once gave an Internet recruiting seminar to a technical recruiting company on the East Coast; not one of the thirty-five attendees had any understanding of the industry in which they were trying to place candidates. This certainly isn't always the case; I've also dealt with technical recruiters who, while they didn't have a techie's knowledge of the industry, knew in a broad scope what skills were required and how they fit with other aspects of information technology, and showcased a genuine appreciation for the brilliance required.

Know Thy Industry!—*Recruiters who have held jobs in your industry generally have an in-depth understanding of what skills are required as well as where the current industry trends are moving. This is a highly desirable quality.*

As an employer or hiring manager, you can increase the probability of receiving the best service by being an educated consumer. Ideally, you should have a good understanding of your own industry. What are the current trends? Who are the power players? What are the names of your competitors? Recruiters whom you interview should be able to hold their own in many of these topics. Additionally, they should have a good understanding of the current rates and perks desired by candidates in your field. On rates, you should listen carefully to the advice you get and compare one recruiter to another; recruiters often note that employers seem to have a somewhat skewed idea of what their industry will bear in terms of salary and compensation. (They talk about clients who want to hire systems administrators for $35K in New York City and similar impossible dreams.) In fact, it's a good idea to be willing to listen with an open mind concerning all of these concerns.

What Are Your Guarantees?

You'll encounter different guarantees depending upon the recruiter. Many recruiters will offer a 100-day guarantee. Perhaps the first 30 days is unconditional; if the person you hire leaves within 30 days, the fee is refunded in full. After that it is assumed the recruiting firm has earned 30 percent of the fee and will continue to earn 1 percent per day for the next 70 days. Other agencies offer a 90-day amortized guarantee; if a newly hired employee doesn't work out in the first 30 days, the full fee is refunded; if the employee leaves between 30 and 60 days, 66 percent of the fee is refunded; and if the employee leaves between 61 and 90 days, only 33 percent of the fee is refunded.

Keep in mind, however, that recruiters can only provide candidates; you are the one ultimately responsible for deciding who gets hired. Always make sure to verify to the best of your abilities how well an individual will fit and perform in your company.

What Are Your Fees?

Fees are certainly an important part of any contract agreement. I have some rather radical viewpoints about them. Normally, recruiters will charge you anywhere from 10 percent to 35 percent or more of the first year's salary to find candidates that you can interview and hire. Sometimes, clients will decide that the fee is 'way too much and try to nickel and dime the cost down.

Personally, I wouldn't do this much myself. I know that for every client who wants to lower a recruiter's fees, other clients will accept them and sign on at that rate. Which search assignments do you think will receive the priority treatment—the ones that pay the recruiter 15 percent as a commission or the ones that pay the recruiter 25 percent? It's simple human nature; people will want to work where their monetary return looks the greatest. When I was recruiting, a client once asked me to find a "color engineer." The client explained that this position had been open for over six months, and they were desperate to fill it. Upon being told of my fee (which back then was rather modest), they insisted on 25 percent less. How much time do you think I spent on that particular search?

This doesn't mean you couldn't negotiate under specific circumstances, of course. If you are planning on using a recruiter for a multitude of positions, you might want to consider negotiating a bulk rate. Just keep in mind that the more you enable a win–win scenario, the more energy a recruiter will expend to ensure your searches are successful.

Making the Choice

Now that you know how to choose a recruiter, the next step is to find one you can use! The process is very similar to the search for résumés.

- Define your industry.
- Browse recruiter directories.
- Utilize search engines.
- Ask your peer network for recommendations.
- Determine which recruiter to use.

These steps are described in the sections that follow.

Step One: Define Your Industry

Quite often, defining your industry is a straightforward process. If you are the manager of a sales team and that is your only responsibility, most likely you would want to uncover recruiters who specialize in sales and marketing. You can target this more specifically, however. Perhaps your sales team consists of individuals who sell computers, or farm equipment, or retail merchandise. In all these cases, you might to consider expanding your recruiter search to one who specializes in that industry as a whole, and then concentrates upon the sales aspect. For example, recruiters in the agriculture field might have contacts within the sales arm, recruiters in the technical industries might have a special branch set aside for technical sales, and the like. You should always explore all your options.

That's all well and good for a single search. But what if your company needs to find professionals in different industries? Some recruiters specialize as generalists, meaning that they handle a number of industries at the same time, while others prefer to specialize and target their skills for one particular niche area. Thus, if you need to find financial, sales, computer, and administrative assistants, you might want to consider splitting up your assignments to those recruiters who have the best successes in those fields, or creating a package deal with one generalist firm. Several large recruiter corporations—**MRI** at http://www.brilliantpeople.com/, **Interim** at http://www.interim.com/, **Kforce** at http://www.kforce.com/, **Robert Half** at http://www.roberthalf.com/, and others—have hundreds of offices under their umbrellas. With a package deal, it's likely that an individual recruiter who doesn't have the candidates you need will peruse the entire company database in order to locate them for you.

Step Two: Browse Recruiter Organizations or Franchises

Once you have your industry targeted, you can then start looking for recruiters who meet your needs. This can be done by the following methods.

Visit several of the recruiter organizations:

American Staffing Association at http://www.natss.org/

Association of Executive Search Consultants at http://www.aesc.org/

National Association of Executive Recruiters at http://www.naer.org/

National Association of Personnel Consultants at http://www.napsweb.org/

National Association of Professional Employer Organizations at http://www.napeo.org/

Net-temps at http://www.net-temps.com/

Recruiters Online at http://www.recruitersonline.com/

Top Echelon at http://www.topechelon.com/

Visit some of the recruiting franchises as well:

Brilliant People at http://www.brilliantpeople.com/

Dunhill Staffing at http://www.dunhillstaff.com/

H.L. Yoh at http://www.hlyoh.com/

Interim at http://www.interim.com/

Intellimark-IT at http://www.intellimark-it.com/

Kforce at http://www.kforce.com/

Snelling Personnel Services at http://www.snelling.com/

Many of these resources will have search engines on their page; this will enable you to query for recruiters in different industries or states. For example, if you want to find recruiters who specialize in the accounting industry, visiting **Recruiters Online Search** at http://www.recruitersonline.com/match/search.phtml will enable you to find only those recruiters that interest you.

Recruiter Organizations and Franchises—*Internet recruiting is one of the fastest-growing industries today. Your challenge will be to find the right ones for your business.*

These are not your only options, of course. The industry is seeing a growth in the number of local and industry-specific recruiter organizations as well. Here are just a few samples:

Association of Staff Physician Recruiters at http://www.aspr.org/

National Association of Computer Consultant Businesses at http://www.naccb.org/

National Banking Network at http://www.nbn-jobs.com/

National Insurance Recruiters Association at http://www.nirassn.com/

If you need to hire employees in these areas, visiting these sites might give you leads on recruiters to check out.

Perhaps after your browsing, you still will not have uncovered the recruiters you need. In that case, it's time to revisit your friendly neighborhood search engine. Before we go there, let's review search engine basics and get them straight in your mind:

What am I looking for? Recruiters.

What are the keywords that I might use? Industry names, such as `Sales` or `Engineering` or `Printing` or `Distribution` or `Metal` or `Lumber` or `Book-publishing` or `Computers` or `Finance`, as well as locations such as `New Jersey` or `Dallas` combined with the keywords `recruiter` or `headhunter` or `executive search`.

Step Three: Utilize Search Engines

Let's say that you are looking for an Information Technology recruiter. Searching on **Google** at http://www.google.com/ for IT recruiter doesn't work, because Google interprets "IT" as the pronoun "it." Thus you might want to search for computer recruiter or oracle recruiter or unix recruiter. All of these searches will return bleeploads of recruiting firms scattered across the country. Thus your next concern might be to target recruiters within your geographic area, especially if you'd like to engage in a face-to-face meeting prior to signing any contact.

Visit **AltaVista** at http://www.altavista.com/ and search for NJ engineering recruiter; one of the sites that might come up is **Xitech Staffing** at http://www.xitechstaffing.com/, an engineering recruiting firm based in central New Jersey, as well as a page that includes **recruiters addresses** at http://aiche.engr.ucdavis.edu/recruiters.htm (but no other contact information). Remember, every search engine ranks sites differently; you can never guarantee that what shows up in the top ten actually meets your specific needs.

Another great way to uncover recruiters who are local to you is to visit **Infospace** at http://www.infospace.com/. This incredible directory allows you to set your own address and then specify a distance in which to search for businesses local to your office. Visit there now and follow the next steps:

1. Click "Yellow Pages." You'll be brought to a page where you can set your city and state.

2. Enter your own town; in my case, it would be Holmdel, New Jersey.

3. Choose "Find." Your location has now been set; now it's time to find the recruiters near you.

4. Enter "Employment" in the field under "Type a category or business name" and click "Find." You'll be returned a number of categories from which to choose, including "Employment Agencies & Opportunities" and "Executive Search Consultants" among several others. Choose one of them.

5. You'll see the results are all within a certain distance of the city and state that you specified.

You can derive even more targeted results if you specify your street address as well in Step 3; in that case, you'd click on "Search Near Address" to enter your own street information. Infospace is a great resource for locating many business needs close to your office. Restaurants, copiers, printers, banks... you name it, you can probably find it via this search engine. It's a valuable resource.

Recruiters have several names by which they call themselves. Some recruiters will use the term *headhunters* to refer to their industry, while others prefer to call themselves *executive search consultants* or *consulting agencies*. You can use all of these key phrases when trying to find these professionals via search engines. For example, perhaps you'd like to consider using a retained search firm as opposed to a contingency office. Visit **Google** at http://www.google.com/ and search for `retained recruiter`; you should be returned several sites that deal extensively with retained search.

Step Four: Ask Your Peer Network for Recommendations

One excellent way of targeting the best recruiter to use is to query your peer network. Poll other hiring managers within your industry and ask which recruiters have brought them a high rate of success. Remember to define "success" of course—as noted earlier, what is successful for one employer might not be important to others.

This will be helpful for you especially if you are not familiar with recruiters. Your peer network might be able to provide useful leads that will assist you in your final decision.

Step Five: Determine Which Recruiter to Use

After you have a number of recruiters from which to choose, how do you make the final determination? There are several points to consider.

Remember, using a particular recruiter is a business decision that should necessitate your taking valuable time in your schedule and hammering out the specific needs of your business. You'll be communicating with your recruiter on a frequent basis. Choose the recruiter with whom you work best.

Another thing to consider is the nature of contingency recruiters. Because contingency recruiters are paid *only* when you hire their candidates, you can opt to submit job orders to two or three recruiters and determine which one delivers on the best service, including understanding your needs, meeting your goals, providing high-quality candidates in a timely fashion, and the like. After some time, it should become apparent which recruiters are those you'd like to work with on a continuing basis.

Concluding Thoughts

Recruiters can be a tremendous resource for your hiring needs. But like all things in life, you get the most out of the relationships into which you put the most effort. Care must be taken to work *with* your recruiter; the more you partner, the quicker your candidates will be found and your available job positions filled.

Remember your end goals. You want to find professionals to hire as rapidly as possible without compromising your needs. Employment should be a long-term proposition; if it turns out that you do need to work with a recruiter, taking the time to create a win–win relationship will result in better candidates in a shorter time.

Internet Resources for Recruiters

The following lists will provide you with clear, concise starting points for many of your Internet recruiting needs. Enjoy!

Candidate Information

This section includes resources for job seeker certifications, professional organizations, background checks, and more.

Business Communities
Inc. Magazine—http://www.inc.com/discussions/
ZDNET—http://techies.zdnet.com/
VerticalNet—http://www.verticalnet.com/portal.asp

Job Seeker Communities
CareerMag—http://www.careermag.com/ubb-cgi-bin/Ultimate.cgi
Monster Communities—http://content.monster.com/communities/
Fast Company—http://www.fastcompany.com/career/

Certification
Computer Certification—http://certification.about.com/
Gocertify—http://www.gocertify.com/
BrainBuzz—http://www.brainbuzz.com/

City Information
USA CityLink Home Page—http://www.usacitylink.com/
CitySearch—http://www.citysearch.com/
Official City Sites—http://officialcitysites.org/

Colleges

ScholarStuff—http://www.scholarstuff.com/

Petersons—http://www.petersons.com/

Alumni.net—http://www.alumni.net/

Expos

Trade Show News Network—http://www.tsnn.com/

Expo World—http://www.expoworld.com/

Expo Central—http://www.expocentral.com/

Netiquette

Netiquette Home Page—http://www.fau.edu/netiquette/

The Core Rules of Netiquette—http://www.albion.com/netiquette/corerules.html

FAQ.org—http://www.faq.org/

People Finders

AnyWho: Find Telephone Number—http://www.anywho.com/

Yahoo! People Finder—http://people.yahoo.com/

Infospace—http://www.infospace.com/

Professional Associations

ASAE's Gateway to Associations—http://info.asaenet.org/gateway/OnlineAssocSlist.htm

Skillbot's Communities—http://www.skillbot.com/community/

IndustryLink—http://www.industrylink.com/

Qualifying

Backgrounds Online—http://www.backgroundsonline.com/

Prove It! Competency Testing Software—http://www.knowitallinc.com/

SkillCheck, Inc.—http://www.skillcheck.com/

Résumé Banks

This section includes many targeted industry resources for all sorts of career fields.

General

A Better Job Fast!—http://www.myjobsearch.com/career.html

Online Résumé Databases: The Riley Guide—
http://www.dbm.com/jobguide/resumes.html

Open Directory—http://dmoz.org/Business/Employment/Careers/

Accounting
Accountingjobs.com—http://www.accountingjobs.com/

AccountingNet—http://www.accountingnet.com/

American Institute of Certified Public Accountants—http://www.aicpa.org/

Actuarial
Actuarial Foundation—http://www.actuarialfoundation.org/

Actuarial Job Postings, Jobs Wanted, and General Discussion—
http://actuarialrecruiter.com/jobs/

American Academy of Actuaries—http://www.actuary.org/

Advertising
Ad Age—http://adage.com/job_bank/

Advertising Job Bank—http://pwr.com/ADJOBBANK/

Ad Week—http://www.adweek.com/CareerNetwork/

Architecture
American Institute of Architects—http://www.aiaonline.com/

Architects Online—http://www.architects-online.org/

Architect Jobs—http://www.architectjobs.com/

Automotive
Auto Dealers—http://www.autodealerjobs.com/

Auto Town Employment Office—http://www.autotown.com/AutoEmployment/

Autobody Jobs for the Collision Repair Industry—http://www.autobodyjobs.com/

Aviation
Aviation Employment—http://www.aviationemployment.com/

American Institute of Aviation and Aeronautics Career Planning & Placement
Services—http://www2.aiaa.org/career/resume-search.cfm

AIR, Inc.—http://www.airapps.com/

Finance—Banking
American Association of Finance, Careers and Jobs Search Firms—
http://www.aafa.com/

CFO Magazine and Treasury & Risk Management Home Page—
   http://cfonet.com/html/cfojobs.html

Jobs In The Money—http://www.jobsinthemoney.com/

Biotechnology

Bio Online: Career Center—http://bio.com/hr/

MedZilla—http://www.chemistry.com/

BioTech—http://biotech.mond.org/Jobs/

Chemistry

American Chemical Society—http://www.acs.org/

Computational Chemistry List jobs—http://www.ccl.net/chemistry/announcements/jobs/

ChemWeb—http://chemweb.com/

Competitive Intelligence

American Society for Information Science Home Page—http://www.asis.org/

Association of Independent Information Professionals—http://www.aiip.org/

Intelligence Brief—http://www.intelbrief.com/

Computers

Developers.net—http://www.developers.net/

Software Contractors' Guild—http://www.scguild.com/

Superexpert.com—http://www.superexpert.com/

Construction

Construction Jobs BBS—http://www.nwbuildnet.com/nwbn/jobs.html

Careers in Construction—http://www.careersinconstruction.com/

Construction Jobs—http://www.constructionjobstore.com/

CRM and Call Center

Association of Support Professionals—http://www.asponline.com/classifieds.html

Building Internet Service Communities—
   http://supportgate.jobcontrolcenter.com/ccn/supportgate/post.cfm

Call Center Careers—http://www.callcentercareers.com/

E-Commerce

Association for Electronic Commerce Professionals—http://www.aecpii.com/

CommerceNet Home Page—http://www.commerce.net/

Ecommerce Times—http://www.ecommercetimes.com/

Engineering
Engineer Search—http://www.engineersearch.com/
IEEE Job Board—http://jobs.ieeeusa.org/
EngCen—http://www.engcen.com/

Entertainment
Actors Web Page—http://starone.com/actorsweb/
Opencasting.com Home Page—http://www.opencasting.com/
The Film, TV, and Commercial Employment Network—http://www.employnow.com/

Executive Management
SixFigureJobs—http://www.sixfigurejobs.com/
CEO Express—http://www.ceoexpress.com/html/career.htm
CIO Wanted—http://jobs.cio.com/

Fashions
Fashion Net—http://www.fashion.net/
Fashion Career Center—http://www.fashioncareercenter.com/
JobsInFashion—http://www.jobsinfashion.com/

Food
Escoffier On Line—http://escoffier.com/
Restaurant Jobs—http://www.restaurantjobs.com/
WebFoodPros.com—http://webfoodpros.com/

Government
Corporate Gray Online—http://www.bluetogray.com/
VetJobs—http://www.vetjobs.com/
Federal Jobs Net—http://federaljobs.net/

Health Care
Absolutely Health Care—http://www.healthjobsusa.com/
HCJobs Online—http://www.hcjobsonline.com/
Health Care Careers & Jobs (Career Center)—http://healthcarejobs.org/

Hospitality

Hospitality Net—http://www.hospitalitynet.org/

Hospitality Online—http://www.hospitalityonline.com/

Hotel and Hospitality Careers and Job Opportunities—
http://www.hotelresource.com/careercenter.htm

HR

Jobs4HR Human Resource Jobs—http://www.jobs4hr.com/

HR FREE Jobs—http://hrfree.com/jobs/

Society for Human Resource Management—http://www.shrm.org/jobs/

Industrial

Boiler Room Careers—http://www.boilerroom.com/

Welding Jobs—http://www.welding-jobs.com/

Iron Steel Society—http://www.issource.org/

Insurance

4InsuranceJobs.com—http://www.4insurancejobs.com/

Insurance Jobs—http://insjobs.com/talent/

Health Insurance Jobs—http://www.healthinsurancejobs.com/

Newspapers—Journalists

The Write Jobs—http://www.writerswrite.com/jobs/

About Jobs for Copy Editors—http://www.copyeditor.com/

American Journalism Review NewsLink—http://ajr.newslink.org/joblink.html

Law

AttorneyJobs.com—http://www.attorneyjobs.com/

Law Employment—http://www.lawjobs.com/

Legal Employment—http://www.findlawjob.com/

Mathematics

American Mathematical Society Employment & Careers—
http://www.ams.org/employment/

Association for Women in Mathematics Employment Services—
http://www.awm-math.org/career.html

Society for Industrial and Applied Mathematics—http://www.siam.org/careers/

MBA

MBA Careers—http://www.mbacareers.com/

MBA Employment Connection Association—http://www.MBAnetwork.com/

MBA Jobs—http://www.mba-jobs.com/

Medical

Nationwide Physician Recruiter Network—http://www.docjob.com/

AnesthesiaJobs.com—http://www.anesthesiajobs.com/

Doctorlink—http://www.doctorlink.com/

Oil

Discovery Place: Oil & Gas Résumés—http://www.discoveryplace.com/ Resumes/

Oil Online—http://www.oilonline.com/recruitment_resumes.html

Oil and Gas Online—http://www.oilandgasonline.com/

Pharmacy

Pharmacy Jobs—http://www.pharmacy.org/jobs.html

MedZilla—http://www.medzilla.com/

Pharmacy Employment—http://www.pweek.com/

Project Management

ALL Project Management—http://www.allpm.com/

Project Management Institute—http://www.pmi.org/

ProjectManager.com—http://www.projectmanager.com/

Real Estate

Real Estate Jobs—http://www.realbank.com/

Real Estate Job Store—http://www.realestatejobstore.com/

RealEstateBestJobs.com—http://www.realestatebestjobs.com/

Retail

Jobsretail.com—http://www.jobsretail.com/

Retail JobNet—http://www.retailjobnet.com/

RetailSeek.com—http://www.retailseek.com/

Sales and Marketing

National Association of Sales Professionals—http://www.nasp.com/

SalesSeek.com—http://www.salesseek.com/

SalesEngineer.com—http://www.SalesEngineer.com/

Science

PhDs.Org—http://www.phds.org/

Science Jobs—http://www.scijobs.org/

SciWeb—http://sciweb.com/

Sports

Health Club Jobs—http://www.healthclubjobs.com/

Sporting Goods Jobs—http://www.sportlink.com/employment/jobs/

Sports Employment News—http://www.sportsemploymentnews.com/

Teaching

Academic 360—http://www.academic360.com/

Higheredjobs Online—http://higheredjobs.com/

Welcome To Teachers Online—http://www.teachersonline.com/

Telephony

GetCommStuff.com—http://www.getcommjobs.com/

Women in Cable and Telecommunications Career Center—
http://www.wict.org/careercenter/

Global Contractor Jobs—http://www.telephonecontractors.com/

Trucking

Job Search Online—http://www.jobsearchonline.com/

Jobs4truckers.com:—http://www.jobs4truckers.com/

Layover.com—http://www.layover.com/jobs.htm

TV

TV Jobs—http://www.tvjobs.com/

Film TV Connection—http://www.film-tv-connection.com/film-tv-jobs.html

TV Careers—http://www.tvrundown.com/sources/resourcf.html

Wireless

BroadbandCareers.com—http://www.broadbandcareers.com/

Daily News—http://www.rcrnews.com/classifieds/

Refreq.com Employment Opportunities—http://www.refreq.com/employment/

Global Job Resources

This section includes some of the most popular international job databases around.

Canada
Workinsight—http://www.workinsight.com/
Job Shark—http://www.jobshark.com/
Canada Jobs—http://www.canadajobs.com/

Australia
JOBNET AUSTRALIA—http://www.jobnet.com.au/
SEEK—http://www.seek.com.au/
Employment.com.au—http://www.employment.com.au/

China, Japan, and Pacific Rim
Asia Jobs—http://www.asia-links.com/asia-jobs/
JobsinJapan—http://www.jobsinjapan.com/
ChinaCareer—http://www.chinacareer.com/

India
Career1000—http://www.career1000.com/
CareersIndia—http://www.careersindia.com/
Jobs.Career.India.Abroad—http://www.employindia.com/

United Kingdom
Top Jobs on the Net—http://www.topjobs.co.uk/
JobHunter—http://www.jobhunter.co.uk/
Jobs Unlimited—http://www.jobsunlimited.co.uk/

United States
The Internet Job Source—http://statejobs.com/
Quint Careers—http://www.quintcareers.com/geores.html
My Job Search—http://www.myjobsearch.com/career.html

Diversity

This section will provide you with great starting points for several diversity resources on the Internet.

African American

Black Voices—http://www.blackvoices.com/

National Society of Black Engineers—http://www.nsbe.org/

Black Enterprise—http://www.blackenterprise.com/

Asian American

ChineseProfessionals—http://www.chineseprofessionals.com/

Asian American Network—http://www.aan.net/

Impacting.org—http://www.impacting.org/

General

iMinorities—http://www.iminorities.com/

The DiversiLink Job Posting and Career Development Site—
http://www.diversilink.com/

Careers Online—http://www.diversitycareers.com/

Handicapped

Project Hired—http://www.projecthired.org/

Training Resource Network—http://www.trninc.com/

Disability.about.com—http://disabilities.about.com/

Hispanic

Saludos—http://www.saludos.com/

Hispanic business—http://www.hispanicbusiness.com/

Latino Link—http://www.latinolink.com/

Gay

GayWork—http://www.gaywork.com/

Gay Job Resources—http://www.skidmore.edu/administration/career/gay.htm

Gay Workplace Issues—http://gaylesissues.about.com/newsissues/gaylesissues/msub4.htm

Native American

Native Web—http://www.nativeweb.org/community/jobs/

Native Jobs—http://www.nativejobs.com/

Native American Journalists Association—http://www.naja.com/

Women

Black Career Women Online—http://www.bcw.org/

Women In Technology International—http://www.witi.com/

Women.com—http://www.women.com/careers/

Résumé Resources

This section will provide you with key links for all aspects of résumés and job seeking in general.

Career Advisers

Joyce Lain Kennedy—http://www.sunfeatures.com/

Barbara Sher—http://www.barbarasher.com/

Pam Dixon—http://www.pamdixon.com/

Fran Quittel—http://www.careerbabe.com/

Interviewing Skills

Career Perfect Tips—http://www.careerperfect.com/CareerPerfect/interviewFAQs.htm

About.com Sample Interviewing Questions—
http://jobsearchtech.about.com/careers/jobsearchtech/msub22-interview-questions.htm

Job Interview.net—http://www.job-interview.net/

Résumé Writing Tips

Rebecca Smith—http://www.eresumes.com/

Proven Résumés—http://www.provenresumes.com/

Professional Association of Résumé Writers—http://www. parw.com/

Salary Surveys

WageWeb—http://www.wageweb.com/

Salary.com—http://www.salary.com/

Yahoo! Salary comparisons—http://verticals.yahoo.com/salary/

Tracking Software

WinSearch—http://www.winsearch.com/

Gopher 2000—http://www.go4win.com/

Skill Set—http://www.skillset.com/

Miscellaneous

The next selection of resources deals with a variety of tools and starting points for your recruiting.

Internet Publicity
Virtual Promote—http://www.virtualpromote.com/
Entrepreneurial Success Forum—http://www.ablake.net/forum/
Friends In Business—http://www.friendsinbusiness.com/board1/

Mailing lists
eGroups—http://www.egroups.com/
Liszt—http://www.liszt.com/
Publically Accessible Mailing lists—http://paml.net/

Newsgroups
Deja.com—http://www.deja.com/
Tile.net—http://tile.net/news/
Master List of Newsgroup Hierarchies Home Page—
http://www.magma.ca/~leisen/mlnh/

Search Engines
Search Engine Forums—http://www.searchengineforums.com/
About.com's guide to Search Engines—http://websearch.about.com/
Search engine tips and techniques—http://www.searchenginewatch.com/

Web Site Design
Poor Richards—http://topfloor.com/pr/website2/
BigNoseBird—http://www.bignosebird.com/
Page Tutorial—http://www.pagetutor.com/

INDEX

A

About.com, 52, 77, 145, 300, 349
Academy of Marketing Science, 84
Accounting.com, 105
AcronymFinder.com, 86
Ad-cast.com, 71, 106, 129
Adcentric, 27
administrative assistants, 174–175
advertising. *See also* classifieds
   forums and, 209, 216
   free, 104, 124–125
   low-cost, 105
   mailing lists and, 224–225
   old-media, 70–71
   posting, on Web sites, 70–72
   recruiting as, 28
   regional job banks and, 165
   targeted, lure of, 102–103
   speed of, on the Internet, 20
   writing, 69–70
AEC Jobbank, 147
affiliate programs, 7
AgentNews, 137
AllAdvantage, 7
AllInOneSubmit.com, 106, 129
AllJavaJobs.com, 145
ALLPM, 125
AltaVista, 14, 114, 126–128, 155, 161, 187, 213, 336
alumni, 11, 114–115
Alumni.com, 11
Amazon.com, 6, 7, 8
American Association of Payroll Managers, 141
American Association of Pharmacy Technicians, 159

American Bankers Association, 149, 302
American Brush Manufacturers Association, 84
American Gear Manufacturers Association, 84
American Institute of Architects, 147
American Institute of Certified Public Accountants, 112
American Marketing Association, 83, 140
American Pipe Fitters Association, 84
American Society for Quality, 298
American Society of Association Executives, 153–154, 158, 160–161
American Society of Bakers, 149
American Society of Health-System Pharmacists, 158
American Staffing Association, 334
America's Job Bank, 112
Anaconda.net, 7
answers, to questions from potential employees, preparing, 65
AOL (America Online), 17, 27, 49, 113, 177–178, 218
   basic description of, 58
   Instant Messaging, 11
   member sites, 186, 192
ArchitectJobs.com, 146
architects, locating, 146–147
area codes, 186
Arlene Rinaldi's User Guidelines and Netiquette Web page, 52
Association for Interactive Media, 161
Association for Manufacturing Technology, 84

Association for Mechanical Engineering, 112
Association for Women in Computers, 161
Association for Women in Mathematics, 105, 118
Association of Executive Search Consultants, 334
Association of Information Technology Professionals, 161
Association of Internet Professionals, 161
Association of Microsoft Solution Providers, 161
Association of Staff Physicians Recruiters, 335
AT&T Worldnet, 58
auctions, 5–6
Australia, 347

B

background checks, 305
BankJobs.com, 137
Bell Labs, 47
Bellovin, Steve, 47
benefits, 39, 40, 93, 94, 280
Beverly Hills Software, 71
Beyond.com, 8
BHS, 104
BigNoseBird, 294
BioCareer, 102
BlackGeeks, 118
Blacklist of Internet Advertisers, 51
blacklisting, 51–52
Bloomberg's CareerFinder, 141
Boiler Room, 17
bookmarks, 61–62
BostonJobs.com, 104

POOR RICHARD'S WEB SITE
Geek-Free, Commonsense Advice on Building a Low-Cost Web Site, 2nd Edition

Poor Richard's Web Site is the *only* book that explains the entire process of creating a Web site, from deciding whether you really need a site—and what you can do with it—through picking a place to put the site, creating the site, and bringing people to the site. It is full of common-sense advice that Amazon.com called an "antidote to this swirl of confusion" and "straightforward information." Praised by *BYTE magazine*, *Publisher's Weekly*, and *USA Today*, *Poor Richard's Web Site* can save you thousands of dollars and hundreds of hours.

❝Poor Richard's Good Advice. With all great new things comes a proliferation of hucksters and snake-oil salesmen, and the Internet is no exception. The antidote to this swirl of confusion lies in Peter Kent's *Poor Richard's Web Site*. The analogy to Ben Franklin's volume is appropriate: the book is filled with the kind of straightforward information the Founding Father himself would have appreciated."
—Amazon.com

❝We highly recommend that you get a copy."
—Marketing Technology

❝Very well written."
—Library Journal

❝Poor Richard's offers clear advice to help you defend against jargon-happy sales people and computer magazines."
—Fortune.com

Poor Richard's Web Site is available in bookstores both online and offline, and at http://www.TopFloor.com/

Poor Richard's Web Site, Second Edition
by Peter Kent   ISBN: 0-9661032-0-3

POOR RICHARD'S INTERNET MARKETING AND PROMOTIONS

How to Promote Yourself, Your Business, Your Ideas Online

Much of what you've read about marketing on the Internet is wrong: registering a Web site with the search engines *won't* create a flood of orders; banner advertising *doesn't* work for most companies; online malls *do not* push large amounts of traffic to their client Web sites. . . .

What you really need is some geek-free, commonsense advice on marketing and promoting on the Internet, by somebody's who's actually done it! Most books and articles are written by freelance writers assigned to investigate a particular subject. *Poor Richard's Internet Marketing and Promotions* is written by a small-business person who's been successfully marketing online for a decade.

Poor Richard's Internet Marketing and Promotions uses the same down-to-earth style so highly praised in *Poor Richard's Web Site*. You'll learn how to plan an Internet marketing campaign, find your target audience, use giveaways to bring people to your site, integrate an email newsletter into your promotions campaign, buy advertising that works, use real-world PR, and more.

You'll also learn to track results, by seeing who is linking to your site, by hearing who is talking about you, and by measuring visits to your site.

"Go now as fast as you can and get this book and soon your Web site will reach the heights of the well known."

—About.com

"This book offers readers the ability to discipline themselves and the resources they need to succeed. It's loaded!"

—The Web Reviewer

Poor Richard's Internet Marketing and Promotions is available in bookstores both online and offline, and at http://www.TopFloor.com/

Poor Richard's Internet Marketing and Promotions: by Peter Kent and Tara Calishain ISBN: 0-9661032-7-0

POOR RICHARD'S E-MAIL PUBLISHING

Creating Newsletters, Bulletins, Discussion Groups, and Other Powerful Communication Tools

E-mail publishing is a powerful communications medium that anyone with Internet access can use. It's cheap, effective, and very easy to use once you learn the tricks of the trade. Electronic publishing is one of the most efficient ways to promote your products or services online, as well as being an excellent way to drive traffic back to your Web site.

Poor Richard's E-mail Publishing is your complete, step-by-step, guide to the nuts and bolts of creating newsletters and discussion groups via e-mail. Whether you're an e-mail novice or a seasoned professional, this resource belongs on your shelf.

You'll find answers to questions such as:

- How do I set up an HTML newsletter?

- Why is e-mail better than a Web site for distributing information?

- How can I communicate via e-mail without spamming?

- What is the proper e-mail etiquette?

- Where do I find subscribers and then how can I manage them?

- Where can I find a high-powered list service?

- What are the insider's tricks to hosting a successful e-mail discussion list?

- How can I generate income through advertising or ancillary product sales?

Poor Richard's E-mail Publishing is available in bookstores both online and offline, and at http://www.TopFloor.com/

**Poor Richard's E-mail Publishing
by Chris Pirillo   ISBN: 0-9661032-5-4**

POOR RICHARD'S BUILDING ONLINE COMMUNITIES

Create a Web Community for Your Business, Club, Association, or Family

Anyone with Internet access can set up an online community—you don't have to be a rocket scientist or spend thousands of dollars. In fact, you probably already have the programs you'll need. But to have a successful Web community where members actively participate you'll need a bit more information. *Poor Richard's Building Online Communities* explains everything you'll need to know, such as:

- What programs are involved and how to manage them

- Where to promote your community so others can find it

- How to protect the privacy of your members

- Ways of dealing with dissension and needless arguments

- How to provide information that people can use

- How to foster a sense of trust and belonging with your members

You'll also learn about the types of systems you can use (mailing lists, usenet newsgroups, Web-based message boards, etc.). The authors explain the advantages and disadvantages of each system as well as how to create and manage each type of community.

If you decide to host a community that is open to everyone, you'll need to invite people to join. This book offers several ways to promote your community.

Finding and getting to know people who share your interests is one of the most interesting and useful things you can do on the Internet. So start building your online community now!

Poor Richard's Building Online Communities is available in bookstores both online and offline, and at http://www.TopFloor.com/

Poor Richard's Building Online Communities
by Margaret Levine Young and John Levine   ISBN: 0-9661032-9-7